FUNDING YOUR DREAMS GENERATION TO GENERATION

Intergenerational Financial Planning
to Ensure Your Family's Health, Wealth,
and Personal Values

CAROL AKRIGHT, CFP

DEARBORN™
TRADE
A **Kaplan Professional** Company

This publication is designed to provide accurate and authoritative information in regard to the subject matter covered. It is sold with the understanding that the publisher is not engaged in rendering legal, accounting, or other professional service. If legal advice or other expert assistance is required, the services of a competent professional person should be sought.

Publisher: Cynthia A. Zigmund
Senior Managing Editor: Jack Kiburz
Interior Design: Lucy Jenkins
Cover Design: Studio Montage
Typesetting: the dotted i
Front Cover Photo: Tiiu Lukk

Library of Congress Cataloging-in-Publication Data

Akright, Carol.
    Funding your dreams generation to generation : intergenerational financial planning to ensure your family's health, wealth, and personal values / Carol Akright.
        p.   cm.
    Includes bibliographical references and index.
    ISBN 0-7931-3713-6 (alk. pbk.)
    1. Aged—Finance, Personal—United States.   2.   Investment—United States.
3. Estate planning—United States.   4.   Inheritance and succession—United
States.   5. Intergenerational relations—United States.   I. Title.
HG179 .A385 2001
332.024′01—dc21   00-011149

Dearborn Trade books are available at special quantity discounts to use as premiums and sales promotions, or for use in corporate training programs. For more information, please call the Special Sales Manager at 800-621-9621, ext. 4514, or write to Dearborn Trade, 155 North Wacker Drive, Chicago, IL 60606-1719.

DEDICATION

With love and appreciation, I dedicate this book to my parents,
My mother, Elizabeth Grace Darling Akright
And to the memory of
My father, James Ritchie Akright
These two taught me the joy of loving and being loved.
Their practice of intergenerational financial planning in our
family gave me the idea to help you and others fund your life dreams.

TEN LAWS OF DREAMFUNDING

1. Money can, and should, be used as a family resource.

2. Sharing money shows you care and want your loved ones to fulfill their dreams.

3. Money is not the goal. It's one means to the goal—of funding your family dreams.

4. The use of money as power and control in families is emotionally and spiritually destructive. It's a dream-killer.

5. Your self-worth is far greater than your net worth.

6. With your family financial resources, help the old, train the young, and take care of your own future.

7. Fund your own greatest dreams to lead a life of purpose.

8. Take control of eventually losing control—plan for your financial transition.

9. Use your money to leave a legacy of values—not just one of dollars and cents.

10. During your life, give money to others—loved ones and those less fortunate. Doing so rewards them and you.

CONTENTS

PART THREE The "Sandwich Generation"—Baby Boomers as Adult Children

PART FOUR Children, the Youngest Generation—They Have Dreams, Too

ACKNOWLEDGMENTS

My special thanks go to Cynthia Zigmund, my very patient, thorough editor, who saw the importance of this topic and convinced Dearborn to publish my first book.

Thank you, Brooke Halpin, of Halpin House West, my publicist, dear friend, and champion, for making this project possible. You are the one who helped bring my idea of intergenerational financial planning to the public. Also, I owe deepest thanks to Mark Litwak, Esq., who most generously shepherded me through the legal aspects of the publishing process.

I am grateful to my clients, colleagues, relatives, and friends, who told me the truths of their family money dynamics and shared the intergenerational struggles they face in funding their family members' dreams. In particular, for submitting to lengthy research interviews, I wish to thank Douglas W. Baker, CFP, Kathryn Ballsun, Esq., Avi Engel, MSW, Elizabeth Gong-Guy, Ph.D., David Grady, Esq., Linda Keegan, Larry Lite, LUTCF, CFP, Raymond E. Makowski, Esq., Robert Mauer, Ph.D., and John Rooks, Esq.

Another source of inspiration in my profession has been my wonderful colleagues at Associated Securities, who shared their expertise over the past decade and added immensely to my knowledge as a financial planner. Special thanks go to former President Phil Gainsborough and to Phillip Kelley for their mentoring and friendship, as well as warm thanks to Neal Nakagiri, Bill Barnard, Max Robinson, Paul Witteman, Shirley Coria, and Anita O'Connor. I also credit Jim Guillou of Sutro and Robert Fash of Smith Barney with introducing me to the fascinating world of financial services.

I owe incredible thanks to Harvey (Bill) Dollar, the computer genius who developed my client spreadsheets and devoted countless hours to working with me on my client cases. I am most grateful to his wife, Nong, who brought our family scrumptious Thai dinners during the months of writing and travel.

Thanks also go to Bob and Paula Burrill, Mary Gardner, Elizabeth Gong-Guy and David Lefkowith, Judie and Phil Nash, Dee Stephenson, and Judith and Tom Wilson for the use of their homes for my writing.

As for the incredible professionals at Dearborn, my heartfelt thanks go to Sandy Thomas, Jack Kiburz, Robin Nominelli, Karla Powell, and all who reviewed, produced, and marketed this book in record time and with great enthusiasm and talent.

I also want to thank Chris Holden of Kinko's for getting my edited version onto disk and off to the publisher.

Margaret Trulock, Tiiu Lukk, and Leonore Blitz, I love you for all those phone calls and for your lifelong friendships. Same goes for Jeri Pollyea, Jan and John Kepler, Mary Gardner, Camilla Carr, Greg Hughes, Frank Hart, Phil Gonzales, Ray Makowski, and Rachelle and Jay Zukerman—I am most grateful for you in my life. Thanks also to supportive neighbors Billie and Dwight McAnally, Doris and Guenther Wagner, Susan Wyatt and Richard Williams. Thank you, too, to Beverly Cohn, Deanne Fahy, Kathryn Peters, Julie Francis, and Mary Fagerstrom for their years of friendship and caring. Special thanks go to Avie Engel, Robert Mauer, and Bob Sullivan for their many insights and wise counsel.

My assistant extraordinaire is Celeise Coca—my right arm, my organizer, and my client support staff all in one. Thank you for taking care of my office, my life, everything that needs to get done. Thanks, too, to Mercy Martinez for the loving way she keeps my office and home neat and clean.

I am most blessed with the love and friendship of my family members: my mother, Elizabeth Akright, who has been my greatest champion and who together with my father shared money as a family resource and inspired many of the concepts in this book; my father, James

Ritchie Akright, whose honorable character, dedication to family and work, and loving friendship are the foundation on which I have tried to build my own life; my sister, Susan Stanton, and her husband, Paul Stanton, who have given their love and support over many decades; my dear mother-in-law, Martha Nash, who fed and nurtured us in the winter months of writing—I love you all and treasure you in my life.

Special hugs to my feline family and computer-side companions—Peaches and our beloved Pumpkin, whom I still miss!

I also wish to express my gratitude to my grandparents, no longer living: Jessie and Lyman Darling and Melva and Frank Akright. It was they who introduced intergenerational planning to my parents, who passed down this great legacy to me and my sister.

Last, but certainly not least, I want to thank my husband, Mark Nash, whose interest, expertise, and savvy about the money world got me interested in this profession in the first place. I love you, appreciate you, and thank you for all that you do to create opportunities for learning, exploration, and adventure in my life.

How Intergenerational Financial Planning Can Help You Fund Your Dreams

We all have dreams we want to fulfill—working at a satisfying career and eventually retiring with financial independence; raising and educating our children; traveling to places we long to see and explore; and surrounding ourselves with the material things that give us comfort and pleasure. Many of our dreams are for other members of our family— our spouse, our children, our parents, our grandchildren. Indeed, some dreams are passed down from generation to generation within families— building a business and seeing it flourish, or making sure each child gets a college education.

How do we make these dreams come true? How do we fund the expense involved in so much of our dream fulfillment? It's a simple but intricate journey, a journey through earning, spending, saving, and investing your money. This book sets you on that journey and helps you arrive at your dreams.

You might think that we all should be able to figure out the path to dream fulfillment. However, many of us never achieve some of our most important dreams—life interrupts our plans, and sidetracks us from the steps we must take to marshall the financial resources needed. Or we try to accomplish too many dreams at one time, and the monies we've accumulated don't stretch far enough. So we ultimately give up on some dreams, settle for less than what we want, and feel that deep disappointment when we know we've failed.

But there are more fundamental reasons that you and members of your family are unsuccessful, so far, in funding some of your dreams. Let's explore these reasons.

First, you think you have to do it all alone. You're operating as an isolated dreamfunder, often keeping your dream ideas to yourself, struggling to manage your money on your own. I suggest you seek advice, counsel, or even financial support from others in your family. Money is a family resource that can be shared in ways that might help you and other family members fulfill dreams.

Second, you and your parents, or you and your children, probably don't talk about money very much, and when you do, it's with guarded concern that you'll either divulge your own private money situation, or that you'll intrude on theirs. Or you think your children are too young to really understand how money works. Well, many families see it very differently. They've got something going for them that all families would benefit from adopting as their own philosophy when it comes to dreamfunding.

Have you ever worried about how your parents, the oldest generation in the family, are faring financially? Have they saved enough to get them through their final years? Do they have long-term-care insurance, powers of attorney, and health care in their will or trust? If so, who is their named executor? Who will make final illness or incapacity medical decisions? Who will step in and pay bills if one or both no longer can do it?

Have you ever sat down with your children for a family money meeting, checking to see how they are spending their allowances, or asking what money they will contribute to paying for their advanced education? Have you taken your children to a bank or stock exchange to explain how savings and investments work? Have you set up an investment account they can follow and through which they can learn more about the money world?

Have you personally thought about what would happen financially in your family if you or your spouse were disabled and could not work? Would you have enough savings to live on for, say, one year? Do you have disability insurance? Do you have a disability clause in your life insurance policy? Do you even have life insurance?

Have you ever thought of money as an intergenerational family resource? Perhaps it is not the best idea to have each generation stockpile assets, sharing them only gingerly during their lifetime, and then passing most of them on through their estate at death. And what about any family members who just are not good at earning, spending, saving, or investing? Would you like to help them learn to be financially independent? Are you willing to help them toward their dreams?

These are the kinds of issues and questions that many families I work with are tackling head on. They open the dialogue about money between the various generations of the family. And they do it in a way that preserves feelings of autonomy, mutual reciprocity, cooperation, and respect among all the family members. We're going to meet some of these families, look at the financial problems they face, and show how intergenerational financial planning helps them solve these problems. We'll see what it means for parents, children, and grandchildren to work together in funding the dreams of all the generations.

The lessons told through these stories offer good opportunities for you to open a dialogue about intergenerational financial planning within your own family. The dreamfunding strategies throughout this book will show you how to cooperate to fund more dreams of each generation in your family. Once you form your own dream team of dreamfunders, you will see that the journey to dream achievement is not only easy but lots of fun as well. So let's get started funding your dreams, generation to generation.

CHAPTER 1

Money as a Family Resource

Money is a dynamic force. It can either fulfill dreams or destroy them. How many families do you know where at least one member of the family is extremely astute in handling money? Perhaps one person is good at finances. The other turns the money management over to the financially savvy person, who guides the family in wise spending, saving, and investing. The holder of the financial purse strings may or may not be the family's top income earner. But in this particular family, the money strategist arranges to set aside enough funds for the children's college educations, encourages the less interested spouse to put aside the maximum into his or her 401(k) plan, and finds vacation bargains the whole family gets to enjoy.

JAN: The Family Financial Leader

One woman I know comes to mind as the financial leader of her family. I met Jan when I was a personal finance reporter and she was a counselor at Consumer Credit Counselors, a nonprofit group that helps individuals and families work with creditors when they are in need of debt management or training in basic budgeting and bill paying. Jan and her husband earned modest salaries. They lived in a nice but small home and had two school-aged children, yet they managed to take wonderful vacations each year. I was amazed at the exotic and educational trips they took, given their family income. One day, I asked Jan how they were able to squeeze seven cents out of a nickel and make their money stretch so far. She replied, "When we got married, I suggested that we each had certain dreams that we wanted to make come true—both for ourselves and for our unborn children. We knew these dreams had price tags, and we were determined to manage our money in such a way that we could pay for our dreams." Jan gave me the idea of the third *P* of the six Ps of funding your dreams—price tags (see Chapter 6).

She went on to tell me that even before she became a credit counselor, she was always good at managing money. Indeed, she was the family's driving force in saving for vacations, college, and retirement. Jan's family is a perfect example of how money can be used as a family resource and play a positive dynamic role in the fulfillment of dreams.

MARY: Family Financial Disaster

Money can also destroy dreams. My friend Mary is the saddest example I have known personally of someone who handled money in a way that can only be called destructive. Only in her late 50s, she is indigent and lies in a near-vegetative state after a stroke.

Mary came from a wealthy family. Her father was a successful architect and developer of commercial properties. At his death he was worth many millions. However, in his trust, he left the bulk of the estate to his two sons and gave only $100,000 to Mary, because she handled money so poorly. Her inheritance was even set up in a spendthrift trust; she would get the $10,000 annual income generated by the principal only if she kept working.

Mary had a heart of gold, but she had some emotional problems, many of which stemmed from having had polio as a child. She had grown up the victim of a disease, and she found that acting like a victim in various ways got her the compassion and attention from others that she never got from her father. She would quit jobs before she had another one; she would underearn given her credentials and talents; she lived like she made twice the money she did earn, and when she got in arrears paying her bills, she would tap her family, then her friends, for a bailout.

Ultimately, $40,000 in debt, she filed bankruptcy, and her trust income was attached by the bankruptcy court. Half of the principal went to pay court trustee fees. Fortunately, Mary did have a few good years after that disaster, working abroad as a college teacher before she was stricken ill and was transported back to the United States to wind up a welfare patient in a nursing home, where she now lives in a comatose state.

Mary's real tragedy is that she never learned to stand on her own two feet financially, and this lowered her self-esteem. She neither understood, nor accepted, that her money problems were created by a lifetime of irresponsibility in handling money in the first place.

JENNY: Stingy Dad Withholds Love and Money

Another destructive money dynamic in families, which I've seen far too often, is the transfer of what I call "emotional money baggage" from one generation to the next.

Have you ever met a rich person who had an impoverished soul? That describes Jenny's father. A self-made multimillionaire, Warren grew up in very poor circumstances. He believes his three daughters should have to work as hard as he did to make money. He feels this so strongly, he's decided to leave most of his $20 million fortune first to his wife, during her lifetime, and the rest to charity.

That would be harsh enough, but there's more. Though he's loath to admit it, Warren really resented his three daughters as they grew up, because they took a lot of his wife's attention. He himself was raised without much outward show of love from his parents, and he needed all the love his wife could shower. He's never once told his daughters that he loves them. He seems to resent Jenny the most, because she was the first child. Also, she followed in his professional footsteps as a lawyer, and he's somewhat jealous of her capabilities. So, while he gave about $1 million in investments to the other two daughters, he's given Jenny no money at all. Furthermore, when he retired recently, he turned over his very lucrative law practice to one of the other daughters, who, frankly, is less capable and less well-liked than Jenny. It was always my view that Jenny went into law in the first place to win her father's love and eventually work with him. She did not succeed at either.

So, how does this impact Jenny? Financially, of course, she has received the least financial support of the three sisters from their parents.

She wound up married to another withholding man, who was stingy with love and who managed to get most of the couple's assets in a divorce. She's never felt loved, and she's never lived up to her earning capability. She has never felt really secure emotionally or financially. In a few words, she feels unworthy, and her financial and emotional circumstances reflect it.

While these three stories may not fit your circumstances, you probably have known someone who fits the profile of one of these people. You may even have members in your own family who might have some of the responsibility or self-worth issues I've described here. And what about you? How well does money work in your life and family?

Financial Health Questionnaire

The following Financial Health Questionnaire will give you clues to your own financial health issues. Take a moment to answer the questions.

1. What were the most important lessons you learned about money from your parents and grandparents? What were the family's "Golden Rules of Money"? (Typical rules are: Money is good; Money is bad; Nobody likes rich people; Money is hard to get; Too much money corrupts the spirit; You can never have enough money; Don't trust people with lots of money; Money doesn't grow on trees; It's only money, honey; The one with the most money wins.)

2. Who handled money with skill in your family?

3. Who handled it poorly?

4. Who made the financial decisions? Did you have a say in money decisions that affected you?

5. Did you feel your parents were generous with you around money?

6. Did your parents encourage you to learn about money?

Financial Health Questionnaire
(continued)

7. Did you have an allowance? Did it feel like enough to meet your needs?

8. Did you have to earn your money through chores or an outside job?

9. Did your parents teach you about how money works? About investments?

10. Do you like money?

11. Do you feel empowered to make the money you want?

12. Do you feel you can afford the lifestyle you want?

13. Do you fight about money with your spouse or significant other?

14. Are you disciplined with money or are you frequently, or always, in debt?

15. Do you pay your bills on time?

16. Do you give money away to others—family members or charitable causes?

17. Do you know about your own parents' current financial situations?

18. Do you talk with your children about money? Do they know the family financial situation? Do they know what you spend on them for the things they want?

19. Are you comfortable handling your money? Do you feel competent in money matters? Is the money world familiar to you or is it a mystery?

20. If you could sum up your relationship with money in one word, what word would you choose? How does thinking about money make you feel?

There's no score to this questionnaire. You don't get an A+ or an F, but as you answered these questions honestly, feelings came up, didn't they? Perhaps you started to feel better and better, as you went down the list—knowing that you came from a family that held positive attitudes and behaviors around money, many of which you have adopted in your later life. Or you may have started to feel crummy, sad, even angry, realizing that there were negative attitudes and dynamics in your early life that are now reflected in the financial status you currently experience.

The good news is that you are not doomed to repeat negative money dynamics of the past. What's more, you have an opportunity to change how money works in your family now and into the future. You can begin to look at money as a family resource, to be used to benefit all the generations, and the more that this family wealth is shared among grandparents, adult children, and grandchildren, the healthier each individual becomes with regard to money and the greater amount of dream fulfillment the entire family can enjoy.

This brings us to the first of our dreamfunding laws:

DREAMFUNDING LAW 1

Money can, and should, be used as a family resource.

HOW CAN INTERGENERATIONAL FINANCIAL PLANNING HELP YOUR FAMILY?

What do most people cherish above all? It is loving and being loved. And where do we learn these precious roles? With whom do we experience more tenderness, disappointment, hope, anger, love, even hate? With our families—our mothers, fathers, siblings, spouses, even our children. And what gets in the way of these relationships being fulfilling, at least to the extent that they can be fulfilling? Misunderstandings, miscommunications, words unexpressed or wrongly expressed, misplaced intentions, futile efforts to make someone be or do something to or for us just because we want them to. Mostly these problems stem from a lack of knowing how to best get what we want and still let others in our families get what they want.

We're probably most unselfish or unconditional in our love with our children. We have so many expectations of our own parents—how they could have shown us more respect, treated us better, liked us better, loved us more deeply—that few could ever measure up. Yet when we become parents, we wonder why our children hold us to task for the same level of superhuman expectation we surely can never fulfill.

However imperfect they are, your family dynamics have more to do with your emotional well-being than any other single influence in your life. As for money, what you saw in your family when you were growing up and what you still see going on today probably has a lot to do with how you feel about money, how you handle it, and how much of it you earn, keep, spend, and share. Some of us get the message that our value as a person is equal only to our net worth in dollars. Others learn that money can be used to buy love or to exert power or influence.

Despite its power within a family, money often is not discussed with candor. Parents don't tell their adult children about their own financial circumstances, and adult children keep their kids in the dark about family money. Conversely, money may be talked about, but with an attitude of fear, shame, greed, contempt, indulgence, or parsimony.

Why is money such a loaded topic in life in general, and in families in particular? Because most of us believe that money is the key to survival in our community and culture. It's how you win importance, prestige, power, independence, and influence. With money, you have more autonomy. Money also shackles our choices, especially when we feel we don't have enough of it. Money buys certain things we value: time, experiences, material possessions, even the company of certain kinds of people. You can show your regard for other family members by the things you do for them, or help them do, with money.

No wonder then, that money is a major source of family conflict. It makes or breaks marriages; it can help or hurt another family member. It can cause power struggles between those who have or control it and those who need to get it.

What's missing in too many families around the issues of money? Honesty, openness, communication, sharing, and responsibility—all the things that build relationships when they're present and break down relationships when they're not. Yet the family is the best place within which each family member can learn the wonder of what money can do to fund life dreams. This can happen when a family decides to open the dialogue about money, to share, and to help one another where financial matters are concerned.

Let's make one thing clear: You really cannot buy love with money. But you can use money in a way that shows your love to your parents, siblings, spouse, and children. Still, no one gives you a road map to chart this intricate journey. In this book I hope to do that for you and your entire family. What I have learned in working with hundreds of families, most of whom had no idea how to begin intergenerational financial planning, is that the journey is not so difficult; you just have to be shown the path.

THE PURPOSE OF INTERGENERATIONAL FINANCIAL PLANNING

When I first began using the term *intergenerational financial planning,* journalists didn't know what I meant. Since I want to make sure you do, let me define it:

Intergenerational financial planning is the use of communication techniques and financial strategies to provide a continuum of financial prosperity and security, generation to generation, allowing all the members of a family to fund their life dreams.

The purpose of intergenerational financial planning is to help individuals within a family fund their life dreams, and, in so doing, to accomplish three things: to be closer to their family, to show their love for their family members, and to be appreciated and remembered as generous and loving members of the family. After all, this is what we concluded earlier that people care most about—being loving and being loved.

Our second law of dreamfunding then is:

DREAMFUNDING LAW 2

Sharing money shows you care and want your loved ones to fulfill their dreams.

You've already started on the journey toward dream fulfillment. You've begun to look at money as a family resource. You can see that perhaps money is not meant to be stockpiled by the older generations and then passed down after they die, with no benefit to the giver to see how this money might benefit his or her heirs. Rather, through inter-generational financial planning, you can use money during your lifetime in a way that brings you joy—the joy of sharing with your family now and helping members of all the generations to fund their life dreams.

THE TRUTH ABOUT MONEY

While your family may have a certain view of money that has colored your own money picture, certain truths about money do not vary from family to family:

- It takes hard work to *earn* the money we need.
- It takes passion and discipline to *spend* it wisely in ways that give us joy.
- It takes foresight and planning to *save* money.
- It takes a few simple but important steps to *invest* money and make it grow.

Unfortunately, many people have never learned the basic lessons in how to implement these truths about money in their lives. Perhaps money was tight in your family and your parents never gave you an allowance to learn about managing even a small amount of money. You saw them working long hours to earn the money to put food on the table, so you understood the hard work it takes to earn money. But did your parents teach you the discipline of spending carefully, or did you have to learn on your own, ending up too many times with more month than you had money? Did your grandparents ever tell you about how they saved money to buy their first house and what they sacrificed to do that? Did you ever have a family member sit you down and show you the benefits and steps of investing?

There is no point in spending a lot of time regretting that your parents didn't train you in all the ways of money management. You're not too old to learn, and that's partly what this book is about. But I have to ask why you and a lot of other people never received basic training in financial education. There are several cultural reasons, and they illustrate the need for more financial instruction within the family.

MONEY: Still a Taboo Topic

In answering the Financial Health Questionnaire earlier, you may have marveled at how little money was discussed with candor and insight in your family. Believe me, you are not alone. While Americans are viewed worldwide as a people totally absorbed in work, getting ahead, making money, and especially consuming, we are also a nation of private earners, spenders, savers, and investors. By private, I mean we don't talk that much about our salaries, assets, or financial status. While everyone is interested in the financial affairs of others, nobody's talking. At least most people are pretty secretive about their money. There are reasons trusts are so popular today. It's not just about saving estate taxes, it's about privacy; trusts do not go through probate, the public administrative process where anyone can go down to the county probate division and read your probated will.

And what's true in the culture trickles down to the family level. Up until the past few years, money was a taboo topic within many families. Children never asked their parents how much income they had or what things really cost; they seldom knew what it took to pay for college; and they never would have dreamed of asking Mom and Dad if they had enough money in retirement to last their lifetimes.

Why the secrecy? We've already observed that money is quite important to survival—both in terms of meeting food and shelter needs, but also attaining status in our social circles. Yet I think the reason people are embarrassed or reluctant to talk about their money, even with other relatives, is the fear they will be judged about how much they've got, how well they handle it, or whether they can provide well for their families. It's the old, "What they don't know won't hurt them—or me" way of thinking.

More important, though, no one has ever taught individuals how to speak with either their parents or their children about money. We weren't given classes in financial management or financial diplomacy. Psychologists I polled agreed that for all the higher education our nation boasts, Americans receive virtually no instruction in the three most important aspects of adult life:

1. How to create healthy, loving relationships
2. How to be successful parents
3. How to handle money wisely

I guess educators feel we can learn these rather significant lessons within the family. But if your parents weren't taught these things, how could they teach you? And if you don't know these subjects, how can you teach your children? Unfortunately, we raise generations of financial illiterates, who lack the basic training to go out and earn great incomes, spend prudently, save regularly, and invest with full understanding of the risks and rewards of the plethora of investment options touted by financial services companies marketing their wares.

The bottom line here is, things have got to change, if families are going to fund every generation's dreams. Financial education begins in the home, supplemented by more formal training in our school curricula. Actually, that's the role financial planners can provide in your family—as money educators, training each generation to open up the dialogue with other generations, so that one by one, family by family, more people begin to take advantage of the wealth of dreamfunding that is possible when family members work together using money as a family resource in intergenerational financial planning.

The taboo against money talk is beginning to fade. More information about money abounds on the Internet, radio, television, and cable programs about money, interest in the stock market continues to grow, and more people are seeking help in individual financial planning. Schools are catching up, too: the College for Financial Planning now has a high school financial planning program, and more students are taking this intensive workshop geared to introduce them to the world of money. As these young people have questions, they ask them at home, often beginning much-needed intergenerational discussions.

GETTING STARTED: How to Open the Lines of Communication

If money is to be used as a family resource to help all the generations fund their life dreams, then grandparents, children, and grandchildren need to talk to each other about money. Open communication and cooperation will be critical if, as a money team, you want to train those who are less skilled in handling money and prepare for the inevitable needs of family members as they grow, mature, and age.

How do you do this? First, you initiate conversations with your other family members regarding their feelings about money. You might start with the Financial Health Questionnaire. Have your parents, your spouse, and school-age or older children fill it out. Compare the responses and see how they differ. These questions are meant to stimulate discussion and sharing. Don't be surprised if some uncomfortable feelings arise. You come from different eras, different family money histories, and you hold different attitudes. But until you can hear and learn to understand and accept where others are coming from with their feelings and behaviors around money, you don't have the raw material with which to begin evaluating dreams of different people and priorities for individuals and the family as a whole. You've got to start somewhere, and these differences actually are a great place to start!

Notice how you feel when you begin to talk with your parents about money. Does it feel strange to ask them how they handled money when they were your age? What golden rules did they learn from their parents? Ask your children what they would like to know about your household finances and about how money works. Do they understand the value of money as well as what the different bills and coins can buy? Perhaps your grandparents would like to know your college plans. Have you thought about what it will cost to go to college? What about saving for retirement? What if you're already 40-plus years of age, and you don't have a dime saved because you're setting aside college funds for your children? Would your own parents, if they can afford to, possibly want to help educate your children, their grandchildren? It may sound intrusive to start asking these kinds of questions. But that's the very myth I'm trying to dispel in this book!

Let's go back to an important point I mentioned earlier: If you ask any member of your family (and you might do this!) who are the most important people in their life, whom would they name? You? Your children? Their own parents? Of course! Now, I will admit, I'm coming from a certain bias—a bias that I think is likely shared by many of you reading this book. If you asked yourself the most important thing you want to do in this lifetime, would you not say that you want to enjoy loving relationships—to love and be loved? And what do you think about when you love someone? You are concerned about that person, right? You want the loved one to be happy, to have wonderful experiences, to get to know and love you, too. Well? Is there any problem, then, in helping these things happen, using money as one, and I repeat, only one means of accomplishing what you most want and what they most want—shared loving relationships? Funding your dreams, funding their dreams—it's all the same thing, just different people with different dreams who love one another. What if, for instance, as a grandparent, you could take your grandson, who is fascinated with the Japanese art of origami (paper folding) on a trip to Tokyo? Or pay for him to take Japanese art classes? What if you know your daughter yearns to be a ballet dancer, and there is a summer internship program with the New York City School of Ballet that she could qualify to attend? Would you spend the money to send her and skip your own summer vacation this year? Or drive to see her perform and make that your vacation? Don't you see the magic in this—the adventure, the challenge, the opportunity built into the very idea of intergenerational financial planning?

Some of this kind of financial cooperation probably already does go on in your family. Still, I reserve the right to ask you if, after reading this book, you don't find there are many more ways you could enhance and expand this intergenerational use of money as a family resource to multiply the dream fulfillment in your own family. I encourage you to read on and discover this for yourself.

WHAT IS A FAMILY?

Many of you don't have the three-generation family I have described thus far: grandparents, children, grandchildren. Your grandparents may not be alive; you may have no children; you may be a child of divorce; you may be the adoptive child of a single parent; one of your parents may have died already; or you may never have married. Rest assured that regardless, all of you may participate in funding the dreams of multiple generations. If you're childless, you may have a godchild or special young person that you mentor. If your grandparents or even parents have died, there may still be a special older-generation relative or family friend whose dreams matter to you, and vice versa. While specific legal rights and benefits accrue in financial and estate planning for blood relatives, married couples, and people with children and grandchildren, believe me when I tell you that most families have some variation on the theme of the intact, three-generation family. Still, you are the child of parents who taught you about money. If you are not married, you no doubt must deal with money in business, in friendships, with some relatives of some sort. This book has a message that goes beyond the lineal ties you have; it speaks to the loving ties you have with the people whose dreams give you joy and the people to whom you are a blessing in their life. I feel certain you can relate to each section of this book, which is divided into parts for the senior generation, adult children, and the young people of today. You will see from the real stories I describe how many of them come from varied family trees. Yet they share the most important theme of all, the cross-generational theme of individuals who want to love and be loved and who would like their money to support the dreams of their loved ones as well as their own.

I encourage you to look at money as a family resource among your own loved ones, whatever family shape they comprise. See what each of them needs to fulfill their dreams. In short, I hope that you, like many of the people you read about here, will put your money where your love is.

DREAMFUNDING STRATEGIES . . .

1. Answer the questions on the Financial Health Questionnaire. Ask your parents, siblings, spouse, and children to do the same.

2. List your own golden rules of money; compare them to those of your parents. Do you live by many of the same rules as they do? Do you want to keep doing that? What are your older childrens' golden rules of money? What are your family's money dynamics?

3. Which family members would you ask for advice about money or financial support? Which members would you be willing to advise?

4. What questions do you want to ask your parents about their finances? Your children? Your spouse?

5. Where are the money problem areas in your family? Between you and your parents? With your spouse? With your children?

Who else in the family might be able to counsel you about these problems?

6. Make a list of your own three greatest dreams. Which of them need funding? How much money might you need for each one? By when?

7. Name the three dreams you think are most important to your parents, then ask them to tell you what they are. Did you guess right? What amount of money is needed for these dreams? By when?

8. Do the same with your children—name the three dreams you think matter most to them, then compare your list with theirs when asked. List funding amounts needed and their time horizons.

9. Ask your parents about their greatest financial concerns right now.

10. Ask your children what they would like to learn about money in your family and in their world.

11. Be the first to open or expand the dialogue about money and the idea of intergenerational financial planning in your family. Approach the person you think would be most receptive and enroll his or her help in reaching out to others. Have a family dream team meeting to discuss which dreams in the family you agree should be funded first, second, and so on. Discuss which family resources (monies) can be used to help fund each dream.

2

The Dreams of the Grandparent Generation

You may think that as people age their dreams diminish. After all, by the time someone has retired or become a grandparent, younger people may view that most of their life is over and that many seniors will just coast until they die. Well, I've got news for the younger folk: the seniors of your family are just beginning one of the most vibrant periods of life—a time when most have the health, money, and time to do exactly what they want. Don't shortchange any person's dream potential just because of age. And for those of you in the grandparent generation, you've still got a lot of work to do and fun to have in fulfilling many of your lifetime dreams. And this is the perfect time to reassess your dreams and see if any of the ones listed here catch your fancy. Perhaps you have never listed your "later years'" dreams quite like this, but let's see which suit you. I cannot list them all, but here are the dream themes I see in my private practice, which includes many members of your generation.

DREAM # 1: To Remain Financially Independent

The prime dream of most older people is to remain financially independent. No one wants to be a burden on the younger members of the family. Everyone wants to have enough money to care for themselves and their health in their later years. This, more than any other concern, is what often keeps the grandparent generation from sharing more of their own resources earlier in life with their grown children and grandchildren. You may feel this way, too. You don't want to give away too much to the rest of the family and end up running out of funds to care for yourself.

What are the ways you can provide your own financial security and yet still have enough money to share with others while you are living or at death? Besides having saved and invested for retirement, which most people do to some extent, I believe the next most critical step you can take is to provide some type of long-term-care coverage for yourself (and for your spouse, if you are married). This can be in the form of a long-term-care health insurance policy, or a rider on your life insurance that provides for use of death benefit funds during lifetime for health care, if needed. Now, clearly, this is a decision you need to make at an early enough age that the premiums on this kind of insurance are affordable. I recommend that you have such coverage in place no later than age 55. Prior to age 50 is even more cost-effective. For example, at age 45 a policy that pays $150 per day for four years of nursing home or at-home care costs $583. This policy would begin paying your costs after the first 100 days of care. (If you're Medicare eligible, it will cover some of the costs on the first 100 days, but it stops after day 100.) At age 50, this same policy would run $685. At age 60, the cost would be $1,142. It would cost $2,449 at age 70 and $6,408 at age 80 (yes, some policies can be issued even at that age).

The alternative to a long-term-care policy or rider on life insurance is that you will pay all costs not covered by your regular health insurance. The worst-case scenario is that you or your spouse ends up with some kind of dementia, such as Alzheimer's disease, requiring round-the-clock care. This expense can drain your family assets very quickly and possibly leave you in dire financial straits.

So, now is a good time to reread your health insurance policy and find out just what it will and will not cover. Find out if you can add a long-term-care rider to your life insurance. Find out what a separate long-term-care policy would cost you. It may be a lot cheaper in the long run to make sure you never run out of your own financial resources. (See Chapter 8 for more strategies on long-term care.)

Next, create a financial strategy for your income and outgo each year—a financial plan. Whether you do this on your own or with the help of a financial planner, this is critical to do immediately, if you have not already. It's also important to revisit this plan yearly, as well as at several important economic milestones of your life.

The first major milestone for seniors is the year you or your spouse retires. That is when many aspects of your finances change:

- You go from having a salary or business income during your earning years to living off either a pension or the assets you have accumulated.
- Your categories of expenses may change considerably. While your need for business attire or having two family cars may cease, you may travel more or spend time doing your favorite sport such as sailing or skiing.
- You may spend more time with your children and grandchildren, treating them to different activities than you had time to do before retirement.

For a married person, the second milestone comes when your spouse dies. At this time, the surviving spouse may get only a portion or none of the deceased partner's pension. So your income may drop, but most of your expenses, such as transportation, upkeep of your home, and utility payments, continue. And food for one does not necessarily cost half of what food for two costs. So now is the time to reassess what will shift in your income and outgo once you're alone without your partner.

Part of your financial plan should be a projection of your income and expenses, taking into account the milestone changes as well as anticipated major expenses (buying a car, paying for a child's wedding, making a business loan to a family member, taking a major family vacation). Take the projection out to age 100 for you and your spouse, and make sure you don't run out of money. Later, in Chapter 7, we'll explore what to do if your calculations show that you will run out of funds too early.

DREAM # 2: To Live in Good Health as Long as Possible

The thing most people dread about growing older and facing the last third of their life (the years beyond retirement) is the idea of getting sick and living with chronic or degenerative diseases. We've all looked around and noticed that while some senior citizens are actively involved in a life filled with social events, physical exercise, and the pursuit of their personal interests, others appear in poorer health, more isolated, and often depressed. To some extent, good health is a function of our genetic fate. However, good health also has a lot to do with having a proactive approach to prolonging well-being through good nutrition, physical fitness, and mental efforts to remain positive in attitude.

You may wonder what this has to do with money. Well, you can use your money to do the things that lead to the more positive description I've outlined. Maintaining a gym membership or participating in certain sports takes some cash. So does buying vitamins and organic foods, which no health insurance will pay for under "prescriptions." Psychotherapy or attending self-actualization seminars, buying books to keep you mentally alert, getting out and staying involved—all require some expense allocations in your retirement budget.

There is little doubt that it costs less money to stay home, remain sedentary, and not take care of your body, mind, and spirit. But what price would you pay to remain vibrant and healthy for most of your remaining years? I remember what my dad said to me, some time after the stroke that left him partially disabled at age 66, "Honey, if you don't have your health, the rest isn't much fun." My father had no financial worries; he had saved well and invested wisely. Yet once illness struck, his money could not undo the devastating effects of the stroke. I am sure he would have traded a good part of his net worth to change the course of his health during his final 16 years.

There are lots of healthy rituals you can continue or begin as a member of the aging senior generation. Spend some of your time and money doing what will keep you healthy. These habits give you a better chance for longer good health—a treasure of such great value, you cannot put a price tag on it.

DREAM # 3: To Enjoy Leisure Activities and Entertainment

During our working years, we seem never to have enough time for recreation. Once you retire, though, you have a lot more free time. Well, you may say it's not "free," because leisure activities often cost money, but at least you have the flexibility to schedule what you want to do when you want to do it. Many retirees, however, worry that they must keep such close tabs on spending that they let the years go by and don't enjoy enough of these pleasures while they have the health. I say, go do all of that now—don't wait. You can budget and prioritize your interests to fit in those tennis games or ski trips.

There are many financial benefits—in the form of discounts—that people over 50 can take advantage of with just a bit of planning. Ask about lower senior rates wherever you go and whatever you do. You'll be surprised how many restaurants, car rental companies, cruise lines, and lodging facilities will give you a break because you're a senior. The American Association of Retired Persons (AARP) has a lot of information about such discounts. Don't forget to give them a call if you have not heard from AARP soon after your 50th birthday. Tell them you've reached that magic number and want to know what benefits you've become entitled to by being in the "over the hill" age group.

Besides sports, there are so many forms of entertainment to explore—theatre, musical events, poetry readings, book signings, seminars, adult education courses, free lectures, the list goes on. Not to mention the computer interests you can pursue: online chat rooms, Internet research, e-mailing your friends and former colleagues. Pursue your passions, your hobbies that were forever on the back burner in earlier years, and share these pursuits with your children, grandchildren, and the rest of your loved ones. You may get someone in your family excited about something you enjoy doing.

DREAM # 4: To Enjoy Your Friends and Family

I'm going to talk about legacy for a minute, which I will discuss in much greater depth in Chapter 10. A legacy is what you leave behind to your children and grandchildren and to the larger circle of friends and community members who are touched by your life. Legacy is not just about money or the financial estate you leave in your will or trust. To me, legacy conveys the idea of shared memories, ideas, and values that you pass down to younger generations in your family and to your peers. Obviously, you have to build this kind of legacy when you're alive. While you may have done a lot of this already, there is so much more to be done now.

First of all, there is your family. How many times have you thought that you'd like to spend some "quality time" with your adult children or grandchildren? Have you really done that much since retirement? Yes, they have busy lives with work and school commitments, as well as obligations toward their spouses. Yet, these are the years when you have the time to enjoy the fruits of child raising. I know one woman, Rita, who takes her son to lunch one day a month—it's their special "date" to get together and keep up with each other's lives and news. At first, she had to coax him to find the time in his work schedule for their one-on-one get-togethers. Now, he looks forward as much as she does to their lunch dates. She picked a time that didn't take away from his wife and kids and yet allowed them some special moments alone. Another friend of mine lives across the country from his widowed father, but Fred takes a solo trip four weekends a year to be with his dad. They reminisce and build new memories while doing things together. The idea is to enjoy the pure pleasure of shared good times with the loved ones who are the true treasures of your life. Sure, there is some expense involved in these efforts, but can you think of a better place to spend some of your money?

And what about your friends? Can you put a price on the close companionship of lifelong friends, those people who know all about you and still like you? Another favorite saying of my father was, "Carol, if you can count on one hand the number of true friends you have, you're a lucky person." I always remembered that, and I saw how he and my mother put effort into staying in touch with their high school and college friends, their cousins, and Dad's colleagues from work. I have tried to build such long-term friendships as well, and I find them very satisfying. My mother remarks that now that she is a widow, her close friends mean a great deal to her. They are her confidants, they share her history, they knew my father, and they make her laugh and delight in these remaining years.

It is a documented fact that lonely people die earlier than people with solid friendships. For those adult children reading this book, if you notice your parent becoming isolated, do what you can to encourage him or her to get out and stay in touch with friends. And if you're the parent living alone, starting to feel depressed, call a friend even in another state, go visit, and make an effort to meet new acquaintances. My grandmother, who lived to be 98, said she took a lifelong friend's advice: "Always have friends ten years younger than you are; then you won't outlive them all!"

There are so many ways you can sustain your friendships. You might consider joining a few friends and spending a month sharing a condo in a resort community—someplace warm in winter, if you live in a cold-weather climate. You can plan a surprise birthday for your best friend, invite all of his or her former work colleagues, and celebrate together. You can share the expense of the party with all those who attend and go together on a birthday gift; it doesn't have to cost a lot of money. Think how meaningful this gesture will be to your friend; can you imagine what pleasure you will get when someone does it for you? The laughter and shared communion at such times promotes happiness and well-being. Life doesn't get much better than that!

DREAM # 5: To Travel and Have Fun

Most people in the grandparent generation want to travel. In earlier periods you may have felt you should spend your money on other priorities, such as educating your children and saving for your retirement. But now it's time to take those trips you've been itching to enjoy. Now, especially, you might want to prioritize your trips, considering when to take which kind of vacations—foreign travel and sports trips in the early retirement years, when you're agile and energetic; educational junkets closer to home and shorter trips later on, when you're not feeling quite so ambitious.

There are so many ways to travel—by plane or car, staying at hotels; or by RV at campsites in national parks across the nation. You can cruise or go on archeological digs or bird-watching expeditions. You may want to go with a tour, or get maps and travel guides and plan your own itinerary. One of the important aspects of travel is to be open to new experiences. Try something you've never done before—to quote a familiar saying, "If not now, when?"

Realize, too, that as a senior citizen, you are the target market for travel agents, airlines, hotels, and a wide variety of travel companies. You should comparison-shop and bargain hard, for these industry folk want you and your money. They'll reward you for being a frequent traveler, and don't forget about those senior discounts.

Travel is a great opportunity to treat your children and your grand-children to special times with you. It's part of that legacy building I talked about earlier. Just think of the possibilities: You could take a family "roots" trip to Scotland and visit the town where your grand-parents lived before emigrating to this country. Or if you share a love of certain sports, such as golf or tennis, you can plan a family getaway to visit and play at a world-class golf course or watch Wimbledon at the scene.

I'd like to reiterate the phrase *don't wait.* You may be in your 60s with living parents in their 80s. If you want to travel together, make sure you do so before your mother's health might prevent the trip. The same is true for the younger generations you may want to include. Some years your adult children simply won't be able to get away because of their own work and family obligations. Your grandkids, too, will one day grow up and be too involved with friends or schooling to get away with you. So a family trip to visit Civil War sites must be timed when they're young enough to be available and yet old enough to appreciate the educational aspects of the vacation. Also, estimate the trip costs far enough ahead to make sure you have liquid funds to pay for the trip.

DREAM # 6: To Help Your Adult Children and Grandchildren

Any parent of adult children will affirm that people do not stop parenting when the kids leave home. There are times when grown children run into financial difficulty. Your senior generation, more than any that has come before, has the savings and resources to help younger family members who need some financial support. While you may not have had the opportunity to get financial help from your own parents, it might well be within your means to assist your own children. Some parents feel no obligation to help their offspring when times are tough, but most parents I've met are willing to help when necessary. Many would like to provide their kids and grandkids with more opportunities than they had in their youth.

The precaution I would suggest, however, is that you have your own financial plan in place, with projections out to the future, to make certain that large cash outlays to help these younger family members will not jeopardize your own financial security. This likely means that when you ascertain such a loan or gift is in the offing, you revisit your own financial situation in light of this expenditure.

Another important point—once you decide to help, determine if you want this to be a loan or a gift, and make certain your child or grandchild understands which it is. If it's a loan, get the agreement in writing, state the interest rate and the date repayment is expected to begin. Also, keep good records of the transactions and determine if you want to offer other siblings the same financial help then or later. I'll address issues of lifetime gifts/loans more fully in Chapter 11.

DREAM # 7: To Make a Contribution to Your Community

One of the great joys for many retirees is the opportunity to support charitable organizations that are doing good in the world. After years of earning and getting, many of us want to give back to our communities. At last you have the time and likely the financial wherewithal to do just that. Perhaps a close friend died of cancer, and you want to help support the local organization that counsels cancer survivors and their families. You could volunteer your time or make a donation now, during your lifetime, so that you can see the benefits of helping fund the dream of supporting families battling this dreaded disease.

Nonprofit groups of all kinds depend heavily on seniors lending time, wisdom, money, and creativity to their organizations. Many of these groups could not exist, nor could they help the many people they serve, without your involvement. They need experienced people with all kinds of expertise to lead their various service activities and fundraising efforts. They thrive on the lifetime gifts and bequests you provide.

One major benefit of charitable giving is the fulfillment you experience in making these contributions. If you are recently retired, you may have discovered already that you have too much unproductive time on your hands—40 hours a week to fill that you didn't have before; volunteering fills those hours with productive work. Perhaps you love children but suffer from the "empty nest" feeling once your own kids have grown up and moved away. There are so many areas of need where you can mentor young people outside your family, sharing your knowledge, your time, and your love. Also, working with groups that help the disadvantaged, you experience the deep satisfaction that comes from giving away to those less fortunate some of the wealth of resources and experience you have to share. Both by writing checks and giving your expertise and time, you add considerable value to your community and derive enormous emotional benefits yourself.

Also, many of my clients who survive their spouse find that volunteer work is one of the best ways to get back out into the world after their loss. While you may not feel needed now that your husband or wife has died, there are people who need your support desperately. Participating in community work gets you out of your home, into the broader world where you can find new avenues of commitment that bring value to your life and that allow you to add value to the lives of others.

You also may want to plan for major charitable gifts during your lifetime or at the time of your death. This is a large part of estate planning that you can incorporate into your intergenerational financial planning.

There are a lot of considerations, including the estate tax implications, income tax issues during lifetime, and your wishes regarding what you give your heirs versus your desire to make the charitable contribution. You should consult a financial advisor and an estate attorney before making any such commitment to a charity.

DREAM # 8: To Invest Wisely and Leave an Estate to the Next Generation

During your working years, you were socking away money in your 401(k) plan or IRA, and in the back of your mind you knew it was helping to secure your financial future. But once you do retire, you start to realize even more how hard it would be to earn back this money if you lost it through bad investments. Not everyone is trained to know much about investing. Perhaps one spouse is better at it than the other. What happens, then, if the less financially savvy person ends up having to take over the family financial reins, due to disability or death of their partner? What if that were you? Do you know where all the investment accounts are located? Have you met with the investment advisor yourself? Do you even know what questions to ask this person?

There is no better time than now to get some professional financial planning advice and to shop for the financial advisor who is right for you. If both spouses are still living, it's best to find someone both of you like, trust, and feel comfortable with in discussing your family finances. This person can help provide a smoother transition when the financial control of family money changes hands. If you are not comfortable with the person your husband or wife had chosen, shop for someone who better suits your needs.

At retirement, as I mentioned earlier, you have a lot of important, sometimes irrevocable, decisions to make about where and how to invest your money. Rolling over qualified (tax-deferred) retirement plans involves making specific elections that will bind both spouses to a certain financial path. Also, the investments you select for retirement funds must provide the income and safety of principal that you need and want. Therefore, wise investing means choosing prudent investments based on your tolerance level for risk and your need for liquidity. Your specific income needs at retirement may determine what types of investments make sense for you. Taxation of investment growth is also important, as you begin to take withdrawals and when the owner of the retirement account dies. The commencement of IRS-mandated withdrawals from some retirement accounts at age 70½ requires preplanning to ensure that investments can be cashed in without penalty or loss due to a downturn in market value of the investments that must be liquidated. When you do withdraw money from your retirement accounts, the previously untaxed portion of the money will be taxed at your ordinary income tax rate.

Not all of your investments may be held within tax-deferred retirement accounts. The taxation of investment growth or income on these funds is an important consideration. Some investments, such as municipal bonds, pay tax-free income. Others, such as mutual funds and stocks as well as government or corporate bonds sold before maturity, may incur capital gains or losses. Capital gains are taxed at a favorable tax rate of 20 percent.

When selecting investments, weigh the potential gains in investment growth with your willingness to take the risk of loss. Your risk tolerance can change as you age. While many seniors start to lighten up on growth investments in favor of more secure income investments such as Treasury bills or high-quality bonds, you must keep in mind the length of time you may be retired. You could well live 30 to 40 years in retirement. Factoring in inflation, you may need to have some growth investments, just to keep up with the rising cost of living. More on that in Chapter 7.

As for leaving an estate, it's a very personal matter. I have had some clients who will never touch principal, spending only their investment income, because they feel the principal belongs to their heirs. It's one dream they have—to pass down significant assets to their children and grandchildren. I had one gentleman, however, tell me that he hopes the check for his funeral bounces! Although he and his wife have over $5 million, they feel they worked very hard to earn this money, and they intend to live it up—down to the last dollar.

So, this is something you, too, need to think about now. The size of estate you might want to pass on to heirs, if you wish to leave anything at all, will determine how you spend and invest your money today. Also, it's important to have this discussion with your spouse, especially if you have a blended family, for you may find that you each have very different ideas about how you want to handle this matter, and such conflicts need to be worked out before you finalize your estate documents. Additionally, telling your children in advance about your estate intentions may alleviate surprises at your death that could cause sibling dissension.

DREAM # 9: To Leave a Legacy of Values to Your Children and Grandchildren

One of the true benefits of being the oldest generation is that you have more experience than anybody else. You know, often better than your children and grandchildren, what is truly important in life. Everyone has his or her own philosophy about that, but whatever yours is, I bet you would like your kids and grandkids to understand these values. Have you thought about what you believe to be so important to you? Have you shared these thoughts with your family? What have you done in your life, or would you still like to do, that reflects these essential values? Maybe you believe that loving relationships give life meaning, and yet you see your son never achieving any lasting involvements. You had or have a wonderful marriage, but have you earnestly spoken with your son about what this lifelong loving relationship contributes to your life? Perhaps you want him to date more and try to meet someone special.

What about your granddaughter? She's decided she doesn't want to go to college; she says she'd rather drop out of high school and get a job so she can be out on her own and not have to be under obligation to her parents for anything, including her behavior. You struggled to get your own college degree and might have some thoughts to share with her about life in the real world without a high school diploma.

It's true that you cannot live your children's lives for them, nor can you protect them from making mistakes, even big mistakes. Yet your ideas do carry weight with the younger generations, for they know you've experienced a lot. Whether they acknowledge it or not, you are a role model for them. The way you can convey the values you find important is to create the opportunities to spend time with the young people you hope to influence—maybe taking them to dinner and the theatre and having a heart-to-heart talk during the evening. You could invite your adult daughter to visit you on a weekend away from kids and responsibilities and find out how she's doing and share some of your thoughts that might help her decide to go back to school to better her career opportunities—and maybe offer some financial help along with your emotional support.

Maybe you'd like your grandson to understand the importance of keeping abreast of public policy. So, you get him to volunteer with you at the precinct voting polls during a presidential election, and you talk politics at the dinner table when he visits.

What's important here is to realize that, regardless of the amount of time we spend with our family members, too often we leave a lot unsaid. We think they'll learn from us by observation. Certainly, our children and grandchildren do learn some of our values by watching what we do. But if you think back to what you most remember about your own elders, perhaps your mother or your grandfather, often it is what they told you, the wisdom they gleaned from experience and shared, that you most remember. I recall my father telling me how much he loved his work, and he would always ask me when we would sit and talk about my life, "Honey, do you like what you do for a living? Do you enjoy getting up every day and going to work?" Fortunately, I could say, "Yes." He also told my sister and I that he not only loved us as daughters but he also liked us as people. These are the values I remember about him—a joyful work ethic and making sure your loved ones are also your good friends.

Your first step in trying to leave a legacy of values is to focus on your hot list of important ideas you want to teach the younger generation. Next is making the time and creating the opportunities to build on your relationships with specific individuals you hope to mentor in your family. Most of all, it's living your values and sharing yourself in words and actions that educate your loved ones in what you want them to value. Here is where "walking your talk" weighs a lot more than philosophy without personal commitment.

DREAM # 10: To Be Remembered with Love and Respect after You Are Gone

Central to our fulfillment as human beings is to know that our lives have meant something to others—especially something beneficial. This dream is about wanting to be remembered by everyone—not just our family members—because of who we are and what we have done for our community and for humanity at large.

That's why your senior years have so much potential for personal fulfillment and recognition. You can mentor the youngsters in your family. You can donate time and dollars to a variety of charities and nonprofit groups. You can promote education at your alma mater. You can volunteer in public policy arenas. You have so many opportunities to give fully and to give back—to share the talents you've acquired, the resources you've garnered, and the wealth of experience, insight, and caring that comprise your lifetime of blessings—and in so doing culminate your life with the richness of your character. You, then, will be well remembered by all whose lives you have touched as an individual who planted many seeds of promise that will ripen for generations to come.

CHAPTER 3

The Dreams of Adult Children

Adult children today, proportionately, are the most populated generation that has ever lived. Predominantly represented by the 76 million American baby boomers born between 1946 and 1964, we have big dreams, and most of us want to have all our dreams come true at once, and now. Unfortunately, we also are the worst savers of the three generations discussed here. We started our families later, have had lots of career and job changes, and we're only beginning to see that delayed gratification might have some merits—and that we're a bit behind in planning for retirement, for our children's college funding, and for some of the longer-range dreams we want to achieve. The good news is, it's never too late to begin dreamfunding strategies, and so, if you are among this age group, don't lose heart. I'll address how to juggle the needs and wants of our elders, our children, and ourselves later in Part Three. Right now, let's take a look at the major dreams of our generation.

DREAM # 1: To Have an Interesting, Profitable Career

Baby boomers are hard drivers, success-oriented achievers. Establishing a career is a top priority for both men and women of this middle generation. It takes a lot of time, energy, and often money to get the training, experience, and the attributes of success. This is a big dream, and many adult children today are focused on this career development process, putting attention on this dream often first and above all others in their quest for professional satisfaction. You, too, may have found yourself postponing marriage, children, even leisure time with friends and family, all in the name of building your reputation, making your mark.

Another phenomenon of this generation is the explosion of entre-preneurship among its ranks. Never before in modern history have so many individuals, men and women, started their own businesses. It takes a special breed of character and inner drive that lead one down the entrepreneurial career path. It is often a rocky road that puts both fi-nancial and emotional strain on the hardy group that goes this route. It also puts stress on their families and friends, who vie for attention from their committed family business owners.

I bring up this often lopsided focus of the career-driven striver not to denigrate the pain and difficulty to which you may choose to subject yourself and your loved ones in the name of success. In many ways, your commitment to achievement is admirable. Yet, I do want to em-phasize that when an adult child is in the early, even middle, years of career establishment and progress, other family members' dreams may go by the wayside. Perhaps your parents want to take the whole family on a trip and you cannot get away from the job or the business. Many seniors may wonder if they'll ever become grandparents, when you hit your 35th or 40th birthday, still unwed and without plans for starting a family. And as you march diligently down your career path, you, too, may wonder if you have given up too many other important dreams to accomplish career success. I know a lot of women, for instance, who hit age 40 and say, "Where is my family? I wanted to have children!"

So what does this have to do with intergenerational financial plan-ning? A lot. Somehow you in the "sandwich generation" have to cope with work commitments, commitments to children if you have them, financial goals, and the desire to be accountable to your parents, stay-ing in touch with their personal and financial concerns and needs. Sometimes, you need to listen when your parents remind you to slow down, take time for the family, even take time for yourself.

Let's talk about time to relax and reflect, time out from your career dream efforts. I know that I have trouble relaxing sometimes, taking moments to just sit, read a book, and stop the mental wheels from turn-ing and strategizing. It is in these moments of quiet, however, that we brainstorm more about all our dreams—what we want out of the nonwork areas of our lives. Without these times of reflection, decades can go by in which we're so immersed in our career achievements that we forget that our parents are aging—that they won't always be able to do things with us, come visit us, travel with us. We let precious years go by, trying to get ahead. Likewise, our kids grow up, leave home, and we've lost our chance to guide and teach them.

The pursuit of career dreams is what allows humankind to progress—these dreams have given us automobiles, airplanes, exploration in outer space, modern conveniences, and a plethora of services that make our life easier. So, I don't knock career dreams in the least; I have many of my own. We all want to find ways to use our talents and training to provide a product or service that we think will be needed by someone. And it's the entrepreneur's commitment to start a business that creates jobs for everyone. But I ask you, if you're in the midst of building your career, what is it that you most want out of life over the long haul? Perhaps career achievement is central to your sense of fulfillment in life. If so, this dream is very important to pursue. Yet, I believe that you need a balance among dreams to be truly happy.

Let's imagine that you find out that you have only one year to live. How would you spend your time in that one year? Staying longer at the office? I doubt it. Remember why you're doing it all in the first place. To make a name for yourself? Maybe. But who will you go out and celebrate your victories with at each milestone in that career? Who are the people in your life that matter to you most? Your parents? Your spouse? Your children? On their deathbeds, few people, I suspect, reflect too much over their wins at work. From my observation, people in their final years cherish their loved ones—their parents, siblings, children, grandchildren—these relationships are what bring them joy. And that gets me back to intergenerational financial planning. What is the point in working so hard to earn money and success that you miss the lives of your loved ones, recital by recital, birthday by birthday? What's more, if you don't have time to enjoy your money or share it with loved ones, what was the point anyway? To stockpile a big number in the bank or brokerage account and then leave it to people you did not have much time for when you were living?

"Making a living" is an interesting phrase in our culture. You don't make a living; you make money, but you have to live the "living" part. Now, I'll get off my soapbox. You get my point. Have a great career, and have a wonderful nonworking life, too! Don't live to work, and don't work to live. Live and work, and seek that elusive balance that makes for true achievement in life.

DREAM # 2: To Raise and Educate Your Children

Having children is not for everyone. Some of you have decided to not have them; others of you weren't able to. However, many of you have taken on the daunting and joyful task of raising a family. One of your prime concerns, besides offering your kids food, shelter, love, and opportunities for learning and pleasurable experiences as youngsters, may be to send your children to college. You dream of giving each child the best possible chance at a good life, and you have decided that the prime ticket to a good future and financial independence is a college degree—perhaps even a graduate or professional degree, too. It's no news to you that a college education today carries a big price tag! Plus, you have to afford the whole ticket price of raising a child from day one.

Here is where adult children have to face one stark reality—it's likely most of us cannot fund all our dreams at once—the dream house, the world travel, the expensive cars, the retirement savings, first-class wardrobes for toddlers, and the college fund. However, you can start prioritizing short-term and long-term dreams. You can see what needs money first and assess what you have to cut in some areas, where can you live with a more bare-bones budget, and where you cannot. Frankly, I know a lot of overindulged children with more clothes, toys, and technology gadgets than they need, or perhaps even want. Yesterday's $50 dress hangs in the closet, worn once. A $70 remote-driven gizmo lies forgotten on the living room floor.

By contrast, I have a colleague who makes a six-figure income and yet buys her kids' clothes at discount stores until the children reach middle school. She commented to me, "They don't need to look like they stepped off the designer runway at age seven. I'd rather send them to summer camp!" Children can read books from the library. They can give away a toy before they get a new one. They can even learn to comparison shop to get the best price on their possessions. Also, they can work at chores or, later, a part-time job to help pay their ways!

Private education in primary grades versus public schools is another choice for parents to consider. If you have a gifted child who is bored in the public programs and needs special advanced classes, you may want to make that a priority. Many public schools, however, offer a fine education. Or you could start private education at the middle school level. You need to plan ahead for this, when private middle and high schools nationwide now cost an average $8,000 to $15,000 per year per child.

It's important to include your child or children in the financial planning that involves them. While you may think they should have everything from piano to tap dancing lessons, from soccer league to architecture classes at the local art museum, you may discover that some of this doesn't really interest them at all. Furthermore, you can keep your children so busy with learning opportunities that they miss out on the social life with their peers.

We will take a closer look at the elements of college funding in Chapter 15, for some specific strategies will aid in paying that hefty price tag. But now, either before your kids are born, or as they're growing, you and your spouse (or ex-spouse) need to brainstorm on the priorities you each place on raising your children. What do you want to emphasize when putting out money for your kids? What experiences do you want them to have, what special kinds of learning, what travel, and how will you begin to train them to handle their own allowances? Finally, how will you keep some of your other dreams alive while you're spending the sums needed to raise and educate your children?

DREAM # 3: To Buy the Home of Your Dreams— and Pay Off the Mortgage before You Retire

Owning a house is a big part of the American Dream. In some major metropolitan areas, however, the price tag of home ownership seems through the roof. Young singles, even married couples today, often must save for a considerable number of years before buying their first home. This is one dream with which the older generation in your family may be able to help, if they have the financial resources to partially or fully fund the down payment. However, several words of caution: whichever parents offer the money, yours or your spouse's, make sure you and your partner agree to accept the money. I've seen one situation where the husband resented his wife's family stepping in with such generosity; he wanted to wait until he and his wife had earned the money for the down payment themselves. Another problem might result if you and your parents do not formalize the arrangement—whether it's an informal written agreement or an actual loan document.

If you're married and shopping for your first home, you and your spouse will soon learn from loan officers the exact price tag of real estate that you can afford. This will be based on your combined income and the amount of capital you have to put into the down payment. What often happens, though, as you get older, you want to "trade up," getting a bigger home as you add children to your family, or you may just want to move to a better neighborhood. Since your home is likely among the largest expenditures you make at any one time, the price you pay and the terms of the loan are going to significantly impact your discretionary spending. Regardless of whether your parents are able to help with the financing, talking with them might provide keen insight from their own experiences in home ownership. So don't fail to tap other family members for coaching on funding this big dream. They may help you decide just how much debt you can afford to take on given other dreams you're hoping to fund.

As you get closer to retirement, other home ownership issues arise. Is the house you're in the size you want, or now that your children have moved out, would you be better off to downsize to something smaller? If you do, you may want to pick a low-maintenance yard or move to a complex where the landscaping is handled through a homeowners association, in which case you have to figure in the cost of a monthly association fee to pay for this service.

Also, once retired, many homeowners want to get out from under a mortgage payment. If you've lived in the house for decades, you may have the mortgage paid off by the time you retire. If not, you have to decide if you want to take a chunk of your capital and pay off the balance. That depends on your retirement income, of course, and the opportunity cost you pay for not investing that money some other way—such as in investments that might be quite profitable. Ask yourself, do you really want to sit on so much equity in a home that is free and clear of debt—just to not have a mortgage payment? Some people do the opposite; they take out a second mortgage to have the equity available to help pay for their children's college educations or for home improvements to make the house more of the dream home they want to live in for the remainder of their years.

DREAM # 4: To Have Financial Independence So You Can Do What You Want to Do

Nothing about work is more stressful than to be stuck in a job or career situation that you hate. I have never experienced this directly, but I know many friends and clients who have been in such a situation. Having the financial ability to get out of a job that is not right for you is a kind of freedom I feel everyone should plan for and create. Maybe your business just is not cutting it; economically it is a strain and a drain on family resources. Yet you feel you cannot afford to close it down, because you need the modest income it does provide, or perhaps it employs family members. By contrast, you may work for someone else but are unhappy with the work, or you are living paycheck to paycheck, just covering your expenses, and you feel there is no time to look for something that pays better or is more to your liking. This is a catch-22: you cannot afford to stay, because you are miserable, and you cannot afford to leave, because you need the paycheck or others need it from you. Often this double-bind paralysis is something you can break, if you just determine that you're going to make the change. That is half the battle won.

The other half of funding a job transition is to make the time to explore new options. You need to brainstorm on what career path really would excite you or compensate you at the level you desire. The best way to do this is to pick a few industries that appeal to you and do informational interviews with people who work in those fields. This is the time to network with your many contacts to help you talk with the right people and find a job opening. In his tape series *Psychology of Achievement,* Brian Tracy has an excellent session on career goal-setting, outlining the specific steps to getting into a line of work you love with a company that better suits you. It's up to you to orchestrate the career move by continuing to search for the right situation and then act on the opportunity that you create, when you're finally offered a position.

If business ownership is your new career dream, then not only do you have to find the industry and type of business you want, you must decide if you want to try to buy a business that is already up and running, or if you want to build one from scratch. Both take capital, and you must have the resources to fund one to three years of living expenses before you start to make money.

That gets us back to the financial resources required to make a career change. From the minute you get out of school and start working, you must start to save and build an investment portfolio. In my seminars, I try to shock people with the time value of money advantage. If you put away $200 each month, earning 10 percent, for 40 years (from ages 25 to 65), you end up with $1.26 million. If you wait 20 years (until you're age 45) to start saving, you have to invest $1,660 per month to get to the same figure by age 65. Obviously, it's easier on the monthly budget to start saving and investing earlier than later. So, whatever you make, save something.

Let's say you want to buy a business and you need $30,000 to seed a loan to buy out the seller. If you're 45, and you'd been saving that $200 per month for the past 20 years and investing it at a 10 percent compounded growth rate, you would have over $150,000. You could afford to take that $30,000 and still have ample funds to continue investing for your retirement.

There are many types of investments, from stocks to bonds, mutual funds to annuities, and I'll explore these more fully in Chapter 13. Just remember, the earlier you begin to save and invest for the long-term horizon, the greater freedom you'll have to make a career change when you want—a move that could bring you expanded opportunities for professional growth, greater work satisfaction, personal development, and more prosperity.

DREAM # 5: To Travel and See the World

As a group, the baby boomers are probably the best traveled generation of all. Perhaps that's because many of us had an extended adolescence, backpacking through Europe after college, even living abroad before settling down to marry and raise a family. Regardless how we got the travel bug, many in this middle generation have an insatiable desire to see the world, to travel and explore, and since we got used to enjoying these pleasures early in life, we want to fund more of these dreams of adventure.

There are many creative ways to finance travel. We can use our expertise to finagle free cruises like my friend who does an art lecture series on cruise ships. Usually as the lecturer, your fare is paid plus that of a second traveler you invite along. Sometimes your job or profession may lend itself to working abroad for a time or taking business trips where you can tag on a few personal days for sightseeing with the bulk of the trip's total cost picked up by your company.

Even if you do pay the whole tab for your trips, there are less expensive ways to travel. Many organizations get group discounts on airfares and hotels if you go on their trip or even if you just pay their membership fee. You can accumulate frequent flyer miles on your personal and business credit cards and use them to pay for many expensive round-trip plane tickets. If you're willing to make last-minute plans—have bags packed, will travel—many group tours and cruise lines will call you when they get last-minute cancellations, telling you to be at the dock on a week's notice. You can try home exchanges, living in other people's dwellings during your holidays. One adventurous couple I know took a year's leave of absence from their jobs and sailed around the Pacific Rim in their own sailboat! Whether you love boating, backpacking, camping, or house swapping, there are wonderful ways to travel and see the world on a budget. I say, go for it! I'm doing the same myself!

DREAM # 6: To Enjoy Your Friends and Family

For members of the "sandwich generation," too often this is the dream that gets short shrift. Caught between raising children, attending to aging parents, and working at their careers, many can't find enough time for some of the simpler joys of life—leisure moments with family and friends, sports, and entertainment. Also, when dollars get tight, the temptation is to work more to earn the additional funds needed and to forego the "break" time that provides the revitalizing of family ties and the refreshment from being overly committed.

If you recognize yourself in these words, I want to tell you something very serious. People get sick when they don't take time to relax. The numbers of people in their 50s today who are experiencing heart disease, cancer, and other life-threatening diseases often come from the ranks of the overworked and underrelaxed. You cannot accomplish all your big dreams at once, and saving and investing for them takes time. Yet, every day you have the opportunity to relax a little, take few moments, call a friend, plan a lunch or breakfast, invite your mother to Sunday supper, or take a walk in the park. Many of these leisure dreams are the least expensive ones on your list. But they do take the other component of dreamfunding besides money—time.

Finding that time is up to you. I urge you to plan right now for the people you want to see and the fun you want to have this month. Make the calls, reserve the event tickets, put the dates in your calendar. And all the while you're focused on your work, in the back of your mind you know that your play days are committed, and you're going to get the leisure time you really want. It's a most freeing experience!

What's more, if you add up the cost of your leisure activities, I think you'll find that they are well within your budget. You may realize that most of the pleasures or leisure you seek—a visit over coffee with a friend, a family picnic in the park, a day at the beach—don't cost very much at all. Now if you're into racing Ferraris, well, that's a more expensive price tag you'll have to focus on earning!

DREAM # 7: To Be Able to Afford Life's Luxuries— Cars, Clothes, and More

One of the reasons we work so hard is to buy for ourselves and our families some of the creature comforts, even the luxuries, that we long to possess. For each of us, the wish list is different, but often they are the accessories our culture dictates a successful person "should" have. I have a good friend in his early 60s who grew up in the 1950s yearning for a sports car. Finally, a year ago, after inheriting some money, he went out and bought an $80,000 Porsche, one of his lifelong dreams. He even moved from a cold climate state to a warmer one, so he could drive the car year-round!

Many women love fine clothes and have walk-in wardrobe closets to accommodate their favorite designer tastes. Whatever your material wants might be, it's fun to plan for and fund these dreams. Sometimes, these items have to take a backseat on the bus to dream fulfillment, because more pressing needs take precedence, such as buying a bigger home to house your growing family, or helping a child go to graduate school.

What is interesting to note is that as we age, the dream list of material possessions changes. Where before we loved numerous clothes and fine furnishings, one day we decide we've had enough of those things, and now we'd rather pay for experiences, such as travel or taking a decorating certification course. Sometimes we have a lifelong passion to have a mountain home near our favorite ski resort, and then we decide that really we'd rather rent a condo during ski season and have a sailboat instead.

My point is that this is probably one of the more malleable dreams each of us has, and the items we covet may change as we change and grow. It still takes money to buy most of these material possessions, but the price tags will vary with our changing demands for satisfaction. Actually, I think it's great to be able to afford a lot of these kinds of things as early in life as they are achievable, because then we can get a lot of this out of our system, and move on to other, perhaps more substantial, dreamfunding, the kind that involves sharing with others rather than addressing primarily our own desires.

DREAM # 8: To Help Your Parents During Life's Transitions

Most adult children with whom I work find that it is important to be able to help their parents in their later years, should the need arise. We remember the sacrifices our mother and father made for us—forgoing some of their own desires to make sure that we had what we needed growing up, that we were educated, and that we got to do many things that they themselves never had the opportunity to do as youngsters. Remembering these gifts of love, we want to give back to the people who helped us grow up to be who we are today.

One problem doing this, however, is not always knowing when our parents might need our help, both emotionally and financially. Members of the senior generation tend to be proud, private people who value their independence. Still, some of them do not have enough money to support themselves as they live far longer than any of them expected.

Here is where you must take the initiative in intergenerational financial planning. While your parents may not say anything about their finances, there certainly are signs to notice. Do they decline invitations to join you out for dinner or to go on holidays when you ask? Do you notice they wear the same clothes year after year, never treating themselves to new ones? Do they skimp on going to doctors because they don't want to pay the out-of-pocket medical costs not covered by

Medicare? Do they ask you not to buy them gifts, because it may be hard for them to reciprocate?

It may not be an issue of too little money that has you worried. You may find that one of your parents is becoming less competent at handling everyday business matters such as paying bills or buying groceries. Perhaps he or she is suffering early stages of an illness that could compromise the couple's financial setup entirely, should the ill one need residential medical care. Or your mother or father may become socially isolated as the result of depression, and you live too far away to notice whether visitors or friends still check in on her or him.

Already burdened with your own busy life, you may be in for a difficult awakening when it starts to register that your parents truly need your help—whether it's to line up medical, housing, caregiving, or counseling assistance from afar, or whether you just need to visit them more often, helping with house repairs or shopping for their clothing, household, or food needs.

Perhaps the hardest part in all this is opening the dialogue with your parents to get them to admit they need some help. You simply start by asking, "Mom, Dad, are you able to manage your expenses right now on the income you have coming in?", "How are you doing with handling your banking and bill paying? Would you like me to help you, or find someone local here who could assist with all this paperwork?", "Are you fixing yourself meals every day, or would you like me to check with the Meals on Wheels group in your town?", "What are you finding difficult to do these days that I/we could help you with?", and "It may be too soon right now, but we'd like to know if you might consider moving nearer to one of us kids, before too long."

What you must always keep in mind is that one of the biggest components of depression among seniors, psychologists agree, is the loss of control over their lives. When people start to need to depend on others for their well-being and care, it takes an enormous emotional toll on their sense of security and happiness. As the adult child, it is important to do all you can to preserve the dignity and independence of the parents you love so much. Just as they taught you to be proud of who you became as you got older, they need to still feel pride in themselves in their later years. It is a delicate, diplomatic role you play as your parents age, and it can also be one of the most satisfying roles you will have the opportunity to fill—at last you can take care of them, as they took care of you.

DREAM # 9: To Teach Your Children to Be Financially Independent

A close friend of mine currently is suffering one of the worst nightmares of a parent; her 30-year-old son is still economically dependent on her and her ex-husband. He has an alcohol abuse problem and can't keep a job. He got into a bad marriage, which likely will end in divorce within the first year. He's almost nonfunctional. As parents, they wonder if he will ever be able to make it on his own. Somehow, he has not learned the skills of economic survival.

Frankly, handling such a problem child is tough. On the one hand, you want to be there for your children when they are down, when they need your emotional and financial support; still, each of us one day must grow up to be responsible for our own lives, our own success, our own support. At some point, a child must become autonomous, for ultimately we are on our own.

While your children may not suffer the difficulties of this young man, you can make plenty of mistakes in the money realm with your kids, if you're not cognizant of a few truths about the way children learn about money survival:

- Children watch what you do with money, and they either mimic you, or do the opposite, depending on how they like the results of your own economic behavior.
- If you don't let your children make mistakes with money, they won't learn the hard lessons of economic survival.
- Children must have some money to learn how to handle it wisely; i.e., you should give them an allowance from an early age.
- Treat your children on issues of money the way the real world will treat them; when they run out of allowance, don't give them more. Later in life, no one will give them a second paycheck when they run through the first.
- Teach them the rudiments of saving for the future, as well how to be a good shopper today. Teach them about sharing money, too.

- Expose your children to basic investments, the concept of retirement accounts, and tell them how you're planning for your own long-term financial security.
- Teach your children about credit, credit cards, and bankruptcy. Get them used to the idea of paying off credit cards monthly to avoid expensive interest payments. Talk to them about mortgages, car loans, and other forms of debt that they may encounter when they're on their own.
- A great way to get them saving is to match dollar for dollar the savings they put aside from their own allowance or earnings. And show them how money compounds with time (the time value of saving money).

Look for more ideas on educating children about money in Part Four.

DREAM # 10: To Be Financially Independent during Retirement

This is the one dream that seems so elusive to late-date savers of the boomer generation, many of whom have barely started saving for retirement. I know countless 40-year-old-plus adults who have poured all their money into their children's college savings accounts, or their homes, or their businesses. If you are in this group, it's not too late to create a retirement nest egg, but soon it will be! The time is now—you have to seriously face this commitment to secure your future financial independence.

This may sound harsh, but I strongly believe that you must start putting yourself first, before college funds, before assisting your parents, if you have no future savings for yourself. Worst case, your children can get scholarships and loans to pay for their higher educations, and your parents would have to rely on public assistance in their later years, if you or your siblings cannot foot their bills. Each generation, first and foremost, must secure its own future. Unless you're planning to inherit a lot from your parents, you had better take this dream very seriously, and now.

For many of you, the situation is not that dire; you're just a little behind schedule, and you need to play catch-up. If you haven't started participating in your company's 401(k) retirement plan, begin this month—whether the company matches your contributions or not. You cannot beat the tax-deferred compounding of retirement accounts such as a 401(k), IRA, or tax-deferred annuity. The way to fund this dream is to carve out something from every paycheck. If you're self-employed, you have to decide if selling your company eventually will provide your retirement nest egg, or if you'll need to establish a pension plan, profit-sharing plan, Simple IRA, or 401(k) for you and your employees. A financial planner specializing in company retirement programs can help you assess which plan is best for your particular business and group of employees.

Now, you don't want to start saving blindly; you need a game plan, a personalized financial plan that incorporates a lot of information about your financial picture. The only way to truly know if you're saving and investing enough to retire and project when you can afford to retire, is to create such a plan. Your financial planner will plug in the numbers and do a spreadsheet projection of your current income, expected increases in income, current expenses, expected future expenses (both ongoing and special big-ticket costs, such as car purchases, replacing the roof, etc.), and you'll be able to see how fast your assets in your taxable portfolio of investments and your tax-deferred retirement accounts will grow. You want to retire at age 60? Such a plan will help you know if you will have the money saved to do so.

Truthfully, you may be all too aware that you have lost valuable years already when saving fewer dollars per month would have let you retire much earlier. That's water under the bridge; you can start now. And you will be surprised, with a regular saving and investment program, how quickly your portfolio of retirement funds can grow. Once you've set aside enough money to live on its earnings, you'll need to revisit your investment plan to see that your specific investments provide the income you will need during retirement.

CHAPTER 4

The Dreams of Young Children

Too often adults dismiss the idea that children have dreams that are of great importance to them. Yet the smallest child can develop a passion that may be the seed of a great accomplishment. Even the youngest member of our family has the right to dream and dream big, and it's the job of parents and grandparents to be on the lookout for clues to each child's special hopes for today and the future. Indeed, as we shall see, many of these childhood dreams need to be funded, too, and they vie for a place in the intergenerational lineup of dreamfunding that takes the whole family's attention and determination to accomplish.

DREAM # 1: To Have a Big Enough Allowance

All children want some money of their own to buy the things they want. They want an allowance, regular money they can count on. Also, an allowance is an important learning tool for them. Having this money gives them opportunities to make good and bad choices, to learn from their mistakes, and to become part of the money world—a world they will have to know and understand before they grow up. Most parents agree that giving a child an allowance is a good idea. The question is, how much money is enough allowance?

This may vary according to the family's financial circumstances, but child development experts I consult with concur that even a few dollars can give a child as young as age 3 or 5 the means to begin their life as a consumer and saver. You might think this is too young, but in my view, the earlier kids get to manage some money, the better. What parent hasn't looked into the eyes of their child gazing up and pleading for money to buy another Power Ranger or doll when he or she has at least four others at home?

These are the moments when you know that a regular allowance makes sense. You can start the lessons about the hard truths of money: like, "You already have lots of Power Rangers or dolls. If you want this one, you'll have to pay for it yourself."

As a child gets older, one rule of thumb is to set the allowance at one dollar for every year of age. You can make that a weekly or bi-weekly allowance. It's best not to give very young children all the monthly allowance at once and expect them to know to save some and not spend it all the first week. As children become more mature, that delayed gratification lesson will be learned automatically, because in-variably kids will end up with more month than they have money. It helps for them to learn how that works early on in life!

You also can teach your children about buying things on sale and comparing prices, as you take them on shopping trips to the store. If your allowance budget is small, let your children read your grocery sales receipts and see what things cost; soon they'll realize that food alone is a big expense! This helps them understand why you cannot always give them more allowance; you have to buy for the whole family's needs.

One of the most important reasons to give children allowances is to give them a sense of control and power over their own lives. No matter how young they are, they know on some level that their very survival depends on you: you pay for the house, their clothes, their food, and that's one reason they feel so vulnerable and dependent on you. A little allowance gives them a bit of independence. As they get bigger, they'll want more and more independence from you, and you'll be glad they do!

DREAM # 2: To Buy the Latest "In" Thing

Kids tend to live in the moment, forgetting yesterday's joys and wanting to immerse themselves in today's new pleasures. That's par-ticularly true when it comes to toys. When your son wants that new techno-gizmo that looks to you amazingly like last year's model, you wonder why he can't enjoy such a toy for at least two years. Well, he's succumbing to the marketing mania that accosts adults and kids alike. Just as your three-year-old car suddenly isn't the "in" model anymore, children see ads on TV and displays on shelves of the newest toys that they simply must buy! I have a good friend whose son loves animals, and I bet he has at least 150 animals in his zoo set—new ones come out every year. The sale of collection items is big business with kids—from Star Wars characters to the plethora of Pokémon toys.

Here again are lessons in the making. You can teach your son about giving away a toy to a friend or church class before buying a new one. And you can add up the cost of all the Pokémon items your daughter now has and let her see how much she has spent already on this particular craze.

The same theory applies to clothes. Boys and girls today want to look "cool." We as parents want to encourage good grooming without giving in to peer fashion pressure at ridiculous designer prices. Perhaps the best way to support your children's dream of the perfect wardrobe is to start out helping them buy what you think looks good on them, but give them choices about color and the right to reject something they respond to with, "I hate it, Mom; I won't wear it!" As they get older, you can let them go shopping with friends ahead of time and then bring you back to choose which items to buy. You'll start to get the drift of what they like. If you hate it, compromise is in order.

That's not to say that children's dreams of buying new things should be squashed. It's perspective on quantity, quality, and price that as parents you want to share. One friend decided that her kids had so many toys; there simply wasn't shelf space for them all. She gave the kids a choice— they could pay out of their own money for a new bookcase to hold all their old toys, or they could give away the ones they didn't use any more, creating space for new toys that she would help them buy. They chose to give away four boxes of old toys so they could get something new.

These lessons seem small, but they're really big. You're trying to teach wise consumer shopping and a perspective on needs versus wants. Your children can learn to be selective about which "in" things they, or you, will buy.

DREAM # 3: To Get a Puppy

Having an animal to love and cherish is a dream of many children. I remember on my 12th birthday my parents gave me a birthday card that read, "This is good for one puppy of your choice." I was so excited that the next weekend we found a breeder of beagle pups in a nearby town and went and got one. His name was Tippy, and he became my very best friend. I talked to him, sang to him, and told him all my troubles. And on days when I was feeling a bit lonely, I would sneak him under the covers so he could spend the night sleeping in my bed. He gave me great comfort. I can still envision his face.

I think every child should have the chance to be a pet owner. Learning to take care of an animal and be responsible for it is one of life's great educational experiences. A child not only learns to love and nurture something outside of himself or herself, but also comes to understand the work and effort involved in feeding, grooming, and watching out for this furry companion. In a sense, children get to practice being in a relationship with another creature who needs their love and who loves them back. The pet also becomes a member of the entire family, and the cat or dog or canary provides a link of love that ties the family together.

You also can teach your child about saving an animal from harm by getting the pet from an animal shelter. You can explain about the terrible problem we have when other pet owners do not take care of their animals. You can show even small children how not to harm the animal by holding it too tightly or doing things that would hurt it. Pets provide excellent lessons in compassion and gentleness.

You can teach your child about animal health and how pets, like people, need regular medical checkups. You show how one must be alert to changes in their eating patterns or behavior—signs that something might be amiss. Children usually will take these responsibilities to heart and become concerned about their animals. They want to protect, love, and laugh and play with them.

That's one of the great joys for children with animals—pets do such funny things, like crawl into paper bags, chase their tails, and play the big hunter when they sight a hare or bird. These antics are a source of joy and fun for your child. Kids with pets laugh a lot and feel the pure enjoyment of companionship.

The death of a pet is also a great lesson for a child. Children need to know in advance that animals don't usually live as long as humans, and when an animal is very sick, sometimes we have to put them to sleep, so they won't be miserable and sick. I just lost one of my cats while writing this book. My little Abyssinian, Pumpkin, Mr. Personality as we called him, was a joyful, affectionate character in our family. When we experience the loss of any loved one, even an animal, we come to understand how much we loved them. This is an important concept for a child to learn early in life. It makes them more humane and more appreciative of the preciousness of life and those we love.

DREAM # 4: To Grow Up to Be . . .

What child has not watched in rapture or admiration some hero in a movie, or in real life, and said to his or her parent most seriously, "I want to be a doctor just like you when I grow up!" Or perhaps, your child sat spellbound at a play, then turned to you and said, "I'm going to become an actor when I grow up." These are pivotal moments or relationships in a child's life that may well define their destiny. As the parent, you must encourage their dreams of becoming something important.

Now I will mention one precaution: You may find that your children want to grow up to be something very different than what you had envisioned for them. You want your daughter to grow up and take over your business, or your son to become a lawyer. Well, those are *your* dreams. These early declarations of intent are *their* dreams. I hope you will support what they aspire to, and put your own hopes for them in second place.

You certainly want your child to have passion for something, and as we'll see in Chapter 6, passion is the first of the six Ps of funding your dreams. Tiny seeds of passion rest in children's hearts, minds, and souls. You must honor that. It may be the key to their future.

That's not to say that you cannot expose your children to many things as they grow up, hoping to influence them in certain directions. I have a close friend whose mother took her as a child to music lessons and musical concerts all during her school years. She grew to love music, majored in it in college, and still to this day enjoys playing in chamber music ensembles while she raises her own children. Now, she's treating her kids to many things to see what strikes a chord of interest with them—travel, sports, and, of course, music. One son seems to love the trumpet; the other, the piano. These family seeds of talent continue to blossom, generation to generation.

If your son or daughter does not talk about any special interests, you might want to draw him or her out with questions like, "Is there anything you think you might like to do when you get bigger? Is there someone whose work or life you admire? What do you like most to do when you have time to do whatever you want?" Sometimes this type of inquiry will start a revealing conversation, and your child will open up and share his or her dreams.

As your children grow, you'll want to try and connect the idea of something they love with someday working at a career. There is always that day of enlightenment when a child realizes, "Gee, I really do have to grow up and find something to do." My moment of reckoning came the day my sister went off to college. I was in eighth grade, and I thought suddenly, "Oh, I must leave home soon and make my way!" From that day forward I started noticing what I liked to do and what I didn't. And ultimately, I found my way to journalism, because I'd always loved to read *National Geographic* and *Life* and *Look* magazines and see what was going on in the world. Growing up to be something you have dreamed about and imagined has got to be one of the true blessings of moving from childhood to adulthood. Help your child do that as best you can.

DREAM # 5: To Be a Young Entrepreneur

Children have enormous creativity and an active imagination. From mud pies to sand castles, from artwork to chemistry experiments in the garage, youngsters seem compelled to make stuff and try their own way of doing things. By all means, encourage these entrepreneurial ventures of your kids. Who knows, you may have a Bill Gates or Mrs. Fields in the making! And they will learn a great deal about what works and what doesn't; what could be better?

For one thing, a child who shows initiative to start a small business— a lemonade stand for instance—may instinctively know she has a knack for concocting a better flavor or being great with people. Kids have an uncanny way of doing what they love to do, doing it the best way they know how, and being very determined to stick with it until the endeavor either succeeds or flops. They also show amazing resilience to start afresh and try something new. Would that more adults could do that!

You can help your children learn various facets of the business world by helping them come up with "business plans," "marketing plans," and evaluations of how it's going after they've been in business awhile. Kids get the idea of customer service pretty fast. If they set up their lemonade stand at the local park during the Saturday baseball game and they've priced the drinks too high, they learn really fast to cut the price to get sales.

You'd be amazed at the success of some of these childhood entre-preneurial efforts. I know of two sisters who gave some crocheted bar-rettes to their girlfriends for birthdays. The gifts were such a hit, they started making them for sale. Soon, the demand was so great, they en-listed their parents' and siblings' help on weekends to make more in-ventory. They had a nice little business going. Another boy created a chocolate chip cookie recipe that rivaled Famous Amos's, and soon his dad quit his job and helped the son expand the manufacturing and dis-tribution. Today the father and son still run the business—and this started when the boy was 11 years old!

Just as when working at part-time jobs, running small businesses, even for a short time, help a child get real-life experience that will pay off later on. They learn about how to market and sell their product or service; they learn how to price something to sell it. They learn about costs and overhead and net profits.

If your child starts making considerable money creating something, you may want to control how much of the money he or she gets to spend right now. You can introduce the idea of putting aside most of the money for something special—a computer, a car, even college.

Entrepreneurs are a special breed of people, and they start young knowing they want to work for themselves. They just want to be in charge. I cannot think of a better way for them and you to identify that there is a budding business owner in your family than to encourage their dream of creating something themselves and letting them run with it—with your guidance and assistance, of course!

DREAM # 6: To Be Financially Independent

Not every child is inclined to start his or her own lemonade stand. Yet, just as a young child needs an allowance, most kids eventually want to be able to earn some extra money, through chores or part-time jobs, so they can have more control over their economic situations. They want to know that they can exchange their efforts for money. This becomes more true as children resist their parents' control over what they buy and when. As a parent, you can encourage a child to try his or her skills at working for you or others, laying the groundwork for them to understand the relationship between effort and financial gain.

Some parents resist the idea of paying a child to perform everyday chores that they expect them to do anyway, such as cleaning up their room, putting their toys away, or doing their homework. Certainly there are tasks everyone must learn to do for themselves and for their families that come with the territory of being a member of the household. Still, there are the extra odd jobs that you can pay your child to do—raking leaves, taking items to the recycling center, or cleaning out the garage shelves and arranging the garden tools neatly on the tool rack. It's a good idea to make the jobs easily doable in a reasonable timeframe, so the child won't get discouraged and quit in the middle of the task. Payment for these chores would be on top of any normal allowance.

Part-time jobs have helped children earn extra money for many years: a newspaper route, baby-sitting, and mowing lawns. There is a fine balancing act between encouraging your child's work ethic and still leaving time for their play and homework. Once in middle school, there may be school-related jobs that give children a chance to earn money. Or perhaps you or your spouse could use some help at your company. My nephew, who was a computer whiz, helped my sister's employer program his entire computer system. He worked from age 14 through high school and saved a lot of money toward his own college fund.

If your child does go out into the community to work, it's important that you spend some time talking about what does comprise a good work ethic and the kind of responsibilities his or her employer will expect: showing up on time, working hard on the job, honesty in all dealings with customers and other employees, as well as getting along with others and showing a good attitude while working. You cannot assume that your child knows these things, and discussing them will help him or her get a good start out in the working world and demonstrate that there is a lot more to a job than just earning the money. You also may want some say in how your child spends the money he or she earns, especially if it is a substantial sum. Here is your chance to convey the concept of saving and investing as well as spending. These topics will be addressed in more detail in Part Four.

It's also important to tie in the idea of working with the idea that one day the child will be leaving home and have to become financially self-sufficient.

DREAM # 7: To Have a Car

By middle school, children seem pretty fixated on cars as the ultimate means of independence from their parents. The question is, what car will they end up driving, and who is the owner? Many parents keep an older car around and give it to their driving age son or daughter when they turn 16. I like this idea better than buying a new car for a teenager right off the bat. In wealthier families, I've seen children getting Jaguars or other fancy sports cars for their "sweet 16" gifts. That's a bit much, I guess. It's sort of like the $30,000 bat mitzvah. How do you follow that act? With a Mercedes when they graduate from college?

If left to buy a car with mostly their own money, most kids will opt for the cheapest thing on wheels that looks decent. It's money they have had to earn, and they do seem to appreciate the more modest price tag of a used car versus the hefty one of a new vehicle. If you truly want your children to know what it takes to own a car, you make them pay for their car insurance and gas and repairs, too. Now, that takes a good deal of saving. Since teenagers are expensive to insure, most parents pay the tab until at least age 25, when the rates drop. It's up to you what costs of car ownership you want your child to shoulder. Keep in mind, though, that this is the first big expense most children encounter. Some prefer to forgo having a car of their own and simply negotiate use of the family car or cars. This takes some preplanning and scheduling, and one thought is that you could tell your child that the family car you now have will become his or hers when the child leaves for college.

I think maintaining a car is good experience for a teenager. Your daughter as well as your son can learn to change a tire, change the oil and filter, and wash and wax the cars. A car is a good opportunity to get children to appreciate that an expensive possession needs care to keep it running and working well for them. Later on, they'll probably just take their cars into a shop for this kind of maintenance, but doing it first will remind them that these tasks must be done, if they're to enjoy the benefits of their "independence on wheels" for very long.

DREAM # 8: To Help Their Parents When Times Are Tough

Children are smart, and they know when you are having a difficult time financially. Even if you don't say much in front of them, they pick up the nuances of stress in the household. What's so fascinating is that most children, if they can figure out a way, want to help. They worry for you and with you, and, small as they are, they may do something so dear as to come offer you the 57 cents in their piggy bank, to help buy groceries, or offer to give you their allowance back.

Kids are pretty resilient and compassionate. They depend on you, and yes, they may be scared about what is happening. But children also have amazing confidence in you, perhaps more than you have in yourself when times are tough. They just know it's going to be all right. At least, they hope so.

Believe it or not, this can be a strange comfort to you, to have your children's understanding when you cannot afford for them what you would like. The daughter of one couple I knew was heading off to college the very year her parents had to file bankruptcy. She didn't complain, didn't whine about what she had to do to pay for college. She moved to Colorado, camped out for the summer, working at a bakery in a mountain resort, went to the college of her choice and applied for financial aid, and this young 19-year-old went to college all four years on her own earnings or student loans. About the time she graduated, her parents' fortunes turned around, and they helped her pay for graduate school. This year, she will graduate with a doctorate and become a college professor.

I've heard countless similar stories. Parents are simply blown away about how their kids will get in there and pitch in, working after school for lunch money, or cutting back on their wants lists. Sometimes, a more compassionate and giving kind of child grows up because of adversity on the financial front in their early years. So I advise against hiding financial problems from your children. Let them know what is going on. Tell them what you're doing to cut back, to earn more, to find a new job, whatever the immediate crisis might be. You can even ask for their ideas about how the family as a whole can spend less right now. They will gladly embrace the idea and try to help.

It wasn't that long ago when young teenagers had to drop out of high school to support their families during the Great Depression of the

1930s. Today, children, too, can adjust and realign their own dreams with what is going on in the household. Here is the perfect opportunity for intergenerational financial planning—where parents and children can join together to solve a common problem and grow stronger as a family because they're worked together to find answers to the current dilemma.

DREAM # 9: To Be the Best at Something

All (not most, all) great men and women started out with a dream to be the best at something—to create something new, to do something old better than had been done before, to do it faster, longer, with more impact, to make a bigger difference. Your child's dream to be the best at something is the tiny seed of greatness.

I think of a story I read about a young boy who suffered terrible injuries as a child from a fire. At physical therapy, he started to walk and then run, to strengthen his damaged legs. Ultimately, he became an award-winning athlete who went all the way to the Olympics and won a gold medal for distance running. That kind of triumph started out as his dream to be the best runner he could be.

You may have a budding Olympian in your family. Or, your child may not have aspirations to become a great athlete; she might dream of discovering the cure for cancer, or uncovering a lost city under the sea, or writing the most beautiful opera that ever thrilled an audience. Whatever her dream, you must encourage her, however unlikely the fulfillment of that dream might seem to you. It's in the dreaming of becoming the best at something that we as children gain confidence that we can accomplish great things. And confidence goes a long way to making sure that we do something very special with our lives.

Find out what your children feel passionate about. If they never mention wanting to become the best at something, then you can draw out ideas of things they might like to try. Since they may not know how to give themselves permission to dream big, your encouragement will be permission enough. You can expose them to stories of men and women who have achieved something significant, the heroes and heroines of history, or those who live today. When your children hear how someone that great was once a child living in poverty, or someone that nobody knew, then their imagination will make the leap that they, too, could do great things.

Once your child has a direction, then you may need to fund some of the exploration, training, and education that will let him or her blossom. This is where you may have to juggle the dreams and needs of yourselves and your parents and of all the children in the family to see that each child's opportunities to become great grow to fruition.

DREAM # 10: To Be Popular and Well Liked by Their Peers

I was in the women's locker room at my gym the other day and overheard two young girls talking about what to wear to the dance at their school that weekend. One of the girls sounded mortified because she "had nothing to wear." "What will Jimmy think, if I show up in that old dress?" she exclaimed. I smiled to myself, remembering how much my friends' opinions counted when I was their age. It's a universal phenomenon that children of all ages want to be liked and accepted by their peers.

How does this affect family finances? Plenty! Not only do you have to look cool (clothes, hair, makeup), but you have to act in a way that wins friends and influences people—even young people. This may involve taking dance lessons, being seen at the right events with the right crowd, and getting asked to attend sleep overs when the other kids get asked, etc. It's all marketing, and acquiring certain behaviors that derive from confidence and from having what you might call "street savvy"—knowing your way around people, circumstances, and things. Teenagers especially spend lots of time and dollars grooming themselves to be "hip" and to fit in. Adults do this plenty, too; we just forget that our children need to learn these social skills at an early age, as we did decades ago.

I bring this dream up because it has a lot to do with how children spend their time growing up. Just as important as gaining a grasp on academics and having desirable real-life experiences, children must learn myriad socialization skills to be accepted by other kids. Just watch a lone child at a dance or school event to know the heartache created if your child is the odd boy or odd girl out. So, as a parent, you can do a lot to create social circumstances that give your children opportunities to experience and experiment with getting along in groups, playing with others, participating in the activities that expose them to being part of the crowd and mixing in. The last thing you want is for your child to be antisocial, with few friends, starting out life on the outside looking in.

This really is an unstated dream of most children, and your willingness to help them get involved in the social life of their school, whether through volunteering at the school and observing the dynamics of your child with others, or by orchestrating get-togethers with other families and helping your child build a circle of solid friends, will help them fulfill this dream of belonging. Many opportunities come to the young person who has developed good social interactive skills, who can walk up to others and introduce himself or herself, who feels comfortable at social and business gatherings, who has learned to express his or her opinions and has learned, even at an early age, the value of networking with peers, and gaining their respect and friendship.

DREAMFUNDING STRATEGIES . . .

For the Three Generations

When planning intergenerational finances in your family, another law of dreamfunding becomes apparent:

DREAMFUNDING LAW 3

Money is not the goal. It's one means to the goal of funding your family dreams.

1. Set aside at least an hour for a meeting with all family members. One of you needs to facilitate the meeting and begin the dialogue about dreams. You can start talking about your dreams, the things you want to accomplish—some of these may be just your own personal goals, some may be goals you have for other family members

or the entire family. Next, invite the others to bring up dreams of
their own that they would like to make come true. One person
should take notes and write down each dream that is mentioned.
Now you have your list of family dreams. (See Draft Family Dream
List on page 60.)

2. Ask family members to help price each dream in terms of time and
   money. Time is how long the dream will need to be funded (e.g.,
   two-week vacation, four years of college, or six months to remodel
   the house). The money is your out-of-pocket cost for the dream.
   Some members of the family will want to participate; others won't
   or are too young to know how. A smaller group will need to desig-
   nate a time to do this; perhaps right then, while the others go about
   their daily business. Soon you'll have a list of dreams with actual
   dollar numbers behind them, and each person's name after the
   dream. You may have some dreams that appeal to more than one
   family member—put all applicable names next to these dreams.

3. At the next family meeting, have the list of dreams for everyone to
   read. It is also helpful if the individual dreams have a target completion date. Then you see how many dreams are targeted for the
   same year, even month. You also need to total up the amount of dollars needed for all the dreams as well as the time (weeks, months, or
   years) that each dream requires. (See Final Family Dream List, on
   page 61.)

4. Now comes the hard part. As a group, you have to study the list and
   see what dreams can be accomplished right now with the financial
   resources and time that the family as a whole can apply to dreamfunding. The grandparents may want to take everyone on a holiday
   vacation, and because of their age or health, this needs to happen
   this year. The adult children and grandparents will see what amounts
   each of them can pay for the trip, the adult children can check their
   work schedules and the kids' school vacation schedules, and the
   family can plan right then on which holiday to take the trip. You'll
   need to discuss the amount of money to spend on this dream and determine where the money will come from to pay for it.

5. Some of these dreams will have big price tags, such as your wish that your daughter go to a private college. You may have saved only half of the money, and she's only four years away from high school graduation. As a family, you'll see where else the money might come from: the grandparents may be able to help; your daughter may qualify for scholarships, school loans, and other forms of financial aid; she also may be able to contribute with her own earnings from summer jobs or a part-time job during high school. If you had never sat down and had this intergenerational meeting, you would not know the total resources you might have to fund this educational dream, which may well be a dream of all three generations.

6. Even young children in the family should have a say in the dreams that are important to them. It could be that your grandson wants a new skateboard; your granddaughter wants to go to a summer horseback riding camp. These dreams need to be looked at with as much earnest appraisal as the adults' dreams. The child may see that his or her dream cannot be fulfilled this year but will be possible next summer.

7. What is most important is to consider everyone's dreams and come up with a schedule and priority of dreams to be accomplished, trying to ensure that each family member gets at least one dream fulfilled before another one gets a second. This way everyone feels included in accomplishing dreams important to them, and they also take pride in helping their loved ones fulfill dreams, too.

   To get started, go only a few years in your dreamfunding time line. Next year, you'll do a longer list, going out at least a decade. As you get better at this, you can tackle a lifetime dream list for each family member. That gets very exciting, and gives you many more years to plan for the largest dreams that need funding, such as retirement and lifelong travel.

8. Once you have your Final Family Dream List for this year, you are ready to figure out financial strategies for funding each dream. The rest of this book is devoted to helping you do just that.

Draft Family Dream List

Dream	Family Member	Price Tag	Target Date
Family Vacation	Jane and Larry (Grandparents)	$7,000	December 2001
Addition on House	Edie and Jerry (Adult Children)	$15,000	Fall 2001
New Bicycle	Cary (Age 10)	$450	Next Month
Have 50th Anniversary Party	Jane and Larry	$2,500	November 2003
Go Back for Master's	Edie	$20,000	Begin Fall 2004
Tennis Clinic	Suzanne (Age 14)	$700	Summer 2002
New Car	Larry	$24,000	Spring 2004
Diving Trip with Guys	Jerry	$3,500	Summer 2003
Ski Trip with Jane and Larry	Cary and Suzanne	$2,800	Spring 2003
Golf Tournament in Hawaii	Jane and Larry	$5,500	Fall 2002
Send Suzanne to Private College	Edie and Jerry for Suzanne	$80,000	Begin Fall 2005
Horseback Riding Camp	Cary	$2,000	Summer 2002

Final Family Dream List

Dream	Family Member	Price Tag	Time	Target Date
Year 2001				
New Bicycle	Cary	$450	1 week	Next Month
Addition/House	Edie and Jerry	$15,000	6 months	Fall 2001
Family Vacation	Jane and Larry	$7,000	2 weeks	Dec/2001
Year 2002				
Tennis Clinic	Suzanne	$700	4 weeks	Summer 2002
Horseback Riding Camp	Cary	$2,000	8 weeks	Summer 2002
Golf Tournament in Hawaii	Jane and Larry	$3,500	1 week	Fall 2002
Year 2003				
Ski Trip with Jane and Larry	Cary and Suzanne	$2,800	1 week	Spring 2003
Diving Trip with Guys	Jerry	$3,500	2 weeks	Summer 2003
50th Anniversary Party	Jane and Larry	$2,500	2 weeks (prep)	November 2003
Year 2004				
New Car	Larry	$24,000	1 week (shop/buy)	Spring 2004
Go Back for Master's	Edie	$20,000	2 years	Begin Fall 2004
Year 2005				
Suzanne to Private College	Edie and Jerry for Suzanne	$80,000	4 years	Begin Fall 2005

CHAPTER 5

The Emotional Baggage of Money
Financial Power and Family Conflict

You probably do not know a family where money has not, at one time or another, caused enormous conflict and power struggles among family members. Money is an emotionally charged issue in our society, and the family unit can suffer as a result. Let's look at a number of families who have faced these kinds of challenges.

MILLIE AND DAVID: Job Loss Creates Resentment and Discord

David worked for one savings and loan for 22 years and then got laid off during consolidations in that industry. It so happened that his third daughter was having medical problems—a congenital heart defect that required multiple surgeries. The first one, when she was age nine, cost $100,000. Fortunately at that time David was still working, and the surgery was covered by his employer's group health insurance. Once laid off, however, David went months without finding work, and soon the 18-month COBRA extension on the health insurance ran out. His daughter now needed a second operation, and they had no health coverage because David's wife, Millie, was a stay-at-home mom with no health policy of her own that could cover the family.

David and Millie started having marital problems, which got worse the longer he was out of work. She blamed him for not getting a job, and she did not wish to go to work herself, for she felt this daughter needed special attention prior to and after the inevitable surgery. Finally, Millie decided she would have to get a job. She found a nonteaching position at their daughter's school, and so the family qualified for new health insurance. The daughter finally had the heart surgery, and she seems to be doing much better.

I'm not sure I can say the same for her parents. For five years David floundered in finding a new career, taking several jobs that didn't work out. The strain in the marriage was evident. At last he took training in real estate and landed a position in realty appraisal with the county in which they lived. He's stayed in this career ever since, but when I ask how he and his wife are getting along, he replies, "Can we talk about something else?"

While this family's apparent problem was discord over David's job loss, the troubles went much deeper. Part of the issue is that, of the two, Millie probably is as, or more, capable of earning good money as her husband. She's extremely bright and talented, having worked successfully as a store manager prior to marriage, but, frankly, she wanted her husband to be the major breadwinner so she could stay home and raise their three girls. She resented the upheaval his job loss created and lost respect for him and faith that he could ever support them again. Despite his obvious turnaround on the job scene, she harbors a lot of anger. He's sort of given up on thinking that the marriage will ever be harmonious again and isolates himself from the hurt of her rejection. Meanwhile, the oldest daughter, now a college graduate, is working and on her own. The second daughter will finish college in two years. The third, because of her chronic medical condition, will have special needs for education that are yet undetermined. Somehow, they've managed the financial aspects of their problems, but not the emotional ones.

If I were to guess at the emotional baggage in this family, I would look to several factors. David just didn't inherit the acute business savvy of his father, an extremely successful railroad tycoon. David needs the structure of a job; he's just not a "make-it-happen" kind of guy. Millie had worked first in politics as a researcher for a prominent politician and then turned to retail management, and she has business sense her husband lacks. On some level, she probably feels, and perhaps rightly so, that she's smarter and could be a lot more successful than David. On the other hand, Millie is representative of what I find true of many women of the baby boomer generation. While they want to have careers and the financial autonomy of making their own money, they are torn about leaving their children at home with other caregivers while they go out and bring home more bacon (money). They want the lifestyle of two incomes on one income, and that's where resentment starts to build.

Still, I want to address the trauma of job loss to more than this one particular family. Losing a job is one of the heaviest financial strains on any individual, and it adversely affects all family members. With more and more companies downsizing, rightsizing, and restructuring, many husbands and wives have faced this difficulty.

It's safe to say that workers have to plan on job interruptions, periods of income or cash flow cutoff, and the need to have savings to fall back on between periods of employment. I believe every individual, or family, needs to have at least six months' living expenses saved in liquid investments—a year's expenses would be better. If you've ever been out of work, you know it could take that long, or longer, to become fully employed again.

As for handling emotional baggage that puts strains on family relationships, at the end of our family stories, I'll give you some ideas to explore.

LILLIAN AND NOEL: Siblings at Odds

Lillian is a twice-divorced mother of grown children, a career woman in her mid-50s, whose financial situation is a far cry from that of her wealthy brother. The two siblings lost their parents when they were in their 20s: Lillian got $500,000 cash from her parent's estate; Noel got the family business, a manufacturing company that was worth considerably more than half a million at the time of their parents' deaths. Now, 30 years later, Lillian has a net worth of about $350,000; her brother's is $20 million. Is it any wonder that Lillian and her brother don't get along and that Lillian carries deep-seated resentment at their disparate lifestyles and opportunities for dream achievement?

Part of the emotional baggage these two live with is a patriarchal family history, in which the father left his business to his son. The message to Lillian was that business is a man's world. Still, she persisted on an independent path and has worked all her life, raising her two children mostly on her own. (Her brother did pay for the children's college educations, since their father could not afford to help, and it would have been a stretch for Lillian as well.) Lillian is an intelligent and capable woman, but she has had to juggle working full-time, being a single mom for much of the child-raising years, and coping with anxiety attacks, recurring depression, and the fear that riddles many successful, entrepreneurial women—the bag lady syndrome. She's terrified that she won't have enough money to live independently in her old age.

In addition, Lillian's parents educated the brother, not Lillian, in financial matters, and so she learned by the seat of her pants, often making costly mistakes. Also, she was raised in an affluent household, with the finest education, and she has striven to provide for her kids, from kindergarten on, the best that she could offer in exposure to the arts, travel, and comfortable surroundings. She has stretched to give them what she felt she should, and meanwhile has not saved enough for her own secure financial future. While Lillian's income from her marketing firm has been substantial by many people's standards (in excess of $100,000 most years), living in New York City has been expensive, and she kept focusing on what the kids needed this year and not on what she will need when she turns 80. In other words, she didn't save much for the future.

Lillian's brother, conversely, was taken by the hand by his father and schooled in the business. This, plus his innate business flair, helped turn a profitable business into a huge company that has made him rich.

Here we see inequitable training and legacy for two children of the same family that has had lifelong repercussions for both son and daughter, probably something neither parent imagined or would have wanted.

Fortunately, Lillian is about to change careers to derive a more substantial and stable income, so that she can save for her future and build on the small nest egg she has managed to set aside. Still, it's scary for a woman at her age to realize she's getting a late start in avoiding the nightmare she's envisioned, being old and living within meager means, or at least not nearly at the lifestyle she now has and wants to maintain. It's especially irritating when she feels that her future might have been much more assured, if her parents had left her half the business as well as some cash, 30 years ago.

CONNIE AND MATTHEW: His, Hers, But Not Our, Money

Connie and Matthew are like night and day when it comes to money. Connie grew up in a somewhat affluent household, where the parents shared their money freely with the kids and still do. Connie has received numerous gifts of cash, including about $100,000 from the sale of a family holding company. She's more of a live-for-today kind of spender, saving some, but not nearly as much as her frugal husband, who, in all fairness, isn't tight but then again isn't loose with money. His parents had known tough times; his mother once told him about not having enough food to eat when she was a child. So, Matthew grew up conscious of the need to save for a rainy day, and his belief is that if his parents could have rainy days, so could he.

When they got married, Matthew felt entitled to have some say in Connie's money habits, and he proceeded to try first to influence, then to control, what he saw as Connie's spendthrift patterns of money behavior and an imprudent lack of foresight about the couple's long-term future. The fights over money escalated in the early years of marriage and then reached a new level when Connie started going underground about her money ways: hiding clothes in the car until Matthew was in bed, readjusting the price of things when she thought the price tag wouldn't suit Matthew's view of appropriate costs for certain things, and building up credit card balances that later caused Matthew to explode in anger. The last straw was when Connie took out a business loan from her mother and only told Matthew after the fact.

He threatened divorce, and at that point, Connie was all for it herself. A medical crisis in the family interfered with separation plans, and when the dust settled the couple, who do love each other, decided to stay together and work on changing the dynamic of money, power, and control that had caused havoc between them.

Money is an emotionally charged element in families. How you use it can make or break relationships. This brings us to the next law of dreamfunding:

DREAMFUNDING LAW 4

The use of money as power and control in families is emotionally and spiritually destructive. It's a dream-killer.

You walk a fine line between influencing other family members, steering them to encounter new experiences or have certain things that you think will benefit them, and manipulating them with money in ways that are destructive or disempowering. One good way to measure this difference is to imagine how you would feel if someone else held financial power over you and did to you what you're considering doing to or for your child or spouse. If it doesn't feel good, don't do it!

Psychologists I interviewed agreed that some of the worst ways of handling money in families take away an individual's sense of independence, initiative, or self-esteem. Another destructive pattern is to make a person feel that his or her value is equated to the money that he or she earns, has, or controls. Therefore, another dreamfunding law is in order:

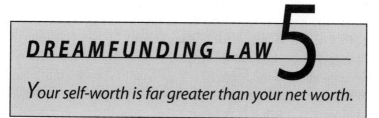

DREAMFUNDING LAW 5

Your self-worth is far greater than your net worth.

This fundamental truth escapes many people, young and old. How many individuals do you know who have spent all their adult lives driven to succeed financially, compelled to earn enough money so that some day they'll feel important, worthwhile, successful? Our culture in particular flaunts financial wealth as the ultimate destination of a life well lived. We define wealth in terms of money, usually. We even ask, "How much is he or she worth?"

In other cultures, however, the term *wealth* is often used much more broadly. I was struck by something recently when I visited the poor (in monetary terms) country of Nepal. While trekking through small villages in the Himalayas, I saw poverty and richness in the same home—poverty in that many children had no shoes, and furnishings were scant. Yet the happiness of these people, who clearly live without much of the material wealth sought by Westerners, was so evident in their smiles, laughter, love of family, and comraderie within their communities. They easily shared what they had, and I felt humbled by the wisdom about life I saw in their eyes, eyes that glinted with laughter and an abundant sense of contentedness.

I ask you to think about the richness in your life and especially about the many talents, skills, and loving thoughts you carry within you, and how important you are to those people who love you, and I think if you tally these nonmaterial treasures, you will find yourself very rich indeed. You, alone, without earnings or any material trappings, are worth a great deal. Stripped of all that money can buy, your self-worth has no price tag. Indeed, it is priceless to you, to your family, and to all your loved ones.

THE MONEY DYNAMIC INVENTORY

Perhaps you've seen similarities of family money dynamics between your family and those you've read about here. If not, you've certainly had occasion to notice that such dynamics do occur and to consider whether you feel good about them. To make this more concrete, I invite you to take the following Family Money Dynamic Inventory and get to the heart of this matter now. If you start to feel uneasy or unhappy about some behaviors, I ask you to suspend those feelings for just a moment and complete the survey. We'll get back to those feelings before you finish this chapter.

Family Money Dynamic Inventory

Answer the following questions about the money dynamic in your family of origin and in the family you are part of today:

Family of Origin

1. Reread the golden rules of money you listed in the Chapter 1 dream strategies. Now ask yourself which were the positive lessons or rules you learned about money in your family as you were growing up. What negative lessons did you learn? What did your parents try to teach you about your own self-worth? Did they say you would only be successful in life if you made a lot of money?

Family Money Dynamic Inventory
(continued)

2. Who held the purse strings in you family? Your father? Your mother? Both? Did you have access to much money as a child? Did you parents use money to control you? If so, how? And how did you feel about it then and now?

3. What have been the biggest areas of conflict around money between you and your parents, and you and your siblings? Did your parents treat all the kids fairly, evenly? If not, who got more, and why? Was it you? Or your brother or sister?

4. What is the worst experience you remember about money in your family of origin? How has that experience affected how you deal with money today?

5. What is the most positive money experience you can remember? How has that affected how you handle money?

6. What did you worry about most in terms of money as you were growing up? What person in your family, or what event, caused you to have this worry?

7. Did anyone in your family use money to control you or other family members? How did that person exert this control? What was the threat behind that control issue? What was that person trying to accomplish?

8. Were there secrets around money in your home? Who kept the secrets? Did everyone have secrets? Why do you think that was true in your family?

9. Were there open discussions about money issues and problems in your family? Were they argumentative, or was there a method of solving family money disagreements?

10. Who was great at handling money in your family? Who was not so good at it? What lessons did you learn from each of these "teachers"?

Family Money Dynamic Inventory
(continued)

Your Family Today

1. If you control the purse strings in your own family, what lessons do you think you are imparting to those who depend on you financially? What is the money dynamic you've set in motion with your family members?

2. What are the golden rules of money you want your spouse or children to live by today and into the future? Do you have some rules today that you'd like to change, or are you happy with the ones you have?

3. If you are the family "controller," imagine how it would feel to be on the receiving end of that control of money. Do you like how it feels?

4. If someone else (e.g., your spouse) controls the money for the most part, what do you like, or dislike, about the money rules you have to live by? Which ones would you keep? Which ones would you change?

5. If you and your spouse share the money control, what agreements do you have about earning, spending, saving, and investing the income that comes into the household? Do you see eye to eye on these matters? If not, where is the discord? Could you sit down with your spouse and talk about making some changes?

6. Are there secrets around money in your household? What are they? Who keeps these secrets?

7. What problems do you or anyone in your family have around money? Does someone spend too much? Is anyone too stingy? Is anyone clueless about how to handle money wisely? What could you teach them about managing finances?

8. What money dynamic do you think runs your family? What theme do you see around money issues? Is it one you like? What would you change about that dynamic if you could?

Family Money Dynamic Inventory
(continued)

9. Are you teaching your children financial responsibility? Do you practice it yourself? Does your spouse?

10. How do you feel about helping outside family members with money problems (sharing with your parents or siblings, or those of your spouse)? Do you and your spouse agree about this? As your parents age, what will you do if they run into money problems? If your children grow up and have financial troubles as adults, have you thought about whether you will step in to assist them? Do you and your spouse agree about these matters?

11. If you wanted to teach your children the most important lessons you've learned about how best to handle money in a family, what would you teach them? And are you practicing those good money dynamics yourself?

After taking this inventory, how do you feel? Discouraged? Encouraged? Did you gain some insights on changes you'd like to make in your own family money dynamic? Most people, by looking back to their family history and analyzing their current money patterns, find there are some steps to take to improve the workings of money among the generations. I hope you've discovered a few yourself.

I think a healthy money dynamic in a family empowers each generation to be responsible to themselves and to the other members of the family in making wise choices around money. The elders need to pass on their experience in what does and does not work, and each person needs to assess the mistakes their parents may have made and the ones they may be making themselves. It always helps to ask yourself, "Is the way I've been handling money with my family accomplishing what I want? Is it helping everyone fund our life dreams?" If not, ask why not, and what could you change to bring about more dreamfunding for everyone. As for those of you who are parents, trying to teach the young, it's important to realize that every individual must eventually learn to be fiscally responsible. In Part Four, we'll look at how you can do that with children of all ages, and the sooner you can start to educate your children about handling money in a responsible way, the better chance your kids have of becoming financially independent and prosperous adults.

So, we've come to one of the most important dreamfunding laws—one that, in my opinion, describes the ideal family money dynamic:

DREAMFUNDING LAW 6

With your family financial resources, help the old, train the young, and take care of your own future.

DREAMFUNDING STRATEGIES . . .

1. If you have not already, take the Family Money Dynamic Inventory featured in this chapter and make a list of five main issues that cause problems in your family of origin around money. Make another list of the five issues in your current family that don't serve you well. In each family unit, do the issues have a theme?

2. Review the two themes you discovered, one for your family of origin and one for your current family—these are one-line descriptions of the money dynamics that were, and are, at work in these two family units. Do you like the themes you discovered? If so, what's good about them? What's bad about them? Are the two themes the same; in other words, have you duplicated the money dynamic of your family of origin in your own family? What would you change about the dynamic you have going right now?

3. If you haven't done so yet, call your first family dreamfunding strategy meeting, and have everyone make their lists of complaints

and concerns. Look for the themes that reveal themselves as part of the family money dynamic. Get agreement on what needs to be changed. Ask everyone to start thinking about the golden rules of money they would like the entire family to live by.

4. Have your second family meeting to hammer out the golden rules of money that all can agree on. Type the list and place it prominently where everyone can see it. It's a good idea to have a dream-funding bulletin board, and make this the first list on the board.

5. Now you're ready to draft the Family Dream List for this year. If you have not met to create this list, now is a good time to do it. Follow the ideas in Chapter 4 about how to come up with this year's Final Family Dream List. Put it on your dreamfunding bulletin board for all to see.

6. To help every family member feel empowered around money, find out how each person can have his or her own money. Kids, too, need to have an allowance (see Chapter 17 for ideas on how much allowance). See which adults need some brainstorming on securing their own sense of financial autonomy. Maybe your nonworking spouse needs to have a specific budget allocation she controls, and that money is given to her at the beginning of each month. Perhaps your older parents need a financial plan to make sure they are spending their savings at a rate that will make it last their lifetime. Perhaps you and your husband need to carve out more investment money from your monthly earnings to save more for retirement.

7. For those of you who are married, take a whole morning one weekend and air all the gripes you each have about your shared money relationship. Each of you should have time to say all you want to say. Look for the problem areas and work to resolve them. You might want to make up your couple's golden rules of money of how you want to deal with each other on money issues, separate from the family's total list of rules. Notice the areas of ongoing conflict and ask each other what each of you can do to create harmony on these topics. Set aside one weekend morning or afternoon each month to bring up anything new or to review your past agree-

ments. I like to call it a couple's money checkup appointment. The more often you do this, the more of a habit open communication about money will become. I've found couples that do this often resolve long-standing money gripes that were undermining their mutual trust and respect.

8. Set up a kid's money training session—again on a weekend morning or afternoon. Ask the children first what they'd like to learn about money. As the parents, you can come up with your own lesson topics for discussion. Make hands-on experience part of the learning—trips to the market can be used to learn about price comparisons or discounts; a trip to the nearest bank or stock exchange can teach your kids about savings and investments. Think about getting your children some books about money that are written for kids.

9. Meet with your parents to discuss any particular money concerns they have and any you might have about how they handle money with your own kids, their grandchildren.

10. If one family member has a real spending or debting problem, have a one-on-one meeting with that person. Try to get the person to talk about and acknowledge the problem. Show how it's affecting the whole family. See what money behavior changes that person is willing to make; get counseling if necessary, especially if the issue is debt-related. The counseling could be psychological, or even involve a debt consolidation team to work through paying off the debt.

11. Set a date for your ongoing intergenerational family meeting, where next year's Family Dream List will be addressed. Put it on your calendar and make reminder calls to your parents, tell your kids, and tell your spouse that this red-letter day must not be skipped by anyone. After all, you're hoping they each get to have new dreams checked off this year's list, because they got funded, and to make room for more dreams of theirs to put on next year's Family Dream List.

CHAPTER 6

The Six Ps of Funding Your Dreams

Now that we've defined terms like intergenerational financial planning and dreamfunding and explored just some of the dreams of the three generations—grandparents, parents, and children——it's time to look at the definitive steps of dreamfunding, which I call the six Ps of funding your dreams.

I mentioned before that dreamfunding involves finding the time and money you need to make your dreams a reality. I also said that funding the expense of dream fulfillment is a simple but intricate journey through earning, spending, saving, and investing your money. But let's look more specifically at the steps you must take to get from your Final Family Dream List to the achievement of your very important dreams. These steps help you find the way from the idea to the money and time needed to bring the idea into reality—the steps guide your way in turning each dream into a dream come true.

Following are the six Ps of funding your dreams:

1. Passion
2. Permission
3. Price tags
4. Priorities
5. Planning
6. Prosperity

We'll take a specific dream and lead you through each of the six Ps. First, though, let's describe each step.

PASSION

Passion motivates you to become someone you want to be, to do something you yearn to do, to get something you long to have. You probably have lots of passions, if you think about it. You have passionate interests that you want to pursue, whether they are exotic travel, sailing, golfing, opera, or research on Celtic history. You may want to climb Mount Everest, or build your own airplane, or become an astronaut, or live in a log cabin in the mountains. Often it takes money to participate in these recreational, professional, or lifestyle activities—a three-week African safari takes a fair bit of cash. So does a degree in aeronautical engineering, or buying your own sailboat.

Your dreams may also take time—time to earn the funds, time to do the activity, time away from working to pursue your interest fully. So, as you're thinking about your passions, you'll want to consider the financial and time resources you will need to pursue them.

Quite simply, passion is the *fun* part of dreamfunding—it's where you discover your dreams. At first you might think your dreams are too far-fetched, too expensive, too time-consuming, or just plain outrageously impossible to achieve. That's where I want to stop before you talk yourself out of your dream. No dream that really matters to you is too big or small or too far out into the future to consider attempting. Now, it's true, as you go through the years, some dreams lose their importance or appeal, and you shed them for other dreams. That's normal "sifting."

You've heard that saying, "Life is not a dress rehearsal." It's true. Even if you believe in multiple lifetimes, this time round you only get one shot at your dreams. You have to discover them now, and sooner than later is better. Also, your happiness depends on knowing what your passions—your goals—really are, and finding some way to pursue them. (Remember, goals are dreams with a deadline.) I cannot imagine that you will be truly happy in your life if you have not discovered what thrills you, excites you, gives you energy, demands your attention, and makes you feel marvelous in its pursuit. So, discover your passions; they define your dreams. That's your first, and probably the most important, step in leading a life of purpose.

DREAMFUNDING LAW 7

*F*und your own greatest dreams to lead a life
of purpose.

PERMISSION

While most of us can discover our passions, not all of us give ourselves permission to pursue these dreams. Accept this now: You do have the right to go after what you want in life. This is the "I *can*" part of dreamfunding. You are a multifaceted person who deserves to experience all the important goals of your life. Give yourself permission to go for your dreams. Block out the doubts, the shoulds, the psychological governors that put brakes on dream achievement. Dream now, dream big, and dream out into your future for your entire life span of possibilities.

You may think you need other people's permission to go after what you desire. Usually that's not true. You may want to get some agreement about pursuing your specific passion. If you're the one with the dream of that large log cabin in the mountain, and you're married, you'll likely want your partner to "buy into" your dream. That does not mean that if he or she says no, that's the end of the dream. Persistence is one of the hallmarks of dream achievers. If you get a negative reaction to one of your dreams, it's likely you have not enrolled the rest of your family in why this is so important to you. Perhaps you'll end up adjusting your dream a bit and buy a family vacation home in the mountains but stay living where you are.

This brings us to another point about permission. If you start to doubt whether you should pursue your passion, perhaps you should re-examine the dream. Ask yourself what aspect of the dream really stimulates you. With the log-cabin dream, maybe you love pine trees and mountain air; maybe you like the visual beauty of the mountains, or they make you feel closer to God. Figure out what this particular dream really does for you—what's the juice that nourishes you about that dream? That's what you have to remind yourself about and convey to those whose cooperation, assistance, and agreement you'd like in helping fund that dream. After you have a clearer resolve about why this dream is so important to you, you'll have more conviction that you really must make that dream come true—you'll shake off your doubts and steadily work your course through the remaining steps of dreamfunding.

Also, many people choose the dream over the relationship when their spouse, or parent, or sibling refuse to go along with the dream. That's a pretty big decision to make, but you could find yourself facing this dilemma. If you come up against such a major choice, you'll have to do some soul-searching to find out which is more important to you— the dream or the relationship, at least the relationship as it now stands. Sometimes, the other person, seeing you take a stand for your dream, will come around. However, you cannot count on that, so be sure that the dreams you stand for are the dreams you truly cannot live without.

PRICE TAGS

Here comes the reality check on dreamfunding, the *dollars and cents* and the *time* part. How much money can you afford to spend on funding your particular dreams? What will each dream cost in dollars and cents, and what kind of time do you need to achieve the dream?

Most dreams do have price tags—money you must have to purchase the shiny red sports car, expand your business, or pay for your daughter's big wedding. You either need money to pay for something, or you need time to do something—time you're free to go on your honeymoon to Australia or study for that second professional certification.

That's why I asked you to estimate the money and the time needed for each family member's dreams on the Final Family Dream List. Those are the price tags you'll have to fund in the remaining steps of funding your dreams.

Here is where a lot of people stop and give up on their dreams. They look at the price tags, mostly the monetary ones, and they cannot see how they'll ever come up with the money. Or they put aside their own dreams in order to fund someone else's dream—their parent or child. Certainly this intergenerational juggling of dreams is precisely what I suggest helps families fund more dreams of more individuals. So, postponing a dream does not mean giving it up altogether. And no one member of the family should get the hog's share of dream fulfillment, leaving the others shortchanged on funding their dreams. As I said before, it's a cooperative effort of assessing time frames, health issues, scheduling conflicts, and out and out negotiation so that you, too, get your dreams funded.

Perhaps you live far away from most of your family, yet you have friends you'd like to brainstorm with on pricing your dreams and assessing how to schedule their achievement. You can have your own dream team of colleagues or friends who share this process of the six Ps with you. Their ideas and encouragement will help you get over the permission part and even keep you from giving up when the price tags seem too high.

PRIORITIES

Priorities are the *choice* part of funding your dreams. More than likely, you cannot fund all of your dreams at once. So you have to make choices, set practical priorities, and decide which dreams to fulfill first. The best way to do this is to make yourself an ABC Dream List—it is your own Final Dream List that you then give to your family or dream team group to review. Obviously, the A dreams are your top priorities, the ones you most want first; the Bs are the second tier of dreams; the Cs are the ones you are willing to postpone for awhile.

I sometimes suggest that people make a Business and a Personal Final Dream List, since these arenas of life often involve different people. Both lists are important if you are working outside the home, but the time frames for business and family dreams may require different schedules. Indeed, your time price tags will have to be juggled between these two lists, for the days and weeks you need for your work or business are time not spent with your family, and vice versa. As for the financial price tags, the budget for professional dreams may not all come from your own pocket if you work for someone else; if you're self-employed, the family does have a vested interest in money that goes into your business versus into the pursuit of family dreams.

Let's get more specific now with your target dates and time frames (time price tags) as you make your Final Dream Lists. You must set actual deadlines for dream fulfillment. On your Personal Final Dream List you might write down that this spring you'll remodel the kitchen (allow two months from start to finish); in 2 years you'll take your family to Costa Rica on vacation (a three-week trip); in 5 years your son goes to college (4 years of education); in 20 years you'll sell the business and retire (it will take that 20 years to grow the business and get the price you want). Remember to list each financial price tag next to the dream: remodel, $12,000; Costa Rica vacation, $15,000; college, $75,000; sale price of business, $1 million.

Only by being specific can you truly get your mind to working on the next strategic steps of dreamfunding. Vague dreams have a way of never coming to fruition. Prioritized lists with target dates, time frames, and monies required put data in your brain to start cogitating and analyzing. That leads us to the next step in dream achievement.

PLANNING

Planning is the *commitment* part of dreamfunding. This step makes or breaks your chances for dream fulfillment. Without planning, the dreams simply won't have a chance of getting funded. You have to figure out where the money will come from and plan how to accumulate the price tag by the target date. If your son goes to college in 5 years and you need $20,000 for his freshman year, that means you have to start saving $260 per month at 10 percent return for the 5 years. If your business can be sold for two and a half times the annual revenues, then you need annual net income of $400,000 per year to sell the company for $1 million in 20 years.

This basic number-crunching is how you begin to plan for accumulating the price tags and determine what funding strategies will help you achieve your dreams by the target dates. If you're an entrepreneur working on business goals, look at your current cash flow, expected revenues this year, what salary and retirement benefits you want for yourself and your staff, what kind of disability and health insurance you'll want to provide, etc.

For your personal dreams, assess your current assets, liabilities, net worth, income needs now and in retirement, estate issues, tax aspects, and insurance needs, and see what your financial picture looks like today. How far are you from funding your short-term, intermediate-term, and long-term dreams? Perhaps you'll want to use some financial planning software or consult with a personal financial advisor to do

projections on how to reach your target funding goals for each particular dream by its deadline.

The bottom line is that either on your own, or with professional
help, you must create both business and personal funding strategies;
then it's up to you to commit yourself to the day-to-day, dream-by-
dream earning, spending, saving, and investing needed for success.
That commitment separates the achievers from those who will fall short
of their making their dreams come true.

PROSPERITY

The dream achievers, then, arrive at the sixth P, prosperity. This is
the *fulfillment* part of funding your dreams. It's getting what you want,
both in terms of financial success and personal satisfaction—what I've
referred to as the *emotional capital* of dream achievement, the fulfillment of the promise of all you are and all you can become, have, or do.
It's the wealth that we talked about earlier, which is greater than your
net worth statement or your accumulation of possessions. It is the deep,
abiding pleasure of keeping your eye on a dream and moving step by
step to make that dream a reality. Such satisfaction brings a kind of
peace of mind, a joy, that begs description but fills the heart. When
you've completed the first five Ps of funding your dreams, you will
achieve the sixth. Although there are no guarantees, you have put in the
time, energy, and commitment to see your dreams fulfilled. You have
methodically taken the practical steps to create the funding strategy.
And when your dream does become a reality, there is no greater satisfaction than knowing you have fulfilled the promise of prosperity.

I mentioned before that dream achievement is not all about ourselves, but also the dreams we have for our loved ones and the ones
they have for themselves. Sometimes the feeling of richness or prosperity grows exponentially when it derives from the fulfillment of the
dreams of those we cherish, for their happiness is central to our own.
How do you feel when all of your son's years of training, commitment,
and countless hours of playing on his high school basketball team culminate in his being named most valuable player and receiving a full
college scholarship? Or when your mother steps down the cruise ship
gangplank onto the turf of her ancestral home, fulfilling a lifelong

dream to see Ireland? These moments no doubt fill you with joy, satisfaction, and happiness for their dream achievement.

One of my colleagues describes money as energy—it flows in that continuum of earning, spending, saving, and investing that I mentioned before. To me, the magic of Prosperity (dream fulfillment) is getting to enjoy all aspects of that continuum, including spending some of the money your success has brought. Remember what I described in dream-funding law # 3—money is not your end goal; dream achievement is the goal; money is just the funding strategy in that achievement. The six Ps lead you down the satisfying path of funding your, and your family's, lifetime dreams. Your destination on this pathway is to be fulfilled in your life and reward yourself with the enriching experience of pursuing your passions, your greatest dreams—and thereby living a life of purpose.

Let's see how the six Ps can work to help one person achieve a particularly outrageous dream. I call it outrageous because it is far-reaching, profound, and fraught with difficulties and roadblocks to dream achievement.

Still, it is a possible dream. If this woman can fulfill this dream, you can fulfill any dream that you give like commitment and energy to achieving.

CATHY: Applying the Six Ps

Cathy is a very determined woman. Her friends tell her she's crazy; her mother worries she's tempting fate to start so late. Even her husband has grave misgivings about her dream. Childless through infertility and a breast cancer survivor, Cathy is determined to adopt two children in the next three years. At 53, she's past the age most adoption agencies would consider her. Many people would say she has no right to pursue this dream, given that she might get a recurrence of the cancer. She has a good life with her husband, works hard at her career in Web site design, fills her time with travel, friendships, and intellectual pursuits. So, why would a woman this age, with so much else to do, want to take on starting a family in midlife?

The answer is quite simple. Motherhood is her *passion*. Since she was 30 years old, Cathy has wanted to be a mom. She has ached for it, dreamed of it, and suffered emotionally and physically for the lack of it. There is a space in her heart that is empty, and she knows that only motherhood will fill that hole.

If infertility and cancer were not discouraging enough, Cathy faces more obstacles than most women in creating her family. Her husband, Marvin, no longer supports her dream. Although he agreed to have children when they got married, a series of career reversals, and probably a change of mind, led Marvin to decide some years ago that children should no longer be part of their family picture. "Cathy, it's passed us by," he said, "and I just don't want to do it anymore." Cathy was devastated. To make matters worse, shortly after delivering that bombshell, Marvin's business failed and he became worried about finances. "Kids cost a mint, Cathy; we can't afford them even if we wanted them," he said. "I don't want to hear about it anymore." When nothing solid developed for his career in their hometown, Marvin decided they should move out of state because there was an opportunity he could pursue. Cathy went along with the move, wondering if she would ever fulfill her dream of becoming a parent.

Then, a year ago, Cathy was diagnosed with cancer. Fortunately, it was caught early, and her prognosis for a full life span is good. Facing this crisis, however, held a silver lining in the cloud—for Cathy took a hard look at her life, her marriage, and her dreams. She went on an extended retreat by herself to make some important decisions. During this hiatus from work and her marriage, she gave herself *permission* to do what she'd always wanted to do—build her family. She decided she would never be truly happy unless she did, and she determined that there had to be a way for her to become a mother. She decided to create an international family through adoption—giving a home to a child or children who otherwise might not have had such an opportunity for a loving home. She also knew the age requirements for some foreign adoptions would not be as strict as for domestic adoptions.

Shortly after her epiphany, Cathy came to me for financial counseling. She said she wanted me to help her with two financial strategies—one if she stayed married; one if she didn't. Marvin's financial circumstances had improved, and now she felt the financial excuse no longer rang true. His personal feelings about being a father at this late age remained an obstacle. After several meetings and doing some income/expense projections, I was able to give Cathy what she needed— the dollar-and-cents data showing that she could afford to pursue her dream, either with Marvin or on her own. She decided to make some changes in her business practices to increase her own income, and she carefully estimated the costs of adoption, the early years of child raising, and her own financial needs. In other words, she discovered the *financial price tags* of motherhood in her particular case.

Next, she thought about target deadlines to start her family. She decided to discuss her dream with Marvin and see if he wanted to participate in this very important adventure—one that would give her immense fulfillment. She went into counseling to get emotional support for this showdown. She set Christmas of that year (2000) to get a decision from Marvin one way or the other. She then targeted a year later, December of 2001, to adopt her first child—since the process can take about that long. She even decided that two years later, in December of 2003, she would adopt a second child so the first would have a sibling, and so she could experience having both a son and daughter. She also factored in taking leaves of absence from work—perhaps two months each time—to travel to the foreign country of the child's origin. Now she had her *time price tags* as well.

Next, Cathy looked at *priorities*. She knew that being a mom, single or married, would be very demanding. She spoke to her part-time assistant, who agreed to work more hours when needed. She also figured in making less money in the first year of each child's adoption. After all, she has waited 20 years to get her dream of motherhood; she plans to spend as much time as she can with her children. They have become her most important priority. If Marvin stays in the picture, she figures she still will be doing most of the child care, but her relationship with him would also be a priority. They will need time to get used to being a family of more than two—time to work out the kinks of becoming new parents.

Cathy, who comes from a family with great longevity, in all good conscience still could not ignore the possibility of the cancer coming back. So she approached another member of the family to see if she would adopt her child if something happened to her as a single parent. Her cousin agreed. Indeed, she said she felt honored that Cathy had chosen her. Cathy assured her that finances would be in place to raise the child. This would come from Cathy's mother's estate, should something happen to Cathy first. One other consideration is Cathy's decision to wait at least two years to adopt the second child. Statistically, the most frequent period of recurrence of breast cancer is within three years, and December of 2002 marks that time frame for Cathy. If she's still cancer-free, she feels she will have beaten the odds and will risk becoming a mother of two, believing that she, like other women in her family, will live many years, certainly long enough to raise her children. Indeed, she hopes to become a grandmother, too!

Now, as committed as this woman is to motherhood, Cathy does have a lot of other dreams. One is to write a book for small business owners about how to design Web sites, and she still has many travels on her dream list. But she now gives lower priority, in terms of time and money, to both of these dream categories. These dreams can wait; taking care of her health and her need to nurture children cannot. Part of her motherhood priority is to start saving for her children's educations, and she plans to reallocate some of her clothing, entertainment, and travel budget to put more aside for these more important college funds.

As you can tell, Cathy is now knee-deep in *planning*. One by one, she's checking off her list of funding strategies—how to pay for the adoption, the early childhood years, and the education years, as well as her own retirement. If she stays married to Marvin, the finances will look even better. Yet she's planning for all contingencies. Our next step in planning is to see how she can broaden her business opportunities without necessarily increasing her work hours. She's been asked to consider a long-term Web consulting contract, and instead of writing a book, she may find a way to use the Internet itself to find, educate, and manage new consulting clients. As you can see, she's carefully planning a way to work out of her home—something she initiated 15 years ago, with motherhood in mind.

For Cathy, *prosperity* won't occur until December of 2001, when she picks up her daughter in China—the country she has selected because of the many Chinese girl babies who need homes. And another treasure will be added to her life in December of 2003, when she hopes to adopt her Russian-born son.

So, I've chosen a dream in progress as my example of how to work through the six Ps of funding your dreams. As I said at the beginning of Cathy's story, if this woman can create her family in her mid-50s, against all odds they might say, can you imagine not achieving your own outrageous dreams? All it takes is a logical, pragmatic sequence of steps, once you've discovered your passion. Oh, it takes something else, I would add—determination to create the life you want and commitment to see it through. Armed with these measures and traits, I do not see how you can fail. I know of so many seemingly impossible dreams that have come true, all because someone did what Winston Churchill admonished a nation at war to do: "Never give up. Never, never, never, give up." Never give up on your dreams, and you will find a way to the rich satisfaction of their fulfillment. So, I urge you to begin this simple but intricate journey—get out your Family Final Dream Lists, both personal and business, and start walking through the six Ps of funding your dreams.

DREAMFUNDING STRATEGIES . . .

1. I've shown you how the six Ps work with one individual's dream. Now it's time to take your Final Family Dream List (let's start with the personal list), and start with the top priority dream, or passion, regardless of whose dream it is. Give each family member several copies of the blank Six Ps of Funding Your Dreams Worksheet at the end of this chapter. Let each person work his or her way through the six steps of funding dreams, working on the family's top-priority dream. You will be amazed at the divergence of ideas in the planning section that the different people in the family come up with. And that's all the better. The person whose dream it is will welcome more input.

   Also, you may find different price tags accounted for, which also may prove illuminating—the dreamer may find ways to cut the financial or the time price tag when he or she sees how someone else arrived at those numbers. Ultimately, it is the dreamer who should set the target date of the dream.

   In the permission section, you want the other family members to state their agreement that this is the primary family goal, and each may have an idea of other people whose involvement (i.e., cooperation), be they family members or not, would help accomplish the dream more easily or more quickly. Again, though, the main focus of the permission section is an affirmation of the dreamer's commitment to turn that dream into reality (i.e., the dreamer has given himself or herself the go-ahead to pursue his or her passion.)

In the prosperity section, the dreamer should state what fulfillment will look like (see the six Ps of Funding Your Dreams: Sample
Worksheet for an idea of what I mean). The dreamer should state in
exact terms what constitutes "success" or "achievement" of the dream.
The more descriptive the dreamer can be, the better. The other family members might write their own descriptions. Compare them all
and you'll see how vested all the family members are in seeing that
the dreamer gets to his or her goal.

2. Now that you've tried the six Ps concept with the family's most important dream, each member of the family should take his or her
own top two priority dreams and repeat the process. If you get stuck
on how to do a section, go back to see what you did with the first
worksheet you completed.

3. Make copies of the worksheets for all the dreams, including the top
priority dream on the Final Family Dream List. Let everyone read
through these dreams. If you have an idea to help someone on one
of their particular dreams, start brainstorming with them right away.

4. If your kids don't quite know how to do this, have an adult ask them
the questions and write down their answers, so they too have a visual worksheet of their dream.

5. Take the dream worksheet, the top-priority family dream and the top-
priority dream for each family member, and tack them to the dreamfunding bulletin board. They'll serve as a reminder to each family
dreamer what they should be focusing on in taking further steps toward dream achievement.

6. Plan your next intergenerational family meeting to have a brainstorming session on all the dreams now up on the bulletin board. Encourage each person to keep a dream notebook—a spiral notebook
will do—where they can write ideas for each step of funding their
dreams. They can bring those ideas to the family meetings.

7. Don't leave out your parents, your kids, or your siblings. The more
heads you put together on creative brainstorming, the better.

8. You'll notice something interesting start to happen—everyone in the family will get excited about their own dreams, and they will become invested in the accomplishment of their loved ones' dreams. Didn't I say that funding your dreams brings families closer together and gives opportunities to show your love for one another? Now you're starting to see how this happens.

Six Ps of Funding Your Dreams: Sample Worksheet

Name of Dreamer: Loren

Passion (Dream)
To build and learn to fly my own private plane.
Target Date: Completion: Fall 2002

Permission
I, Loren, give myself a full go-ahead to build and learn to fly my own private plane. I will get Penny's [wife's] agreement that we will save the money to pay for the plane parts and for my flying lessons. I'll ask Hal [brother-in-law, also a pilot] to recommend a training school and manufacturer. I'll tell the neighbors about the construction project that will be going on in the garage next to their house for the year it will take me to complete building the plane.

Price Tag
Financial: Plane parts: $50,000
Time: One year, starting 10/1/01; 40 eight-hour days, on weekends—my best estimate

Priorities
Will have to give up golf games on Saturdays, since Sundays are family days. Will take my bonus this year and put half toward the plane parts purchase (get Penny's OK). Must continue investments schedule, so remaining funds will have to come from discretionary budget. Ask Penny to take less-costly vacation this year and put those extra funds into plane—promise her a trip in the plane for our vacation in 2003—wherever she wants to go (that I can fly to!).

Six Ps of Funding Your Dreams: Sample Worksheet
(continued)

Planning

With bonus ($15,000) and vacation cuts ($5,000), I still need $30,000 for the plane alone. Find out about putting that much down and do installment payments on the remaining balancing—say $1,500 per month at 8 percent interest for two years and two months would pay off the plane (balance with interest: $38,899.78).

Hal says he's got an instructor's license and can teach me, so I'll only have to pay for getting my flying hours plus the cost of the license. Call general aviation office at airport and ask about hourly costs for plane use until mine is finished. Schedule first lesson with Hal by March 2001—take off Thursday afternoons so I don't miss time with family on Sunday.

Get Penny involved in setting up garage for building the plane; we'll need to use the tool closet for some of the parts and move the furniture to a storage unit. Decide on extra tools needed for assembly and purchase. Ask Hal if he has any, or what his cost is.

Prosperity

I'm flying "Bentley" [my plane] with Penny, Peter, and Amy to Costa Rica on our vacation in spring of 2003. We're soaring over the Pacific; I'm confident of my skill and safety for my family. I love the adventure of being up in the clouds piloting my way to a new adventure.

Six Ps of Funding Your Dream: Worksheet

Name of Dreamer: _____

Passion (Dream)

Target Date:

Permission

Price Tag

Financial:

Time:

Priorities

Planning

Prosperity

7

Funding Your Dream of Independence

I do not know a single senior citizen who does not dream of financial independence in his or her later years. They do not want to have to ask their children for financial assistance, or they may not have any children to rely on to take care of them as they age. Fortunately, most members of today's grandparent generation have saved for their future. Now in their 70s and 80s, this group comprise the wealthiest generation that has ever lived in this country. A great majority of this group are World War II survivors, who lived through two global wars and the Great Depression. If you are a member of this sturdy bunch, you remember bread lines of unemployed workers who could not feed their families. You remember participating in food rationing, gas rationing, and patching silken hosiery because new hose were too expensive. Your generation lives on interest, rarely touching principal.

Yet, even though the grandparents of today are savers, many of you are living far more years in retirement than you ever expected. Your longer life span, averaging 76 years for men and 79 for women, means you are funding more years of independence after your working years than any previous generation. Furthermore, you realize that not all these later years will be spent in good health, and health care costs keep rising. So you face stretching your dollars to cover a longer period. You may even have decided to keep working and retire from several jobs before quitting work altogether. Since not outliving your money is an uppermost concern, let's examine the important financial strategies needed to fund the dream of independence and meet some families who are working to achieve such security in their own lives. Perhaps one of their situations will reflect what you or a loved one in your family may be facing.

AL AND JESSICA: Multiple Retirements— Expensive Lifestyle

Al and Jessica are approaching their third retirement. Al, a renowned research physician, keeps getting job offers each time he retires. A workaholic who loves what he does, Al is still employed at age 66, despite several heart attacks. His wife, Jessica, who did not work outside the home and has no retirement income of her own, loves to travel. So, to appease her about his still working, Al arranges for them to take multiple trips abroad each year, often tying them into his keynote speeches at medical conferences around the world.

At the time of his second retirement from a major research hospital, Al and Jessica came to me for financial planning. With his various pensions, which he is already collecting, plus his current income, Al and his wife can afford their expensive lifestyle now. They spend $8,000 per month, $96,000 per year, to pay their bills, excluding taxes. However, when we ran the projection numbers for their postretirement period, we discovered that after Al's third retirement, the couple is going to have to trim their lifestyle budget a bit. We looked at three variables that affect whether they will outlive their money:

1. Al's age at death; we looked at ages 75, 80, and 85.
2. Lifestyle cost (income required): we looked at $96,000/year and $90,000/year.
3. Rate of return on their invested capital: we used 8 percent and 10 percent pretax.

By looking at the following chart, you can see there are nine possible outcomes; in only three instances will the money last past Jessica's age 100—that is, the couple likely will not outlive their money:

	Income Required $96,000/Year		Income Required $90,000/Year	
Al's Age at Death	at 8% ROR*	at 10% ROR	at 8% ROR	at 10% ROR
		Jessica's Age When $ Runs Out		
Age 75	Age 87	Age 91	Age 90	Age 99
Age 80	Age 91	Age 98	Age 95	Does Not Outlive $
Age 85	Age 94	Does Not Outlive $	Age 98	Does Not Outlive $

*ROR = Rate of return on investment

*Assumption = If Jessica's money lasts past her age 100, she does not outlive her money.

By reducing their lifestyle costs after retirement by just $500 per month, or by $6,000/year, Jessica will have enough money to live well into her 90s and, in the case of 10 percent ROR (rate of return on the investments), will not outlive their money. You can see she will be substantially better off if Al lives at least until age 80. This is because two of his three pensions will cease when he dies. Also, a 2 percent greater rate of return, 10 percent versus 8 percent, makes a big difference as well.

Another consideration in this couple's projections is that Al is approaching that magic age of 70½, when the IRS insists that he start withdrawing money from his individual retirement accounts (two of his retirements included lump sums he rolled over to these IRAs). Al can wait until April of the year after the year in which he turns 70½, but once these withdrawals begin, we must refigure his projections to include income tax payments on the withdrawals. Also, we'll determine how much beyond the mandatory withdrawal amount he may want to take from the IRAs versus from the taxable portfolio investments the couple has saved. As I mentioned before, one of the big milestones in a senior's life is at retirement. The probable distributions from previously tax-deferred retirement accounts and taxation on the monies withdrawn are important factors to review at this time.

The important point about Al and Jessica's story is that sometimes an expensive lifestyle can be maintained after retirement; sometimes it has to be adjusted, as in their case. If you're approaching retirement, you'll want to know if such changes apply to you. Income/expense projections are a must in retirement planning if you're determined not to outlive your money.

LINDA: Divorced with Too Many Eggs in One Basket

Linda's financial future looks much less rosy than the story above. After her divorce 15 years ago, she began living with her new boyfriend, Art. This significant relationship lasted a decade, and then they broke up. Linda had received only a modest financial settlement from her divorce. She went back to work as a therapist, but her practice still has not taken off in terms of her income. During her ten years with Art, that didn't matter. Now it does. Art was generous with Linda as they split—he gave her $350,000 worth of a registered stock, a biotech company that looked promising. Unfortunately, the stock not only did not increase in value, but its stock price was starting to head down by the time Linda came to see me. Except for a small investment portfolio she had managed to save, this one investment was her biggest asset.

At this point, I want to discuss risk tolerance and the risk scale. I give clients certain psychological tests that show their comfort level with risk. I use a scale from one to ten with ten being high risk (someone who might be comfortable investing in orange juice futures contracts on the commodities market, when nine out of ten people lose money investing in commodities) and a one on the risk scale meaning they're likely hiding money under the mattress at home, because they don't trust banks! It's very important that you know where you stand on the risk scale because your investments should match your comfort level with risk. Linda was a seven, and I would estimate her investment in this at a nine—in other words, she was invested in a stock too risky for her comfort level. She knew that, but she still felt her ex-boyfriend was a sound investor, and she trusted that he would tell her if he thought she should sell the stock. He never did.

I strongly urged Linda to sell most of the stock and diversify the proceeds in a portfolio divided among different asset classes of investments. She wavered on what to do, but then decided to keep her stock, hoping it would start to turn around. Finally, as it began to plummet in price, she sold one-fourth of it. We diversified that, choosing a variable annuity with a variety of mutual funds. About a year later, the restrictions on the stock lifted, and we sold another quarter of it. We broadened her range of investments once again. Two years later, the stock is nearly worthless. Her original $350,000, including the two pieces she let me diversify, is worth about $85,000. She's heartsick, and so am I. We could have built a significant portfolio from the original asset amount; now it will take much longer. At age 62, Linda must look forward to making a go of her therapy practice and working until age 75 to be able to afford to retire.

Sadly, this is a case of a grandparent generation single woman with too many eggs in one investment basket, an investment basket that was too risky for her situation and temperament. Also, outside the stock, she had too small an investment portfolio saved at her age for being able to retire at the normal retirement age (62 to 65).

ROGER AND MONA: Big Cash Expenses Can Compromise Security

Roger and Mona have a considerable amount of money, and Roger has just retired at age 62. Both have pensions, and Mona has Social Security disability income as well, following a near-fatal bus accident that left her with chronic back pain, unable to work. What has been interesting as we've done retirement planning together is to see how a few big cash expenditures in the early years of retirement can drastically change your long-term financial future.

Roger and Mona are not particularly interested in leaving a large estate for their children. It's a second marriage for both, with a total of seven children from the prior marriages. When we first began talking, they planned to gift $40,000 split among the children during their lifetime, beginning in 2005 and every five years thereafter. They also planned to purchase a family vacation home for $75,000 in two years and also spend about that same amount taking all seven kids and ten grandchildren on a major holiday in China four years from now. When we did their projections, we plugged in these numbers for the gifting and the two big cash outlays. Finally, they thought they would each buy a new car every four years until they each reached age 85, and then keep one car for the two of them after that, buying their last car at age 90.

Even though they started with a nest egg of $2 million, including Roger's retirement and some investments that came from inheritances, they were shocked to realize that they would run out of money by their mid-80s, if they made these big cash outlays—especially the two $75,000 chunks in the next four years. We massaged the numbers a bit, reducing the gifting to $20,000 from $40,000 every five years, and we eliminated the two $75,000 chunks. Also, they stretched the car purchases to every six years. That did it. They ended up with plenty of money for the rest of their lives, and plenty either to give away through lifetime gifts to their kids or charity. I ran the spreadsheets several ways, and it was clear that the two $75,000 expenditures were what really "broke the bank." These early outlays were the prime reason they would have run out of money.

After seeing these numbers, Roger and Mona decided to eliminate the vacation home altogether and find a less expensive all-family vacation than the original dream of going to China. They do plan, however, to take this family trip soon, as Mona's back condition is getting worse, and they feel their travel days are numbered in terms of how many more years she'll be able to take major trips of any length.

With these stories, we see how important it is to figure the amount and sources of retirement income and the expenses you will encounter in different years of retirement. You may not have figured how many years you have to fund, but with the expectation of longer lifespans, I think it is wise to project out until age 100. I know in my family, both grandmothers lived to be 98 and 99, respectively, and one great-grandmother lived to be 103! You'd rather have your money outlive you than vice versa. So, let's take a close look at the components of dreamfunding in our final decades of life.

RETIREMENT INCOME

There are five sources of income in retirement:

1. Retirement benefits from former employers (pension income or lump-sum distributions)
2. Self-employment retirement plans
3. Social Security
4. Income from private investments
5. Working in retirement

It's critical for you, by age 50 at the latest, to start thinking which of these income sources will apply to you and how much income you can anticipate receiving from each. It's also important to know what happens to each source when the wage earner who earned these benefits dies. Often, in case of a company pension, the surviving spouse experiences a sharp cut in this income, or it may terminate. The average "haircut" is about 50 percent of the wage earner's benefit.

As for Social Security, check your most recent Social Security Earnings Benefits Statement (Form 70004) to see what income benefits are projected for you and note the difference in monthly benefits depending on whether you choose to begin receiving Social Security at age 62, 65, or 70. Nonworking spouses will also get Social Security when they turn 65; it is usually about half of what their retired spouse gets. When that spouse dies, the nonworking spouse gets the Social Security income of their deceased husband or wife. If both spouses worked and one spouse dies, the survivor should get the greater of the two Social Security amounts.

RETIREMENT EXPENSES

Your expenditures in retirement are a key factor to long-term financial security and the dream of independence. When I start working with a preretirement client, I insist that they fill out Cash Flow and Retirement Income/Expense Statements (see sample worksheets in the Appendix). First, I ask them to fill out what they are currently spending in all categories, and then in parentheses next to each item, I have them fill out what that expense will likely be in retirement. Some expenses will remain the same; some won't. Then we total the three categories of expenses: fixed expenses (ones that don't vary much month to month), fixed/variable expenses (ones that occur every month but may differ in amount (phones, food, gas), and variable expenses (discretionary expenses that are optional altogether). Most clients are amazed at what they're actually spending every month; only a few seem to know their monthly expenditures almost to the penny.

Totaling all three categories of expenses, we have what I call their "monthly nut," their monthly lifestyle costs now and the projected lifestyle costs of retirement. We multiply the monthly number by 12, and that's how we get retirement income needed, a critical number for the retirement income/expense projection. I usually inflate this income needed by 2 percent for inflation. If inflation starts to rise, I increase that inflator factor accordingly.

Next we look at major expenses. These might include any of the following dreams that you want to fund:

- Child's wedding costs
- Purchase of vacation home or other real estate
- Replacement of cars
- Gifts to children or charity
- College tuition or other educational expense for child, grand-child, spouse, or self
- Major vacation or irregular travel expenses
- Home repairs/decorating/remodeling
- Purchase of recreational vehicle/equipment/club membership

You may think of something else that fits this category of expense. You'll need to know or guess in which years these expenses will occur, and you will plug them into your spreadsheet. It's always a good idea to write notes at the bottom of the spreadsheet to identify what each such expense is for—a few years from now, when you review the projection, you may forget what the large expenditures were to cover.

Also, these major expenses may use sizable chunks of your capital. They are the ones you have to look at carefully when you do your projections, to see if they blow your lifetime security budget—that is, cause you to run out of money early, as we found in the first projection done for Roger and Mona.

PROJECTING YOUR OWN RETIREMENT FIGURES

If you're computer savvy, you can run your own projections on an Excel spreadsheet, using separate columns for each source of income, as well as for the various investment accounts you have. You should at least separate your taxable monies from your tax-deferred retirement assets, because you will treat the growth rate on those portfolios differently, due to different tax treatments. I mentioned that I use a 7 percent after-tax rate of growth on the taxable accounts and an 8 percent to 10 percent rate on the tax-deferred amounts. I always use two rates of growth on the latter, one more conservative than the other.

If you're not good at creating spreadsheets, you can use any number of the prepared retirement plan software packages, such as Vanguard Online Planner, or go to the Financial Engines Web site (www. financialengines.com) and work with their retirement planning program. Each software program is different. If you're still not sure you can work the numbers, hire a Certified Financial Planner to run these projections for you. It will be well worth the expense to make sure the calculations that help determine your future financial security are correct.

WILL YOUR MONEY LAST YOUR LIFETIME?

Regardless of how you create your spreadsheets, these income and expense projections show you a lot. You'll be able to see if your money will last. What can you do if you see that you will run out of money? It's pretty basic. You'll need to work longer to save more, or you'll need to cut your lifestyle expenses, your major expenses, and do whatever tax planning you can to minimize the tax bite on your accumulated investment and retirement accounts.

WHEN YOU HAVE MORE THAN ENOUGH FOR YOUR LIFETIME

Perhaps you have the opposite problem. You have too much money that's accumulating and you discover that you are going to have a large estate that will incur substantial estate tax upon your death. There's no better time than right now to begin a serious review of your estate documents and talk with an estate tax attorney and your financial advisor about how to play that tax game in a smarter way. Again, you see that retirement is a key milestone on your economic pathway. It's critical that these calculations be done well before your expected retirement date to allow the opportunity to redo your estate plan and reconsider who will be titled on what accounts, with who will be named as beneficiaries. (Your beneficiaries may be trusts rather than your spouse or children.) Also, while you usually can change beneficiaries later, some decisions you elect, such as setting up an irrevocable trust or deciding whether to take a pension income or lump-sum distribution from your employer's retirement plan, are irreversible, one-time decisions. You want all the information you can get before making these important choices. They may affect the amount of retirement income you will have, the size estate you can accumulate, and the amount of both income tax and estate tax you may have to pay.

While there is a lot of speculation about the viability of the Social Security system and whether it will run out of funds to pay full retirement benefits to workers, today the system is viable, and you should make sure you collect all you are entitled to. Recently the federal government started sending Social Security Earnings and Benefit Estimate Statements (Form 7004) to all workers ages 25 and older. You should have received such a statement already; if you have not, call the nearest Social Security office and request one. You have to estimate future income between now and retirement on this form. It's probably a good idea to do this anyway; otherwise you're relying on the government to estimate your future earnings based on past earnings, and that may not be appropriate in your situation.

PRESERVING YOUR CAPITAL

The retired clients I have who are truly financially independent, fund a good third to half of their lifestyle costs through private investments. Because they were the "saver" generation, and invested their dollars conservatively, protecting against loss of principal, the seniors of today constitute many of the nation's millionaires. Most of them use a portion of their investment income to cover lifestyle costs, but far more still save some of their investment earnings, which means their estates keep building. Still, with longer life spans and ongoing inflationary erosion, you need both growth and preservation of your capital in retirement.

Protection against Inflation

You may think that investing for growth and preserving capital are polar opposites. I disagree. You have to consider the erosion of capital from inflation and know that your retirement period could well exceed 30 years. Do you know of any 30-year period in history where what you bought in the 30th year cost less than it did three decades before? Well, maybe handheld computers will be a fraction of their current cost, but overall, don't you need more money to live the same level of lifestyle than you did even 10 years ago?

My point is that every retiree needs to find a way to invest for long-term growth that preserves the value of their capital in lifestyle dollars. Few of us want to scale back our lifestyle a little every year while our money stands still and loses value.

Protection against Market Volatility

But what about loss in the kind of volatile investment markets we've seen in the early years of this new century? The answer, as you've no doubt guessed, is having a diversified portfolio of different asset classes, so that no matter what sectors of the market are doing well or doing poorly, you don't have too many of your retirement eggs in one basket as Linda did in our earlier example. One thing to comfort you about diversification is the performance of different types of investments over decades. No one class of investment has remained at the top of the performance rankings, nor has any single class always been at the bottom. Nearly all asset classes were at the top of performance at one time or another, and most hit market lows. The comfort aspect of this is that by spreading your money among different asset classes, you also spread your risk.

Equity versus Fixed-Income Investments

It used to be that financial advisors would tell you that for every decade you get older, your breakdown between the two main investment markets—equities (stocks and stock mutual funds) and fixed income (bonds or bond mutual funds, whether corporate, government, or municipal)—should change by percentage allotment. If you were 50, you would have 50 percent in stocks, 50 percent in bonds. At 60, you would move more into fixed income because you would want to take less risk, so the allocation would have been 60 percent in bonds, and 40 percent would have been in stocks. At 70, the bonds would increase to 70 percent, with 30 percent in stocks, and so on. But that was before people lived so long, thereby increasing the erosion factor of inflation on your retirement portfolio. And that was before the 100- to 200-point daily swings in market indexes such as the Dow Jones Industrial Average, the S&P 500, and the Nasdaq. Today, we cannot use such a simplistic approach to investment growth and preservation.

This brings us back to risk. As you retire, and especially if you do not plan to work even part-time after retirement, you need to realize that it will never be easy to make back the capital once you lose it through inappropriate investments. Therefore, you must choose appropriate investments and be comfortable with the risk involved. Some of you will want 80 percent of your investments in the stock market because you're used to stock investing, you know that short-term fluctuations in the market are inevitable, and you're willing to ride out the interim valleys because you believe that the five- or ten-year trend is upward (I'll give you a hint: that is my belief as well). However, if you cannot stand to see your money fluctuate daily, even weekly, you may not be a candidate for stocks or stock mutual funds at all.

Annuities

If you're mostly worried about preserving capital so you can leave a sizable estate for your heirs, you might want to look at a relatively new investment vehicle, the variable annuity. These insurance policies with mutual funds within, usually have a guarantee on the principal—your heirs will never get less than the premium (purchase) amounts you paid into the policy, even if you die in the year the market is down and your portfolio is down. Some of these policies have a "step up in basis" clause that ratchets up this "floor" of policy value every few years, and then your heirs will never get less than the new, raised amount. These guaranteed death benefits do not apply to the policy value if you, the owner, pull money out of the investment before death. Then, the value will be whatever it is at that time—more than you paid in if the market is up at that time and you have gains, or less than what you paid if the investments have performed poorly or the market is down. So you must think in terms of your various pools of money and consider which pools you are likely to drain for spending during your lifetime, and which you will leave in your estate.

Another type of annuity, which is a fixed-income instrument, is the more traditional fixed annuity, with a specified interest rate that may change as interest rates change. Many people choose this over other fixed income investments because the earnings again are tax-deferred until withdrawn. However, these quite conservative investments tend to lag adjusting to new interest rate changes compared to some other fixed-income vehicles, because the rate can be changed only once a year.

Fixed-Income Investments

You might want to allocate the percentage of your funds that are not invested in equities among bond mutual funds, fixed-income unit investment trusts, and individual bonds, whether corporate, government, or municipal. But a word of caution about bond funds: As you probably know, there is an inverse relationship between interest rates and bond values. If you have a ten-year bond that pays 8 percent, and then interest rates rise so that new ten-year bonds pay 9 percent, your bond is worth less money because a new investor would not pay you the original amount you invested to only get an 8 percent return in the new interest rate environment. If you sold the bond, you would lose some principal. So, here I will state a bias I have in favor of individual securities instead of mutual funds.

If you buy an individual bond, you can decide whether and when to hold it or sell it. However, in a bond mutual fund, the portfolio manager buys lots of bonds, and it is his or her decision when to sell which bonds. When interest rates rise, that fund manager wants to compete for new mutual fund investors' dollars, so the manager likely will sell old bonds to replace them with newer bonds that pay the higher interest. That would mean the current shareholders of the old bonds sold would lose principal. You don't control those decisions. I learned this lesson the hard way in the mid-1980s when inflation went crazy and interest rates rose rapidly. I saw principal erode rapidly in every long-term bond fund I had purchased. I have never bought a bond fund again for any of my clients. Not everyone feels the way I do about it, but I'd rather control the purchase and sale dates of my client's bond portfolios, and I do that by holding individual bonds, not bond funds. You, or your investment advisor, can do the same.

Obviously, if you need to draw a lot of income right now from your investment portfolio, especially in volatile markets, you will want to have more fixed-income securities. You can have your advisor take the amount of money you would like to earn in monthly income from the investment portfolio and figure what dollar amount of your capital would be needed, invested in bonds, to produce that income. That way, you do not have to sell equity investments in a "fire sale" environment (i.e., when the stocks or stock funds are down in value) just to get your next month's income check. The remainder of the portfolio, not needed for current income production, can be invested in equity assets.

A Word about Liquidity

It is critical to know when you expect major expenses to hit and to know the lifestyle income you will need the first year of retirement and out into the future. Of course, to some extent, you are guessing on the income. But you want to anticipate which month of which year you need to have liquidity (cash) that you can get your hands on for major expenditures. Then you and your advisor can plan to liquidate (sell) the best investments at the time to create that cash flow. If you're talking about fixed income, you would want those investments to "mature" (convert back to cash) at the right time.

Certainly, you'll have unexpected expenditures pop up. The furnace might need to be replaced, or you might get the chance for a once-in-a-lifetime trip you had not anticipated. So, for these instances, it's a good idea to have some emergency cash in money market funds to cover these unexpected outlays. How much you leave in cash is a comfort-level decision only you can make.

Real Estate Investments in Retirement

The long-standing rule about investing in real estate is trite but true: location, location, location. Whether it's a second home you're considering buying after you retire or a piece of land that you feel certain is located at the edge of the next boom town, you really have to know what you're doing in real estate, and you had better plan on holding that investment for quite a while. Never take cash you might need for expenses that you already know about and plunk it down in real estate.

The exception is rental property, and I do have some clients who over the years have methodically purchased rental real estate (apartments, duplexes, houses) with the idea of supplementing their retirement income from employer plans with rental income from properties they own and manage. If you don't mind dealing with tenant problems and maintenance, or you can hire responsible property managers to handle this aspect, then, OK, do it. Eventually, though, people usually hold such property for a portion of time in retirement, and then they either tire of the work involved or they need the equity for other purposes. Still, for the vast majority of people, owning their own home is about as much real estate as they want to consider in retirement. As for liquidity, real estate is about the least liquid form of investing you can do, other than owning a business.

There is one liquid form of real estate investment, however: REITs—real estate investment trusts. They're kind of like a mutual fund of properties, but unlike the old real estate limited partnerships that were hard to get out of, REITs trade on the stock market. You can buy or sell units any day the stock market is open. Again, you have to know what you're buying, who the manager of the trust is, what kind of properties they purchase, and if you want to be in partnership, so to speak, with them.

Still, real estate has long been viewed as a viable inflation hedge, because when overall prices rise, often so does the price of real estate, if, and that's a big *if,* the location is one that is not flooded with unsold property. So, we're back to location again. Always know as much as you can about the market where you buy, if you do buy real estate investments.

MONITORING YOUR INVESTMENTS AND ASSET ALLOCATION

Once you arrive at the best asset allocation for your investments at the time you retire, this is not the end of retirement planning—it's only the beginning. Your circumstances will shift as you get older. Your lifestyle budget will need revision as you change your activities or as health issues arise. You should have a financial team to help assess your tax situation and guide you in monitoring and repositioning your portfolio to adapt to your changing lifestyle and expenditures. I suggest a once-a-year financial checkup with your financial planner and your accountant. You should revisit your estate documents every few years as well, especially if changes in federal or state law might affect the estate plan you've created. You should begin to educate your children about your finances as well (see Chapter 9), so they can help out where needed as time goes by.

DREAMFUNDING DURING RETIREMENT

As we saw in the grandparent generation list of dreams in Chapter 2, older people have lots of dreams to fund. If you're in the grandparent generation, don't you wake up each day with the idea that there is still much left to learn, enjoy, and do?

If you've planned your financial independence as I've talked about here, you will have the resources to spend on some very important dreams in this final third of your life. I say a third, because many retirees will live 30 to 40 years after retirement, depending on the age when they quit working. That is a lot of time to make dreams happen to fulfill your life of purpose.

DREAMFUNDING STRATEGIES . . .

1. Use the Cash Flow Statement and Retirement Income/Expense Statement in the Appendix to gather information you'll need to do your own retirement projections.

2. Review your Social Security Earnings and Benefit Estimate Statement (Form 7004). Make certain it includes records of earnings for all years you have worked. If anything is missing, ask the local Social Security office what they'll need to prove your income. Usually past tax returns or 1099s will do.

3. Gather your investment account statements, including all retirement accounts at your company, taxable mutual fund or brokerage account statements, and IRA or pension/profit-sharing plan statements. Review the amount of income you now receive from these accounts as well as the total annual rate of return you are now receiving from these investments.

4. Get retirement planning software or help from a financial advisor to do a preliminary projection of retirement income and expenses. You will need to estimate the number of years you'll continue to work, the year you plan to begin collecting Social Security, as well as your annual living costs now and into retirement, and major

expenses you expect to incur. Note which year these expenses will happen, going out at least ten years for these major outlays—longer if you know them.

5. Look at the Risk Scale Chart at the end of this chapter, see where you fit, and what might be the likely division of equities versus fixed income for the asset allocation of your retirement portfolio. You must tailor this decision to your own understanding and comfort level with each type of investment. We're looking for an educated guess on portfolio returns based on the percentages of investments you put in these two major categories of investments: equities (stocks and stock mutual funds) and fixed-income investments (bonds or fixed-income mutual funds). If you're considering annuities, you'll need to break down those assets between the two categories as well.

6. After taking your first stab at your retirement projection, see if your money lasts until you and your spouse are both age 100. That should give you a good idea if you have enough saved for retirement now. If you fall short of a lifetime income, go back and see what you can adjust. Will you work longer to earn more money for savings and investments, or will you trim expenses, especially large outlays in the early years of retirement? Then redo your projection.

7. As for projecting portfolio returns, I use 7 percent for taxable accounts (that's 7 percent after tax) and 8 percent and 10 percent for growth-oriented retirement accounts (that assumes at least 60 percent in equities). The two rates of returns are to give you a more conservative and more aggressive option, depending on how aggressive you are willing to be and how markets perform. If the investment markets change substantially since the writing of this book, you'll need to adjust your percentages accordingly. For portfolios that are mostly fixed income, I use a conservative 5 percent rate of return. Again, if interest rates change either direction substantially, adjust your rates in the projections.

8. Once you've made your retirement projections, you'll have a much greater comfort level, because you now have a place to begin estimating how close you are to financial independence. I hope you're

already there, and then you can retire when it suits you. But, if you're not, do not get discouraged. You can always trim your lifestyle, even if you don't plan to work any longer.

9. As for anticipated inheritances, I recommend you not put these in your projections. A bird in hand, they say, is a safe bet. Until you actually receive the money, don't count on it. Anything you get will be extra to add to your financial comfort.

10. Before retirement, review the liquidity of your current investments—how quickly can they be turned into cash, without suffering fire-sale losses in market downturns or when interest rates rise? You want to have enough money to cover your lifestyle costs without suffering losses when markets or interest rates change.

11. Have your financial advisor discuss the tax consequences of drawing income from your different accounts (taxable versus tax-deferred accounts). Discuss your mandatory retirement account/IRA withdrawals, so you will know how much income tax to anticipate in that first year after you turn age 70½.

12. Review your estate documents and plans regarding beneficiaries. Make sure the entire estate plan is updated for any recent changes in tax laws and discuss with your estate attorney and financial advisor the naming of beneficiaries to any retirement rollover accounts you set up. Your estate plans may affect whether you take your employer retirement monies as a pension income or a lump-sum distribution to a rollover retirement account. These irrevocable decisions could save, or cost, you lots of estate tax dollars.

13. Review your own personal Final Family Dream List for your last third of life. Look to see the price tags, target dates, and priority schedule for funding these dreams. Again, these "major expenses" will need to be planned for in terms of liquidity—having pools of money in cash to pay the price tags when they are due. See which dreams are "musts" to do first, equating to the richness of prosperity in these next decades of your life.

Risk Scale of Investing

Risk Level   **Comfort with Investing/% Levels**

1   Extremely risk-adverse; 100% fixed income; may need maximum income from portfolio

2   Very risk-adverse; 90% fixed income, 10% equities; may need significant amount of income from portfolio

3   Risk-adverse, but wants some growth; 75% fixed income, 25% equities; can afford to take only partial income from investments—have other sources

4   Tolerate risk better; definitely wants growth component in portfolio; 60% fixed income, 40% equities

5   Comfortable with some risk but wants ability to draw income and wants equal balance between 50% equities and 50% fixed income

6   Risk-oriented, growth-oriented, but may need some income portfolio; 60% equities, 40% fixed income

7   More risk-oriented; moderate growth needed/desired for retirement portfolio; 75% equities, 25% fixed income

8   Risk-oriented; desires more aggressive growth in portfolio; 80% equities, 20% fixed income

9   Extremely risk-oriented; needs no income from portfolio; 90% equities, 10% fixed income

10   Most risk-oriented; takes no income from portfolio; 100% equities; may invest in commodities or options

CHAPTER 8

Looking Ahead to Long-Term Care
The Dream of Managing and Paying for Health Care

I mentioned in the grandparent dream list that one of the biggest worries is how to afford the health care you need in the final years of life. Most of us dread the idea of losing our financial independence because the escalating high cost of health care erodes our money. None of us want to end up in a nursing home, on Medicaid, without choice and without control over the type and level of care we receive. We don't want to end up broke, outliving our money because health care costs use all our capital and dissipate our estate. We want to achieve the dream of managing and paying for health care for our entire life. This kind of long-term care planning is a form of "wealth protection," which is especially important if we want to leave a financial legacy for our heirs.

There are three basic steps in financial planning that anticipate the costs of health care and ways to fund them:

1. Take a look at your family health history—your parents', grandparents', and your own. Unfortunately, many chronic diseases of aging have a genetic component. If your grandfather died of heart disease and your father also has a bad heart, you stand a greater chance of developing a heart condition yourself. The same goes for cancer, Alzheimer's disease, and diabetes.

   Part of what you're trying to estimate is how many more years you might live and the likelihood of incurring the costs of a major illness, sooner than later.

2. Look at your financial picture and see how well you're insured to pay for health care costs—whether that's being self-insured by having enough assets to cover the high costs of long-term care, having multiple health insurance policies that will combine to cover most of your health care costs, or purchasing long-term-care insurance coverage. This latter kind of coverage could be an individual long-term-care insurance policy or a rider on your life insurance that allows you to use death benefit proceeds during your lifetime to pay for your health care costs. You should also become familiar with the government insurance programs, Medicare and Medicaid, to understand what they might cover so you can assess the Medigap—what costs Medicare plus your insurance policies will not cover.

   If you plan ahead, you can do a lot to protect your financial assets from erosion through ongoing health care costs. If you're married, it is especially important to know how to protect the lifestyle of the well spouse, should one of you become ill and need extensive long-term health care services. You would hate to face the terrible dilemma of knowing that caring for one spouse means the depletion of assets that would support your partner.

3. You will want to know who will help you when you become incapacitated and need others to make important financial and medical decisions on your behalf, when you are no longer able to do so. We will look at the legal documents you will want to put in place to ensure that your designated person or people will have authority to make these all-important choices.

Let's take a look at some stories of people who face different family situations and have made individualized choices to try to fulfill this dream of planning for, and funding, long-term care.

MARGARET: Long-Time Widow Self-Insures and Protects Her Estate

Margaret was widowed early, at age 54, and has never remarried. Her grown son and daughter worried about her long-term health care. While Margaret has enough money to last her lifetime without major health care costs, these funds would evaporate all too quickly if she were to go through a long-term-care health crisis. Her son Matt, who is financially astute, suggested a rather aggressive way to protect Margaret's assets and estate and still cover potential health care costs. His sister Audrey has agreed to be the physical caregiver, should Margaret need one. In fact, mother and daughter already live together in Margaret's home.

Financially, the family has taken a somewhat high-risk approach. They have removed Margaret's name from all her accounts. The monies are kept separate and are treated as hers, used as she wishes, but Matt invests Margaret's money for her, sends her checks when needed, and his name alone appears on the accounts. Audrey also has one joint account with Matt, for the money Margaret wants to go to her. Since Matt manages the family finances, he is also named on that account—to control how much of the money Audrey uses and when.

This family has decided to let Margaret spend down just so much of her money held in the children's names, and then she would qualify financially for Medicaid, because the assets have long been transferred out of her name. Both Matt and Audrey intend to see that Margaret gets excellent care in a Medicaid-qualified facility, if her condition prevented Audrey from providing the level of care she needed at home. They will spend whatever amount of "her" money she needs to receive quality health care while she is alive. They figure, however, that most of her estate will be protected from erosion, and Margaret will be able to do what she wishes, leaving some of her assets to her two children.

VICTORIA: Betting on Good Health

Victoria is 63 and in great health. She believes such good luck will continue. Married to her second husband, she has three children from a previous marriage. Her whole family, husband and kids, promise to take care of her in her old age. She's betting they will. So far, Victoria has not purchased any long-term-care health coverage. The irony is that Victoria can afford the premiums of such a health policy on her ample retirement income, especially since her good health qualifies her for an attractively low premium. I think she should buy at least three years of long-term-care coverage, since the average stay in a nursing home prior to death is two and a half years. She's considering it, but likely will look to her family to supplement the costs of health care, should she run short of money. Also, she is relying on the fact she will stay married and that her husband will outlive her. Right now, none of his pension income will go to her at his death, and his estate will go to his children. Betting on good health can be a high-risk scenario. Still, some people choose to do that, hoping they won't have an extended illness.

ABIGAIL AND RAYMOND: Choosing a Personal Representative

Abigail is a widow with five children, all of whom squabble about what is best for her. Weary of these conflicts, failing in health, and wondering who would truly look out for her interests, Abigail found an elder-law attorney to act as her personal representative (PR). This lawyer, sympathetic to the family dynamics, now acts as the power of attorney for both health care and financial matters for Abigail. The attorney's assistance already has been needed, because Abigail has congestive heart failure and is no longer able to live alone. Her PR found a quality skilled nursing home that would take Abigail. Her children visit her often but have no say in their mother's medical or financial decisions. While the kids are a bit miffed about it all, Abigail feels better, knowing she has removed herself and her care from family conflicts. She plans to leave her estate equally to her five children, but they will have no say in how she spends her money while she is alive.

For 20 years prior to his death at 98, Raymond had a PR who drove him to the airport, took care of his investments during his last two decades, took him to doctor's appointments during his chemotherapy for bone cancer, found a life care (continuing care) center for him in the final weeks of his life, and handled his funeral arrangements and the probate of his estate after death. Because Raymond had become a widower early and had no children, he was a perfect candidate for having an outside (nonfamily) PR take charge of his financial and medical affairs, so he did not have to worry about these matters himself.

FUNDING YOUR LONG-TERM CARE

Once you have reviewed your own family health history and made a good guess at your potential life span and health concerns, you will want to review the kinds of health insurance coverage you have or may want to purchase. We'll look at both private and public health programs.

Private Health Insurance

Now, no matter what your age, is a good time to review your health care coverage and see how well positioned you are to pay for your long-term health care. Get out your health insurance policy manuals and see what is covered and what is not. See what services are covered for home health care as well as care in an assisted living center, skilled nursing home, continuing care facility, or hospice program. If you have more than one health insurance policy, find out at what levels of expense one policy stops paying and how much the secondary policy covers. Also, find out the lifetime cap that most policies maintain—meaning at what point they stop paying altogether. For many policies, the cap is at $1 million; for others, it's lower. Many health insurance policies limit coverage for drugs as well, and this can be one of your greatest medical costs as you age.

Medicare and Medicaid

You may already be signed up with Medicare. However, there is an excellent manual available at no cost that thoroughly explains Medicare and Medicaid coverage. You can obtain it by calling your local Social Security office and asking for *Medicare: Why You Need to Know*. It's a good idea to refer to this manual to maximize the benefits to which you've contributed.

Estimating Health Care Costs

To get some idea of health care costs, you have to consider the location and level of care you might need. To have someone come into your home to help with activities of daily living (eating, dressing, toileting, transferring, and bathing) costs on average $100 to $250 per day. If you cannot stay at home and instead choose an assisted living center with a private room, the cost depends on the level of care needed and the size of the accommodations. Typically a studio apartment would start at $1,500 per month and go up to $2,500 per month; a one-bedroom could range from $2,000 to $3,800 per month. Skilled nursing care, on the other hand, which is driven by the amount of necessary medical care, ranges from $30,000 to $60,000 per year across the country. These prices vary according to location, but today's figures will give you some idea of the annual costs you might face in paying for long-term care. Don't forget to add the inflation factor of a 1 percent to 2 percent increase per year.

Funding the Gap: Long-Term-Care Insurance

If you can see that monthly costs of long-term care, together with your other lifestyle costs of living, would drain your assets too quickly, you will want to consider obtaining long-term-care insurance coverage to fund the gap, the gap of what you would pay out of pocket beyond what Medicare and all your insurance policies together would cover. I've already mentioned that some life insurance policies will let you attach (and pay for) a rider for long-term care, in some cases only for terminal situations. Here's where you are spending your heirs' inheritance, since you would use some or all of the death benefit monies to pay for your long-term-care health costs during your life. The money you spend will be deducted from any life insurance proceeds paid to the beneficiaries at your death. This option is especially good if you now have health conditions that would disqualify you from obtaining a competitively priced long-term-care individual policy, or from obtaining one altogether.

If you choose a separate stand-alone long-term care policy, you have a wide range of features in policies that cover different levels of daily benefit and different periods of coverage. Estate planner and long-term-care specialist Larry Lite lists the most important benefits you should consider when buying long-term-care insurance. Ask if the policy you're reviewing includes these features:

- Provides all levels of care in nursing homes and home care.
- Pays for assisted living facilities, shelter care, adult congregate living facilities (continuing care), and Alzheimer's facilities.
- Allows for care by family members.
- Provides unskilled homemaker services and personal care attendants.

- Covers caregiver training for family members.
- Covers adult day care, respite care, bed reservation, hospice care, and Meals on Wheels.
- Provides a survivorship benefit for spouse.
- Offers benefit periods from one year to lifetime.
- Offers daily benefits from $40 to $250 per day.
- Has a nonforfeiture option.
- Provides indemnity plans, a pool of money, or payment for actual charges.

The younger you are, the lower your annual premiums for long-term-care insurance. You also can manipulate the premium costs by changing certain features. If you take out coverage for only three years, the cost is much less than for lifetime coverage. If you lengthen the elimination period (the amount of time after a triggering event before the policy starts paying your health care costs), you also lower the premium. If you reduce the amount of the daily benefit you want, that, too, trims your cost of purchase. Once you lock in the premium, most companies will maintain that annual premium amount for as long as you own the policy. Usually, though, there is a clause that allows for premium increases if major changes in costs of health care occur.

NONFINANCIAL ISSUES IN LONG-TERM CARE

Once you have planned for and funded the cost of long-term care, you still have many issues to resolve in ensuring that you receive the best possible care. Most of these involve choosing people to help you if you become chronically ill or suffer some mental incapacity.

First, you need to decide if there are members of your family who can step into these roles. Perhaps your daughter is an accountant and understands financial matters well. You may want her to have the ability to manage your financial affairs when you are no longer able. In that case, she needs to be appointed with a *durable power of attorney,* which gives her legal rights to act in your stead. Yet you may feel that you want all three children involved in deciding on medical matters, such as whether you should have surgery or not, or when to discontinue life support. In this case, you would have to sign a *health care power of attorney,* naming your children or your representatives.

You may have heard of a *living will,* a legal document in which you state your preferences on life support, nutritional support, and other terminal illness matters. However, a living will, indicating to your physician what your wishes are, may not cover all situations that could occur. You still should give someone the health care power of attorney to cover these other potential medical crises.

These legal documents should be drawn up by an attorney who specializes in estate law. Although books on estate planning and some do-it-yourself legal associations or workshops provide prototype documents, I would still advise that you have any such document reviewed by an estate attorney before you accept and sign it. If the document won't stand up in court, it's worthless. Your signatures on any such document should be notarized.

Some hospitals and doctors have a document called a *directive to physicians,* which are valid at that medical facility. Still, this document may not be honored if you are out of town when you become ill, whereas the health care power of attorney is a legally enforceable document that must be honored in any state at any facility. I feel everyone should have a health care power of attorney as well as a durable power of attorney in place. It's wise to have copies of both with your estate attorney, in your safety deposit box along with your will or trust, and with a family member who could fax these documents to any medical or financial institution so that the appointees could act on your behalf very quickly.

If you are in a situation like Abigail's, where you feel there are family conflicts about your potential long-term care choices, or like Raymond's, where there is no immediate family member in your hometown to help, it may be wise to select a local *personal representative.* This person must be someone you trust to look out for your interests and who has the skills to handle your financial or health decisions. This may be a friend, a former colleague, or someone at a financial institution's trust department whom you have interviewed and like. This person could be your estate attorney or accountant. Whoever it is, this is a reversible decision, if you later decide to appoint someone else.

A PR does a lot of work for you, whether it's during your lifetime or at death. You must inform the person before he or she accepts the position that this role could last years, not months or days. You and they must not underestimate the extent of this job. You must plan to pay this person for this effort, and these arrangements should be put in writing. You can pay an hourly rate for services rendered or a percentage of your estate. Sometimes a combination of the two is appropriate. You also would cover the PR's out-of-pocket expenses for work done for you. Be sure to give the name and phone number of your PR to your relatives, and the PR should have phone numbers and addresses for your closest of kin. You can direct your PR regarding how much contact you wish him or her to have with your family and what information you want disclosed prior to death. Your will or trust will inform your heirs of your estate after death, although your PR will likely coordinate your funeral arrangements and handle some, or all, aspects of your estate settlement. For this reason, your PR must have copies of all your estate documents and a means to notify institutions where you have accounts and relatives you want informed about your death.

FAMILY CAREGIVERS

If you are lucky enough to have a spouse, siblings, or children who will help with your long-term caregiving, it is important that you tell them early on what your wishes are regarding your care should a health crisis occur. This is where intergenerational planning talks become so important.

If your spouse is still living, consider whether he or she is in good enough health to be able to really assist you. Perhaps you need to bring in someone else to assist in your care. You might have a younger sibling, who also is retired, and could stay with you during a short-term medical crisis. If your siblings are deceased, which of your children is most geographically and physically available to drop what he or she is doing and come to your aid? Perhaps your children could take turns to come live with you and help out for short periods. Who can best leave his or her home or work situation first and get things rolling in terms of lining up services you will need? Who in the family would you like to take charge, coordinate service providers for the long term, and perhaps even do some of the physical care for you?

You need to let your other family members know what kind of care you would choose first, such as home care, and how you can afford this care. If you don't have enough money to cover your health care costs, this becomes a family problem that others might help fund. The sooner you reveal this financial situation, the better.

If you have selected nonfamily members to hold the powers of attorney, you need to inform your children or siblings about that. They will need to know who is supposed to make the critical decisions about your health care and who would be handling your financial affairs.

Thinking about all these matters may be the last thing you want to do when you're healthy. However, once a crisis develops, you are much better off to have discussed and planned these issues in advance. You will have more peace of mind, and so will the other members of your family. Planning for long-term health care long before you need it means you will not have to worry about the thing you may dread the most—losing control of your health care destiny as you age.

DREAMFUNDING STRATEGIES . . .

1. Think about your family's health history and how it might indicate your own potential for longevity and specific health problems. At what age did your grandparents or parents die? Of what illnesses? Did any of them have long-term disabling diseases or acute illness that required hospitalization or nursing care? Look for a history of heart disease, stroke, cancer, diabetes, multiple sclerosis, Alzheimer's disease or other dementia. These may be clues to potential health crises you could one day encounter.

2. Review all the health insurance programs for which you currently qualify. Are you eligible for Medicare? If so, do you have both Part A and Part B coverage? Do you qualify for Medicaid? Do you have private health insurance, long-term-care insurance, or life insurance? What services does each provide? Does your life insurance carrier have a rider that can be attached to your life insurance, allowing the use of death benefits for long-term-care costs?

3. Look into local costs for various levels of long-term-care services. Call nearby assisted living centers, nursing homes, home health care providers, hospice programs, shelter care facilities, adult day care

programs, and ask for price lists from each. These will help you estimate the costs of health care services you might one day need.

4. Call several insurance companies that offer long-term-care insurance and ask them each for an illustration that would cover you for several different benefit periods: 1, 2, 3, 4, 5 years and for lifetime. Ask how the premium would differ if you select different elimination periods before benefits kick in—one month, three months, six months, and 1 year. Also suggest a $150-per-day benefit and a $250-per-day benefit—see the difference in cost for each. Ask to see the maximum daily benefit amount offered and what that costs in yearly premium. Ask what the best premium would be if you bought the policy at your age today. Then ask about the "cost" of waiting—if you bought the policy in 5 years, 10 years, 15 years. Finally, compare the annual cost of long-term-care insurance with the annual costs of self-insuring—that is, paying for the Medigap amount not covered by Medicare or your other insurance, if you became seriously ill and needed maximum care in a skilled nursing facility or with skilled home care.

   Then, ask yourself two questions: Can I afford to buy long-term-care health insurance today? and Can I afford not to buy it?

5. Consider who could help you today if you became ill and needed caregivers to assist you. If you are married, is your spouse physically able to be the caregiver, or would it be too taxing for his or her own health condition? Could your spouse take over handling your financial affairs? Would you want him or her to do that? Is your spouse the person you want to make life-determining medical decisions if it came to that? If not, who would fill these roles? A child or several children? Your brother or sister? Would you want to find a nonfamily member such as a friend, colleague, or institutional representative to take on one of these roles? If so, who might that person or company be?

6. Have you formalized these appointments in your estate plan, naming the designated persons to hold the durable power of attorney, health care power of attorney, or to act as your personal representa-

tive? Do you have a living will or the need for one? Have you signed a directive to physicians or do you want to do that now?

7. Have you told your spouse or children how you feel about remaining at home with home care versus going to a residential facility, such as an assisted living center, shelter care home, nursing home, or continuing care center? Have you decided yourself what you truly want to happen if you need care that you, your spouse, or any other chosen caregiver cannot provide?

CHAPTER 9

Talk with Your Children about Your Finances before It's Too Late

Just as we said that money is often a taboo topic in families, most grandparents exercise privacy when it comes to money matters. Perhaps you like to keep your personal finances to yourself. You and your spouse (if you are married) may share such information freely between yourselves, but the thought of telling your children much about your income, expenses, assets, and liabilities may feel awkward.

Keeping your financial affairs private might be fine for now, but what if only one of you really knows much about the money? Or, perhaps you are single, whether by choice, divorce, or death of your partner. What if you were to become ill, mentally incompetent, or even die suddenly? Who would step in to handle your finances, health care decisions, or your funeral? Also, whether they say so or not, your children may worry about your financial situation as you age. The less they know, the more concerned they may become, since they have no idea about how financially secure you are, and if you have enough money to take care of yourself for the rest of your life.

I encourage all seniors age 60 or older to think ahead to the day when you may grow tired or be unable to manage your money or even the most basic of personal needs, such as taking care of your home, paying your bills, even performing the necessary tasks of eating, dressing, or making crucial medical decisions. In the last chapter, I asked you to decide to whom you would give over important legal, medical, and financial decision-making responsibilities.

What does your transition team of helpers need to know? A lot. You may be surprised at the amount and kind of information you should provide. I hope you can get over any preference you have to keep everything about your money secret. From the following stories, I think you'll see how important financial disclosure is to providing a smooth transfer of control when the time is necessary.

RANDY AND SARAH: Sudden Death Leaves Wife in Chaos

Randy and Sarah had what I would describe as an old-fashioned marriage. Randy made and managed all the money. Sarah was the homemaker, who raised the couple's four children. While Randy's political career as a state senator brought them financial success, his outside business ventures were a disaster. Sarah was shielded from worry about these money matters. Randy never discussed his business failures with his wife; he also ran up debts on outstanding personal loans from his cronies who put money into the bad deals. The couple lived in the limelight, but as far as finances were concerned, Sarah lived in the dark.

One afternoon, Sarah got a call that Randy had dropped dead at age 62 of a heart attack while filibustering his latest bill on the Senate floor. Dazed and hardly able to believe her husband was gone, Sarah got through the funeral. Then her troubles began. First of all, she had no checkbook of her own. She always charged the household expenses or paid cash her husband doled out to her; Randy had balanced the checking accounts and paid all the bills. Sarah didn't even know where all their money was—in what banks and what brokerage accounts, and she was not certain if they had a safe-deposit box. Randy's financial advisor called to give his condolences, and learning that Sarah was clueless about the money, met with her to start tracking down what was where.

While awaiting this information, Sarah received a call from Randy's creditors in a deal that had gone bankrupt. Randy owed them $50,000, and the note was coming due in two months. In the next few weeks, Sarah, to her consternation, learned that Randy and she were deeply in debt. Also, she discovered he had borrowed heavily against his life insurance policy, leaving her only a $100,000 death benefit on a $500,000 policy. If it weren't for the rather generous pension she would get from the state, Sarah would have been in terrible straits.

The kicker to this sad story is that it took Sarah and her advisor seven years to locate all the assets that the couple jointly owned. Fortunately, they uncovered a safe-deposit box with two other insurance policies against which there had been no borrowing. They found an overseas commodities account with silver coins, and another brokerage account in a city where they used to live that even Randy's financial advisor did not know about. I'm happy to say that Sarah ended up with about $500,000 in liquid assets, after paying off the business loans. She is now investing the balance to secure her future.

The point here, though, is that Sarah should never have been kept so ignorant of the couple's financial status. You could blame Randy for not telling her more; you could blame her for not asking more. The result is the same: she lived through several stressful years wondering how she would ever pay off the business debts and still have enough to live on into her old age. The state pension got her by in the early months after Randy's death, but it would not have sustained her in the lifestyle to which she was accustomed.

JUDY AND ANDY: A Notebook Tells It All

Another couple who are clients of mine have tried to prevent the problem of one spouse knowing it all and one knowing nothing. Andy is the only income earner, and he's done quite well in different scientific research positions that have paid him handsomely. Judy, his wife, has absolutely no interest in knowing about financial matters other than the monthly allowance Andy gives her for the household and for the extras she wants for herself, her children, and her grandchildren. When they came to me for financial counseling, Andy knew his health problems would shorten his lifespan and that Judy would one day likely survive him. He was worried that she knew so little of their financial affairs.

To start, I asked Judy to come to as many of our meetings as possible. I observed her to be extremely intelligent but bored to death with the details of investments. I worked with both of them to come up with an investment strategy that met their needs yet was simplified from the multiple accounts and types of assets that Andy had selected before.

Then we took an idea of Andy's that I think is terrific. He wanted to create a financial notebook with every bit of financial information Judy would need if something happened to him first. It includes a list of all the couple's bank, brokerage, and outside investment accounts, the policy numbers and location of their insurance policies, the list of contact persons, addresses, and phone numbers of all these financial accounts, as well as the location of their will, trust, and deed to their home. I suggested that each December Andy put the most recent statement from all accounts and policies in the notebook.

Other important items Andy wanted in the book were his military records (he's entitled to burial funds from the Air Force), a copy of his company retirement benefits with a page telling what Judy will get when he dies, his Social Security number and recent benefits statement, his Medicare information, as well as copies of the declaration pages on all his insurance policies—health, auto, homeowners, liability, and life insurance.

Andy has included copies of the durable power of attorney and health care power of attorney (his wife, then his daughters, are named as the appointees). He even has written out what his preferences are for type of funeral, coffin, music, military rifle salute at graveside, and what's to be written on his gravestone. I must say, when this man goes through his last illness and dies, there will be few unanswered questions about where things are and what he wants done in his final stage of life and at death.

I suggested we add the cost basis to his brokerage statements so that Judy will have information for her half of the assets that will not get a step up in cost basis at his death. He's also including information on the purchase date and price of their home and has added a page with a recent appraisal of his gun and coin collections. If all my clients were this organized and prepared for the transition of financial reins during illness and at death, I would be thrilled!

The one thing Andy hasn't done is to bring his two sons into the information circle. If something were to happen to both him and Judy, the boys have not been told anything about this couple's estate plans or documents. Also, Andy feels that one son is more financially astute and should probably be in charge of handling the estate. Right now he has both sons named as successor cotrustees, but he needs to have a discussion with the two of them about how he hopes they'll work together, even if the one son knows more about the money world. I suggested the couple call a family meeting to discuss everything they feel the boys need to know and to tell them where the financial notebook is located in the house, going through it when everything is complete. Also, I asked to meet the boys the next time they were in town, so that Andy could introduce me and advise his sons that he wants me to act as the intergenerational financial advisor, at least during Judy's lifetime.

AURORA: Splitting Duties among Several Children

Aurora is an extremely bright 80-year-old who has a large estate. Her four children are her designated heirs and will inherit equally, receiving amounts of equivalent dollar value, although the assets may vary as to what each child will get—some may get stock, some mutual funds, some cash, and so on. Also, all four children will jointly share in decisions that affect Aurora's health care in her final stages of life. However, Aurora is splitting other duties unequally, drawing on each child's special expertise.

Her son, Duncan, now helps Aurora with her investments. A bit of a stock buff himself, Duncan advises his mother on asset allocation and changes in her $2 million investment portfolio. He has annual meetings with his siblings to go over the portfolio and update them on what he and Aurora are doing. Still, she looks to him before making decisions in all her financial matters. It helps that he is an estate attorney by trade.

All too familiar with sibling squabbles of his clients, Duncan drafted Aurora's trust so that the other three children all share in and must concur with major financial matters, such as sale of Aurora's rental properties or residence. The trust even requires Duncan to give an annual reporting of the investments to his three sisters, and by inference, they are to object if they have a problem. Otherwise, saying nothing implies consent to what is being done in the portfolio. Duncan reminds me that you don't want to hamstring the active trustee in managing the portfolio, but you want something in writing that requires accountability to the other interested parties. Obviously, Aurora is present at all such family investment meetings and gives her consent as well.

Right now, Aurora is still in charge of her financial affairs, although she leans heavily on Duncan for advice. The trust provides for Duncan to take over as the main successor trustee, with the same approval process continuing after Aurora's death.

As for other assistance Aurora might need, the family has agreed that the three girls, who live closer to their mother than Duncan, will be on first call to help Aurora during a health crisis. One daughter, a civil attorney, will be the one to arrange health care providers, if there are services the three sisters are not qualified to provide. So you can see that Aurora is tapping her children for various kinds of assistance, according to their special skills and geographic proximity. She has tried to provide for a smooth transition, letting her family take over different functions as advisors and helpers, yet trying to be fair in the way she passes down her financial legacy.

From these stories, you can see how some families have planned poorly for the financial transition, while others have done their best to anticipate problems. So, we've come to another law of dreamfunding:

DREAMFUNDING LAW 8

Take control of eventually losing control—plan for your financial transition.

In planning your own financial transition, I suggest you put together a financial notebook or file and make sure the people you have selected to assist you know where it is. This could take you some time to gather all the papers and information your caregivers will need, but you'll see that you have most of this data at your fingertips. To trigger your thoughts of the kind of information you should provide, I'll review the most important areas to cover.

LOCATION OF ASSETS

For all accounts listed below, provide your family the following data: type of account (savings, checking, brokerage, etc.), account number, name of institution, contact person, address, phone number, who has title on the account (is it individual, joint, or in your trust?).

- Bank accounts (checking and savings)
- Brokerage and other investment accounts (include purchase documents that show the cost basis of individual investments)
- Safe-deposit box (list contents and location of keys)
- Deeds to all real estate, including cemetery plots
- Retirement plan documents, including Social Security information
- Military documents, including date of discharge, death benefits, medical or retirement plans
- Insurance policies and information, including medical (Medicare and private insurance), long-term-care, disability, and life insurance; also business continuation insurance, if applicable
- Estate documents, including wills, trusts, powers of appointment (durable power of attorney, health care power of attorney, and personal representative documents), living wills, medical directives to physicians; codicil to will or trust that lists personal property and the persons to inherit them
- Last year's tax return
- This year's cash flow and retirement income/expense statements
- Contact list, including name, address, and phone number of your estate attorney, accountant, broker or financial planner, insurance agent, and banker(s)
- Your address book, with names and phone numbers of relatives and friends (for notification of illness or death)

You may decide to keep the originals of some of these documents either in a safe-deposit box or with your estate attorney, but a copy of each of them should be located in your financial notebook or file. For your address book, put a page in the notebook stating the location of where you keep this book for daily use.

A WORD ABOUT POWERS OF APPOINTMENT

It is critical that your children know whom you've appointed to hold durable power of attorney (to manage your finances) and health care power of attorney (to manage your medical situation). Your children may or may not be these appointees. Also, your children or close friends should know the names and phone numbers of your doctors, and the basic coverage you have in private health insurance, Medicare, disability, and long-term-care insurance. They should know if you can afford to pay for home care or nursing home care yourself, or if you have policies that will help pay these bills.

RESIDENTIAL AND LIVING COSTS

Your children or caregivers need to know the names of, and how to get in touch with, any household personnel you might have—housekeeper, gardener, or other maintenance companies—as well as the phone numbers for your local utility companies (gas, water, phones). They need to know about your pets, their needs, the name of their veterinarian, and to whom you would want to give your pets if you can no longer take care of them.

Whoever is handling your finances will need to know where you keep your checkbook. A review of your most recent checks will show the regular payees you write checks to for household services. Looking through your checkbook register for several months will give them an idea of your monthly costs, which will be important so that your appointee for durable power of attorney can keep enough cash on hand to pay your monthly bills.

You will want someone to screen your calls, listen for messages, and handle any important items while you're not available or cannot respond. If you're going to be hospitalized for some time, perhaps a relative can change your voice message to indicate to friends and relatives the best person for them to contact if they want to reach you.

As you start to think of all these things, I imagine you are realizing just how many details are involved in running your household and taking care of day-to-day business. The further ahead you think about these matters, the better prepared your caregivers will be to assist you in all the important ways.

BUSINESS CONTINUATION PLAN

If you own a business and have to stop working, either for the short term or permanently, your children need to know who can step in to fill your shoes. They should know about any buy-sell agreements or disability or key-man insurance that the company may have taken out for you. They especially need to know if you are thinking one of them should take over the business.

Buy-Sell Agreements

These contracts make it possible for your business partners to buy out your share of the business, usually with the proceeds of an insurance policy the company holds on your life. If you die, the death benefit will buy out your family, compensating them for your share of the business's value, and taking them out of the partnership (as your heirs). It is likely your business colleagues do not want to end up in business with your wife, husband, or children.

Key-Man Insurance

If your talents and activities are central to your business operations, that is, you are key to the company's success, this kind of insurance, owned by the business entity on your life, gives the surviving employees and partners working capital to keep the business running and find a replacement for your talents so the business can continue.

Disability Insurance

This is one of the most important types of insurance you can have during your working years. If you are an entrepreneur with no group disability policy, you must have a private disability insurance policy to cover the contingency of your becoming temporarily or permanently disabled. Usually this replacement income kicks in after 60 or 90 days and starts paying you a partial income (usually about 60 percent of the income you stated when you bought the policy). At a time when your family is concerned about your health and recovery, they will have this supplemental income to help pay the bills while you are not working and earning anything.

Succession Planning

Often, business owners are so concentrated on building their businesses that they do not think ahead to the future of the business once they want to retire or if they die. Creating a business succession plan is critical if you want your heirs to acquire the value of your share of the business once you're gone. You need to consider who would replace you as head of the company—another family member, a long-time employee you've been grooming to take over, or an outside buyer. There are many estate and tax ramifications to business succession, whether it is exercising your stock options, selling the business outright, or closing it down at your retirement. Take time now to consider your options and express your desires in concrete written terms in enforceable legal documents. If most of your net worth is in your business, you owe it to your family and heirs to plan for this important financial transition as well.

TAXES

Your children should know the location not only of last year's tax return but also the supporting documents for the current year's tax return. If you don't have a file labeled "this year's tax return," I suggest you make one, and drop in every item that comes in all year long that would be needed to file your returns, both personal and business.

Also, be sure your accountant's name, address, and phone number are included in your list of contacts in your financial notebook. Your executor and family will need to contact the accountant to notify him or her of any illness that might require an extension or to let that person know when you die.

For tax purposes, it is important that the person handling your finances know the value of all your assets on the date of your death, as well as the date that is exactly six months after your death. The executor who handles your final year income tax return as well as the filing of your estate tax return (IRS Form 706) will need this information for the accountant who works on both returns in the year of your death. The executor can choose either the date-of-death value or the value of the estate exactly six months after the date of death as the preferred date for your estate tax return. As for your heirs, when they inherit your assets, they will receive the cost basis that is the value on your date of death. Thus, they receive a "step up in basis—cost basis," which means when they sell or liquidate the assets, the capital gains (appreciation) that happened during your lifetime is wiped out, and no one has to pay tax on those deleted capital gains.

The best way for your heirs to capture the date of death value is to save the next morning's business section of the local newspaper or the *Wall Street Journal,* which gives the previous day's closing prices—the date of your death. This is something you might want to mention to your children now, so they will remember at that hectic, emotional time, when you pass away.

ESTATE PLANS

Once you have selected your various appointees and had your estate documents drawn, it is helpful to inform your primary heirs of the essential content of your estate documents. You want them to know as much as possible in advance to provide a smooth transition. This disclosure is especially true if you plan to use a sizable portion of your estate to make charitable donations, or if the provisions of your estate might cause conflict among the heirs. Now, I will say that some estate attorneys I interviewed expressed the opposite view, saying it's your money, do what you want with it, do not concern yourself with informing them in advance, and don't worry if anyone gets upset. However, I have seen situations where considerable intergenerational strife occurred because of surprise clauses in wills and trusts that led to great embitterment in some heirs. I have observed far fewer cases of this when the grandparents' estate intent was disclosed earlier to all parties involved. You don't have to give details of dollar amounts, if you prefer not to, but I think it is preferable to disclose to your main beneficiaries, who are likely your children, the major assets of your estate plan and which persons are named to serve in the handling of the estate (executor, trustees, personal representative). Also, if you have favorite personal possessions you want to give to specific children, grandchildren, or other heirs, you should put this in writing (in a codicil to your will or trust) or give the items away during your lifetime.

FUNERAL PLANS

Most people make funeral plans in their later years. If you have done so already, you should let your children know the location of cemetery plots and deeds as well as the existence of prepaid funeral, burial, or cremation plans. You should also advise them of any specific wishes you may have about the funeral service, whether you're entitled to military honors or funeral allowance, what information you want included in your obituary, the groups you prefer as recipients of memorial donations made in your name, the wording you want on any cemetery plaque, and how you intend for all related costs to be paid. Even if you think your spouse will live longer than you, it's a good idea to tell the next generation about these private matters, in case your husband or wife dies first.

If you are in the early senior years, all this may sound like a lot of private information to divulge just in case something happens, especially if your family is blessed with longevity, and you expect to live many more years in good health. But remember, we must consider several possible scenarios in which you might have to relinquish some or a lot of control over your financial and health matters:

- Short-term disability
- Long-term disability
- Mental incapacity
- Physical incapacity
- Death

Frankly, any of these could occur at any time due to an accident or a deviation from good family genetics. You and your family need to be prepared for all possible situations.

Your loved ones will appreciate that you thought ahead to plan for a smooth transition of financial control.

DREAMFUNDING STRATEGIES . . .

1. First, think in terms of suffering a short-term disability during which you are unable to do anything at all about your finances for nine months—go to work (earn), buy your necessities, pay bills, balance your checkbook, review your investments, and so on.

   - Who would be able to do these tasks for you (financial matters as well as the physical caring)?

• Do you have disability insurance to cover this interruption? If not, do you have cash in liquid accounts to pay for your lifestyle during this period? Or, is there a family member who might help you with this?

2. Now, consider a long-term disability—worst-case scenario. You're in a coma and live for a long time.

• Have you assigned to someone the appropriate powers of attorney (durable and health care)?
• Which family member will step in to visit you in the nursing home, see to your needs, act as your advocate for the best possible care? Do they know what you would want or not want done in terms of medical treatments?
• Is your spouse well informed about the location of all your financial assets and accounts? Do you have the equivalent of a financial notebook or file? If not, begin to put one together—give yourself a deadline and complete all the items I listed in this chapter. When the notebook or file is complete, tell your spouse where it is and go through the information it contains. Select an additional person to be part of this information loop in case you and your spouse are injured together. If you have children, bring them into these conversations and tell them as much as you can about what responsibilities you hope they can fulfill in helping your spouse, or just you.

3. Now, consider, that you walk out of your house today and get hit by a car and live for three months in a critical condition before you die. This kind of final health situation can be very, very expensive, especially in an intensive care unit or skilled nursing facility with 24-hour supervision.

• Do you have insurance to cover this kind of situation? Who knows about your health policies?
• Since you will die in this case, do your current estate documents reflect what you want to happen? Are they outdated because of recent estate law changes? Have they been reviewed in the last two years? If not, now is the time.

- Regarding your personal property, have you decided which items (such as jewelry, coins, special collections, even cars) you want to leave to certain family members? Is that written down anywhere?
- Have you asked anyone to take your pets if something should happen to you? You might want to think ahead to who would be willing to care for the pets during your final illness and adopt them when you're gone.
- If you still own a business, do you have a business succession plan that satisfies you?
- If you have not told your family what your wishes are regarding your funeral, burial, or cremation and have made no financial arrangements for these expenses, think about what you would want, and then go take care of this business. You'll feel better once it's out of the way.

CHAPTER 10

The Dream of
Making a Difference

What would you like your legacy to be? Do you want it to be reflected solely in the dollars you leave in your will or trust? Probably not. Most of us want to be remembered, but usually not solely in terms of money. We have something much more meaningful in mind. It has to do with the people we care about—what they think of us, what we value, and how we can pass our values down to our children and grandchildren, even to our community.

Now is the time to think about this legacy and how you can utilize your financial resources while you're living to build this foundation for your heirs and the wider family you wish to influence. You can begin by taking your legacy work very seriously, putting thought, effort, even money into leaving behind opportunities, experiences, and memories future generations will appreciate. We talked about everyone's basic desire to be remembered with love and gratitude and how intergenerational financial planning can help make that happen. Here is your chance to make such a dream real—the dream of making a difference. Much of this legacy work can and should be done in the early part of your senior years. If you have not yet started, now is time to begin.

The word that comes to my mind when I think of a legacy I would like to leave is that of mentor. Many of us dream of being mentors to the people we love, especially the younger members of our families. We want, somehow, to help them learn from the life lessons we have experienced. Much of this oral history gets passed down in conversations. When was the last time you consciously created the occasions for discussions like these? You need time spent with your children and grandchildren—time not sandwiched in between holiday festivities or attending a graduation. And what about the values you want these loved ones to learn from you? Have you given this much thought?

If not, you are not alone. Too often we plan activities and even vacation events with our family, but we leave a lot unsaid. Yet when you think back, what is it that you remember about your own parents? I remember my dad telling me, over and over again, "Carol, if you can get up every morning, look in the mirror, and like the person you see, then you'll always take pride in the person you've become." Through comments like this, he wanted to teach me about integrity and being responsible.

So, what is the best way to find the right times to convey the values you want remembered? Well, you can use your money now to create shared memories with your loved ones, times when there are plenty of moments to talk and share your deeply cherished thoughts, and reciprocally, to hear about theirs. You can travel together on a family cruise that perhaps only you can afford to fund. You could buy a vacation home for the whole family, like my friend, Lena, whose family has been going annually to the lakeside cabin her great-grandfather built. Lena's eyes shine with joy when she talks about all those summer times together. Indeed, every member of her family plans to have their ashes scattered on the nearby lake, so they can all be together forever in a place they love.

Many grandparents find ways to leave legacies of values beyond the financial assets that pass down as part of their estates. Let's see what some of them have chosen to do.

JERRY'S LEGACY: A Love of Nature

Jerry was an executive who loved the outdoors. Employed as a corporate lawyer, he spent the early morning hours of his weekends duck hunting and skeet shooting. He brought his daughter, Sherry, on some of these outings and even took the whole family on camping trips to share his love of nature. Sherry and her sister Carla soon started exploring the outdoors on their own, hiking down to a nearby river, outfitted with bowie knives, but armed mostly with a sense of adventure and curiosity about wildlife. Both girls went camping as teenagers, learned to ride horses, hiked, and have expanded their outdoor adventures to include scuba diving, rafting, sea kayaking, skiing, and backpacking. Even after the girls were grown, the family spent a Christmas in Aspen, enjoying the beauty of the snow-covered peaks of Colorado. Now, Sherry's boys are following in the nature-lover footsteps—both are skiers and hikers, and the youngest has started rock climbing.

So, not all one's values are conveyed by conversation. Part of your legacy may be to involve your family in experiences such as Jerry's outdoor activities. Your enthusiasm and pleasure in whatever your passions may be will be observed and likely modeled by your children and grandchildren. And, of course, such outings usually offer unscheduled downtime when conversations about other values may occur.

JENNIFER AND LYLE: A Legacy of Higher Education

Jennifer, born in 1886, graduated from Fairmont College (now Wichita University) in 1908. Her husband, Lyle, also finished college and attended two years of law school at Yale University. This couple and their eight brothers and sisters, first-generation Americans, all attended college, even though it was a financial stretch for their immigrant parents. The older generation believed in higher education; they wanted their children to have opportunities they did not have in the old country.

So, Jennifer and Lyle sent their own three daughters to a state university. These women, now the grandparent generation today, carried on the family tradition of higher education for their own children. The family urged the five grandchildren to go to college. All did. Two went on to get master's degrees; two more received law degrees. These are now the adult children of this family.

The grandchildren's children have recently entered or graduated from college themselves. Two have engineering degrees; one is working on her master's. Two others are doing their undergraduate work now; one just completed a year studying French at the Sorbonne in Paris, France, as part of his university's international exchange program.

Higher education, an important value to Jennifer and Lyle's parents, remains vital four generations later. So much so, that not only have the parents of each generation funded this dream, but in several cases the grandparents contributed significant sums to support their grandchildren's academic training. As a result, the current generations are gainfully employed in established careers or are receiving the education they need to advance their professional opportunities upon graduation. Their great-grandparents' dream has come true.

So, you can see from these stories that leaving a legacy involves more than stockpiling the most money until the end of life and then passing it to heirs at death. Your most important legacy is a legacy of values, and you must consciously assess what your values are and how you want to convey them to your loved ones. Let's explore how you might do that.

TAKING A VALUES INVENTORY

Let's say that your grandchild looks up at you one day and asks, "Grandma, what do you believe in?" First, you're probably shocked that a 12-year-old could ask such a simple but profound question. Next, you might pause and wonder, "How can I possibly answer this earnest inquiry?"

You could start by reflecting on your *inventory of values.* If you had to enumerate the things you feel are most important in life, they likely would reduce to a simple one-word list. I'll give you mine:

- Love
- Laughter
- Family
- Friendship
- Health
- Adventure
- Honesty
- Integrity
- Loyalty
- Responsibility
- Joy
- Freedom
- Commitment
- Caring
- Compassion
- Inner peace

I wrote those down in the order they came to mind. Everything I can think of that I would want to tell children and grandchildren is pretty much summed up under these categories, these values. Now, your list may be different than mine, but without much deliberation you probably could come up with your inventory of values in a few minutes. If you could impact or influence or make a difference in the lives of your loved ones, it will likely be by sharing this inventory of values in ways that illustrate why they are important to you.

TEN RULES OF LIVING YOUR DREAMS

By listing your inventory of one-word values, you've focused on the most important ideals you may want to share with younger generations. I find it helps to go one step further in stating how you've tried to live by these values. I call this process the *ten rules of living your dreams.* Your ten rules are very personal to you, and you'll need to take some time to really think about these. The best way I know is to imagine that you want to teach your children and grandchildren your personal commandments for living a good, productive, and fulfilling life—ten rules that, when followed, have helped you fund and realize your dreams. I'll give you my ten rules:

1. Be true to myself and my innermost values.
2. Love deeply, build lasting family ties and friendships.
3. Use my talents and skills to serve others and make a contribution to my community.
4. Laugh often, play a lot, and savor the bounty of life.
5. Take responsibility in all areas of my life—for maintaining good health, for being a loving person, for creating financial independence and prosperity, for fulfilling all my commitments to others and to myself, and for helping others less fortunate.
6. Appreciate the beauty of nature, spend lots of time enjoying it, explore the world, and learn about the diverse peoples and cultures therein.
7. Count my blessings every day and thank God for them.
8. Be open, honest, loyal, and caring in all my relationships with others and with myself.

9. Live each day to the fullest, learning from the past and looking forward to the adventures of tomorrow.
10. Look in the mirror each morning, and live my life so that I like, love, and respect the person I see in my reflection.

I would like for each of you to write out your own ten rules of living your dreams. These are the values you live by—the ones you want to share.

TALK TO YOUR CHILDREN AND GRANDCHILDREN ABOUT YOUR VALUES

While in many cases the way you live your life conveys your values, do not underestimate the impact of the spoken word in illustrating what your values, your passions in life, are all about. In short, you are sharing your dreams and hoping that some of what is important to you will also become important to your descendants and to the community in which you have lived.

With your children and grandchildren, I cannot think of a better time to share values than moments planned away from the hustle and bustle of day-to-day life—vacation or personal one-on-one time. We do see each other for Thanksgiving, Christmas or Hanukkah, at weddings, birthdays, funerals, and christenings. But I'm talking about time when you and a child or grandchild are free of the frenzy of meal making and gift wrapping—time when you can take a walk in the woods or on the beach, talking in earnest, or on a special trip you take with either or one of your parents, your niece or nephew, or your own children.

I mention travel a lot, because I think it creates a kind of time and space for people to build memories, strengthen family bonds, and share values—occasions that are difficult to achieve any other way. You are removed from your familiar environment, suspended really, and your relationship with your travel companions is the tie that links you together. I have experienced some of my best memories with my mother on trips she and I have taken alone, without anyone else around. We sit up nights and reminisce about her life as young girl, the things her parents taught her, her early years with my father, and she tells me stories of my own childhood that I do not recall. You can do the same, reliving important moments, milestones in family life, and creating new ones you'll recall for years to come. I cannot say enough about the benefits of finding time for this kind of encounter—the realm of values cherished and conveyed to loved ones.

Another benefit of multigenerational family vacations is to teach the value of cultural diversity, piquing the interest of younger family members in peoples around the world, and sharing your appreciation of the natural beauty of the planet—both values that can be enhanced by international travel. Travel also exposes youngsters to the variety of art and architecture around the world.

Now, I do not want to convey that you have to travel abroad on expensive vacations with your children and grandchildren to convey values. You might decide to spend a summer with the whole family at a small rental cabin in the mountains of Colorado, hiking and exploring meadows of wildflowers and teaching them botany or nature photography. You can stretch your funding to cover many less expensive ways to share your ideas of what is important in life.

WHO DO YOU WANT TO HELP, GUIDE, INFLUENCE?

While you hope to share your most important values with all the members of your family, you may feel a special bond with individual family members. It might be your oldest granddaughter, because you developed a very loving relationship while she lived near you in her first five years. If you're without children of your own, it might be a niece or great-nephew. As you watch them grow, you may see they have certain needs that you could fulfill—guidance about making and keeping friendships, tutoring in a subject you're especially skilled in, an interest in a sport that you love to play.

It's important to consider whom among your family members or in your community you would like to directly affect. Think about whom you want to influence or make a contribution to, whether in time or money. Think about how you can best make a difference in their lives. Make a point to initiate these efforts now.

If you're drawn to a certain charity, start planning now how you can make a difference. Perhaps it's volunteering at their local chapter, sitting on their board of directors, contributing to capital and annual campaigns, or setting up a charitable trust with them as the beneficiary. It may be that a community shelter for battered women may close down without additional funding, and you could rally support from some of your women friends and make a significant contribution yourself. It could be that the private liberal arts college you attended needs ongoing support or a major bequest you could provide. There are so many ways you might be able to share some of your money and time now, to help in dreamfunding for the younger generations, and you can enjoy seeing these dreams come true during your lifetime.

This brings up one point that may be sticky for you and your family. If you decide to contribute a sizable donation to nonfamily beneficiaries, either during lifetime or at death, your heirs may express concern that you're "giving away the farm," that is, monies that would normally have passed down to younger generations of the family may be designated for your charitable dreamfunding. You need to find the best solution to blend leaving a legacy of values to both your heirs and your community. One simple way to handle this problem is to set up a life insurance trust. You take out a life insurance policy on your life with the death benefit going to your heirs in an amount equal to the size of the charitable gift. You can make the gift (which is irrevocable) to the charity or charities of your choice now, taking advantage of the tax benefits of such donations. (You may donate appreciated assets such as stock or real estate to a charity without paying taxes on the capital gains, and the asset is removed from your estate, thereby avoiding federal estate taxes.) At your death, the life insurance proceeds, with your heirs as beneficiaries, replaces the money that you gave away earlier. This is a win for everyone—you, the charity, and your heirs.

Charitable giving is, in my mind, the best example of putting your money where your love is—supporting the causes that represent your values in life. You can explore a variety of charitable giving techniques by consulting with your estate attorney. You'll want to inform your family about your charitable dreamfunding strategies.

As you see, your legacy can include a lifetime of sharing—sharing your part of the family money resources and sharing yourself in time and values. Give your loved ones, whether family or members of your larger community, the gift of adventure, education, good ideas, and guidance. Strong values build character—yours and theirs. You will get to enjoy your money a lot more now, while you are alive, and what greater assets can you leave behind than younger generations of cherished people, who bring joy to your life and who are filled with admiration, respect, and gratitude for you when your life has ended—when they are left with your legacy of love?

So, I will conclude this chapter with two more laws of funding your dreams:

DREAMFUNDING LAW 9

*U*se your money to leave a legacy of values— not just one of dollars and cents.

DREAMFUNDING LAW 10

*D*uring your life, give money to others—loved ones and those less fortunate. Doing so rewards them and you.

DREAMFUNDING STRATEGIES . . .

1. Take your inventory of values. Make a one-word list.

2. Write out your ten rules of living your dreams.

3. Decide with whom in your family you want to share your values, which individuals you most want to mentor. Plan an occasion this month to be with each person and begin sharing your thoughts and special interests.

Funding Dreams through Gifting

Most of us like to be generous with our children and grandchildren when we can afford to do so. Certainly, this concept of gifting to younger generations is a premise of intergenerational financial planning. Still, we must take care not to undermine younger family members' funding of their own dreams by giving them too much, too soon, or in ways that take away their independence.

This is a ticklish area of family politics. Often parents will offer to help with big price-tag items, like paying for college, a wedding, or a down payment on a first home, and there is nothing wrong with assisting a young member of your family to get started in life by providing financial support for these major expenses. However, you may question the advisability of such gifting, wondering how much is too much. You may feel torn between wanting to gently shove your youngsters out into the real world, so they can learn to fly on their own financial wings, and wanting to help them have a "soft landing," so they will be sheltered from the stark financial reality you yourself may have faced without much support. Or you may see your adult children or grandchildren taking on big expenses, debts, or responsibilities without much forethought, understanding, or planning.

Let's look at a few stories of gifting under varied circumstances.

ELLEN: Gifting Helps Fund College Dreams

Ellen was a child of the Great Depression. Her parents scrimped, saved, and did without new cars, clothes, and vacations so she and her two sisters could go to the state university. Ellen remembers how proud her father was that all three of his girls graduated with college degrees. With this background, Ellen herself came to appreciate the value of higher education. She and her husband paid for both their daughters to go to college and graduate school. Soon, they decided they wanted to contribute financially to their grandchildren's college tuition, and so they started thinking about how they might do this.

Once their two daughters were married and the first grandson was born, Ellen and her husband, Jeff, began gifting $10,000 per year to each daughter. They could afford to, now that Jeff's salary was increasing, and they lived on much less than he made. Plus their investments had done well, and they felt they could spare these gift monies at this stage of their lives. They sat down with their daughters and sons-in-law to express their wishes and explain why they were starting the gifting program. They told their children that part of this money should go toward a college fund for each grandchild that was born. One daughter never had children, and Ellen suggested she use the gifts for retirement savings. The second daughter's two sons graduated from expensive private colleges, with at least two-thirds of the funds paid from their grandparents' gift money that was passed down, saved, and invested over many years as these children grew to college age. This is an example of intergenerational financial planning and dreamfunding at its best.

BARRY: Gifting Helps an Ailing Son and Floundering Daughter

Barry is a grandfather with a son who suffers from multiple sclerosis. He just learned last year about his son's illness, and the family is looking ahead to how this devastating disease might affect the family finances. Divorced and retired, Barry is fairly comfortable with enough assets to sustain him as he ages. But he's terribly worried about how MS will affect his son's ability to keep working, support his family, and educate his son. As Barry's financial planner, I've taken a hard look at the reality that his son can work now but may eventually have to change careers to accommodate his disease, or stop working altogether.

One plus is that Barry has tons of equity in his house. If he sold the house and downsized, he could capture another $250,000 of investment capital, even after buying a condo. Since that is money Barry doesn't need to live on, it could be invested to provide a supplemental income for his son's family, should they need it. For the time being, Barry is staying in the house, for its location is desirable, and it likely will increase in value over the next few years. But he's more than willing to make this move and help his son if the illness progresses to the point where he can no longer work.

On the other hand, Barry's daughter is a struggling artist who is not in good financial shape herself. Barry has let her move back into the family home with him to save her paying rent for an apartment. She's very frugal, but her dad has offered to pay her health insurance and buy her some of the equipment she needs for her painting and sculpting. My concern is that this 27-year-old woman has yet to face the reality of supporting herself. Her father cannot continue to do so forever, and I think it's time Barry give her a deadline for when the financial support will stop. He has hinted that she needs to find steadier work, even in her field of art, and she claims she is trying to do that. If she doesn't, the day will come when he'll have to cut the cord and send her on her way. It is one thing to assist a child with a major illness; it is quite another to support a child's lifestyle that may not be viable over the long run. You want your children to become financially self-sufficient. This is one of the fundamentals of becoming an adult.

HELPFUL KINDS OF GIFTING

We've already mentioned college funding as a helpful kind of giving. If you have ample funds to contribute to loved ones, another smart way to give is to share more than material gifts—give your children educational experiences and adventures that help shape their character or their view of life. Good examples are a summer program abroad, or two weeks on an Outward Bound type of wilderness challenge. Or start a stock portfolio, teach them about stocks and bonds, and get them excited about the investment world. On big-ticket purchases, suggest that they match you dollar for dollar when acquiring computers, cars, and other major items they might want or need. That way the recipient will share responsibility in paying their fare share of the purchase.

So far I have just talked about the immediate younger generation, your children. What about when you want to give to your grandchildren? How will your own children, their parents, feel about the gifting you intend to do? They might resent money or gifts bestowed on the grandchildren, for you may well outspend and undercut the sharing they want to do with their own kids. Delicate family dynamics come into play when funding some of your dreams for your entire family. The helpful way to begin is to run your ideas about giving to grandkids by their parents. They might not approve of the type of gift, the amount it costs, or the manner in which you want to be generous. Including all affected family members in discussions will help find the best way to share with all the generations of your family. That's why the intergenerational financial meetings are so important; there won't be any surprises on the Final Family Dream List, which will include some gifting to both your children and grandchildren. It's the most helpful method of being generous to all.

HURTFUL KINDS OF GIFTING

Sometimes gifting can be extremely hurtful in the long run. I've seen this happen a lot with the World War II generation, who have accumulated great wealth as a group. They were so thrifty with their money, and wanted to give their adult children more than they themselves had growing up. Perhaps you have watched friends fund an extended adolescence of their adult children, who stay in school for years, changing majors several times, trying to decide what they'll do when they grow up. Or they head off on a parent-paid holiday that grows into several years of backpacking and staying in youth hostels, with money getting wired to wherever from mom and dad.

One successful parent I know finally got tired of supporting his son, who at 22 still had not gone to college. Frank was a great kid with wonderful people skills but no education or career training. His dad had a heart-to-heart with the boy and said, "Frank, when you're 23, that's it. You'll be paying your own way." Amazingly, in a matter of a few months the young man decided to become a chef, talked it over with his father, and they agreed that his father would pay the tuition at the culinary arts institute where the son had been accepted. After graduation, Frank would have three months to find his first restaurant job, and then all financial support would stop. Not only did this young man prove himself a straight-A student in culinary school, he was offered a job before he graduated to become the sous-chef at a nearby resort hotel restaurant. Here was a case where the dad refused to keep hampering his child from getting out on his own; he created deadlines for performance and withdrawal of parental financial aid, and the child met them.

Sometimes gifts with no strings can be harmful, if a young person doesn't know the least thing about long-term financial goals or investing. For example, when young adults get used to receiving annual money gifts from their parents, such as the $10,000-per-year annual exclusion that incurs no gift tax to the parent, the children start to depend on that money, not to save for their futures, but to pay off their basic bills and credit cards. Then, if the parent decides for whatever reason to cease this practice, the child panics, because he or she is living beyond his or her own income and is overextended. So, if you have been gifting regularly but decide to stop, it's best to give plenty of notice to your child. Also, if you give $10,000 to each grandchild, you can suggest that you expect each to put these funds in investment accounts or use them for special expenditures, not for monthly expenses. You could recommend to your older grandchildren that they put $2,000 into a tax-deferred IRA and another $5,000 into growth mutual funds; the remaining $3,000 could be spent more immediately on something special. Still, you should know that a gift is a gift, and you may have no control over how the money is spent.

Giving too much to very young grandchildren falls into the "hurting" category as well, for it places too much cash in inexperienced hands and can lead to overspending as a child and adult, resulting in lifelong debting behavior. This size of gift is usually best given to parent to be invested on the child's behalf.

Also, I especially recommend against giving your grandchild your credit card to use without restriction. The time for keeping the card should be limited, and it should be to pay only for specific expenditures you approve ahead of time. It is better altogether for you to be along during the credit card purchases, and that creates a great opportunity for you to teach how credit cards work and to explain that a credit card is a form of borrowing money for a short period of time. The grandchild must learn the money has to be paid back.

TIMING YOUR GIFTS

It is difficult to generalize about the "right" time to give. Certainly, many parents and grandparents want to help out when funding for college is a concern and when helping a child get started in life is both advisable and appreciated. Parents of adult children should think long and hard ahead of time about the kind of financial assistance they want to provide and when to give it. I think the sooner your children are able to pay their own way, the better. It builds their confidence that they have become independent adults. It builds your confidence that any "extras" you provide will not undermine the child's feelings of security that he or she is capable of taking care of himself or herself.

In giving to grandchildren, it's best to plan in advance for those occasions for which you know you will want to help, get your children's approval on the matter, and be judicious in the amount you offer. Sometimes grandparents who are financially able to be generous will lavish sumptuous birthday gifts, cash gifts whenever they visit their grandchildren, or even "bribe" them with promises of unique adventures that the parents cannot afford. Now, I am not saying that giving to your grandchildren is a mistake; indeed, I encourage it. However, the way you make these gifts is important. Your children may have their own plans for educating their kids about money, and as the grandparent, you could thwart their goals if you don't balance what the parents want with what you want for your grandchildren. Clearly, this type of generosity merits intergenerational planning conversations and agreements.

Also, you already may have found out that some children and grandchildren are not at all shy about asking you for money, especially when they are in need of quick cash for something important to them. Do not make it a habit to succumb easily to "emergency" requests for money from family members, when you have not had time to think it through. Even when the reason seems legitimate, at least tell them you've got to mull it over and you'll get back to them shortly.

Of course, one of the biggest issues about timing is whether to give money away to your family while you're living or to wait and pass your assets to them at death. I'll admit right now I have a bias in this area. I think if you can afford to give money to your loved ones while you're alive without jeopardizing your own financial security, you should. Why? Because you'll enjoy the giving of it a lot more now!

GIFTS VERSUS LOANS

As I've said before, when you give money to a loved one, you need to be clear about whether it is truly a gift, which you do not expect to have repaid, or a loan, which you do want paid back. In the case of a loan, even to a child or grandchildren, document the agreement in writing, state the interest due, the time period when repayments begin, and the date on which the balance is due. That way there are no misunderstandings that would cause hard feelings later on. Loans without specific repayment instructions are really gifts, so do not be surprised if the recipient does not pay you back in a timely manner, or at all.

Also, if you can afford to give the money, don't need the interest or the capital, and really don't care if it is repaid, then give it freely, gladly, and don't think about it again. One of the true joys in having money is to be able to share your resources with loved ones in helping them fund their dreams, and when it feels right to give it away, then enjoy doing so.

HOW MUCH SHOULD YOU GIVE?

Perhaps a good solution is annual gifting of a specified amount that suits your means. It could be $500; it could be $10,000, or more. The idea, if it's affordable, of course, is to provide your family with some amount they can count on receiving. Additionally, lump sums of larger amounts for particular dreamfunding can be discussed at your family intergenerational planning meeting. You can offer, or they can ask, and you can take a pause and come back later with your decision, sharing at the level that feels right to your pocketbook, their needs, and the occasion at hand.

I will pass on my own observation in working with numerous families: uneven gifting to siblings, whether children or grandchildren, can cause havoc in family relations, unless the other siblings agree that one person has special needs for the larger amount. Still, you may decide that one child or grandchild merits special favoring, and you'll just have to live with the consequences. What you hope not to do, however, is to take away the joy of giving for you and to create bad feelings instead of good intergenerational dynamics, which is the goal of gifting in the first place.

DREAMFUNDING STRATEGIES . . .

1. Review your retirement projections to see what gifting you decided you could afford and have already planned in your Retirement Income/ Expense Statement (in the Appendix). Next review your Final Family Dream List. What dreams of other family members do you want to help fund that are not included in your expenses? What target dates for these dreams require you to provide funds in certain years? Recalculate your projections, plugging in these additional gift expenses, making sure your money still lasts for your projected life span. If you can afford this gifting, find out which funds will provide the money when it's needed. Do you need to adjust your investment strategy to create liquidity when the dreams need funding?

2. If you've indicated you could help with certain dreams and find you cannot after all, let the dreamer know immediately, so he or she can look to other avenues for dream support. Perhaps you can provide partial funding, but not all the money that is needed.

3. If you cannot do all the gifting you wanted, put your head together with other family members who might be able to share in the dreamfunding with you, and jointly plan your gift monies.

4. If you find you do have ample funds and you want to begin annual gifting, for example, to your children, set a time to talk with each one, indicating your intention, your parameters (restrictions or preferences) on the uses for the money. It's also best to let everyone (siblings) know if there is some reason that one child will be getting more than others.

5. If you're planning to give more than small gifts or amounts of money to your grandchildren, run the idea past your children first.

They may want to restrict the gift process in some way. If you can agree to that, let them know. If not, you may decide to postpone giving and think it over.

6. When trying to help adult children who are just going out on their own, make sure you and your spouse agree on how much to give and for how long. Clue your kids in to what you're thinking once you've decided. They may be expecting more help than you can or want to give, or they may have expected no help and will be able to plan ahead better, knowing that your gifts are forthcoming. Have in mind your own deadline date or age, when you think enough is enough and you no longer would be willing to supplement your children's financial situations. Let them know your thoughts on that, too. Before any family member asks, think of the circumstances under which you would be willing to make a loan to a child, parent, sibling, or grandchild. If a situation comes up, get a written loan document that all parties agree to and sign. Make provisions in case the borrower defaults on the loan. What recourse can you, and would you, pursue?

7. Having reviewed all these issues once, go over in your mind your relationship with every family member or potential heir. Have you done right by them? Have you created a gifting strategy that takes care of each of their individual needs and makes you feel good about what you're doing, or not doing, for them? Is there more you could do now, while you're living, to share your resources in ways that help your loved ones? With your current plan of gifting, have you overdone it with anyone—undermined their independence, or hurt any relationships by being too generous and upstaging someone else? If so, think about how you can change your gifting to provide the most good for all.

8. Most of all, enjoy sharing your money. Let your family know how much it means to you to be able to give away some of what you have so they can fulfill some of their dreams. Give them a chance to show their appreciation for your generosity. Express your own pleasure at seeing the results of gifting during your lifetime. That's your greatest reward of giving to your loved ones!

CHAPTER 12

The Middle Generation
Caught between Dreams

Baby boomers, those individuals born in the United States between 1946 and 1964, make up most of the middle generation today. They are "sandwiched" between caring for their aging parents (the grandparents) and taking care of their own children (the grandchildren). You could say they are sort of caught between dreams, constantly juggling their own earnings and savings to help fulfill the dreams of all three generations. Sometimes their own money resources do not seem expansive enough to address all these commitments. Consequently, financial stress is a way of life for many such adult children.

Certain demographics and historical trends make this all the more true. While the baby boomers' parents, today's seniors, are the wealthiest generation as a group, they also may live a very long time, due to medical advances in treating the diseases of aging. I know people whose parents are in their 80s, in great health, and likely to live far into their 90s. Although many of these seniors are well-fixed financially due to their tendency to save money, some are not so fortunate. They are living for more years in retirement than they expected, and, in many cases, spend these later years in the costly domain of long-term care. Most of these elders have Medicare and some private health insurance carried over from one spouse's former employer. However, Medicare covers only the early months of a long-term health crisis. What's more, the kind of long-term-care insurance available today was not around earlier when the cost was affordable for this aging group. So, for instance, if one spouse develops a lengthy final illness or disabling dementia, the couple's funds may be drained, leaving the surviving spouse without enough money to last his or her lifetime, much less the ability to help fund dreams of other generations in the family. Also, quite a number of these older couples took the retirement pension income for the husband's life only (instead of for their joint lives). When he dies, that pension income stops for his wife. If either parent runs through all their retirement assets, with only Social Security to live on, he or she may need financial help.

That brings us back to the baby boomers. At the very time this middle generation enters their peak years of career commitment, trying to save for retirement and wondering how to pay for children's college educations, they may see the need to provide financial support for their parents. This might mean sending a monthly check to make up the difference in bills the parent cannot cover with their reduced income or assets, or it might necessitate having a parent come live in their home or helping pay for residential care at an assisted living center or nursing home or for home care. Contributing this kind of support can be quite a financial burden to the adult children, even though they feel responsible and want to help.

So, of all the generations, today's baby boomers have the strongest need for knowing the total family resource picture. If your aging parents admit they may be heading for financial disaster, this becomes a major family issue that must be addressed among the generations. If you're not facing an immediate crisis, it's good to take things slowly and wait to offer what help you can give until you have a better idea of their problems, your limitations to solve them, and how offering help will alter your own financial picture.

Financing seniors' long-term health care is one major problem. While your parents are still in good health at somewhat younger ages, it may pay for you (and your siblings, if you have them) to pitch in for the rather expensive premium it would cost to buy them long-term-care insurance. Even for seniors in their 70s, this may make sense; the purchase price would still be cheaper than funding the yearly costs of long-term care later on. If either parent is now uninsurable because of a preexisting condition, you might investigate to see if a rider can be added to his or her current life insurance allowing use of death benefit monies for long-term-care expenses.

You'll want to brainstorm with your parents about their housing options, too. They may have enough space in their home to take in a boarder, whose rent money would supplement their income. They might be able to take out a reverse mortgage, which pays them a monthly income out of the equity buildup in the home.

So far, we've just talked about helping out parents in dire need of assistance. Yet there are other dreams adult children may want to help fund for their mothers and fathers—paying for special occasions, such as a golden anniversary trip or party, or bringing them to visit for holidays. As the adult child, you want to think ahead about what special treats you would like to finance. That has to be figured in to your yearly budget as well and can add to the price tags you're looking to fund.

An important aspect of financial obligations to parents has to do with the expectations some adult children have about how they should live their own lives. Whether it's wealthy elders who expect you to live up to the standards of their own economic lifestyles, or ones who struggled to give you an education and opportunities so you could rise above their modest beginnings, adult children today feel some pressure to keep up with the Joneses. This is particularly difficult for adult children who choose to live in big cities with higher living costs than their parents contended with in smaller communities. The end result is the idea that they often can't escape the pressure to succeed and spend. They've got to make their parents proud—be successful—and live the good life.

Still, another financial squeeze on the sandwich generation is the income instability baby boomers have experienced as a group. Following World War II, their parents experienced unparalleled prosperity and job security for decades. Baby boomers on the other hand have lived through a series of job interruptions and economic ups and downs, due to the Vietnam War, inflation, corporate downsizing, and technological innovations that have replaced people with computers. In funding their own dreams, much less those of their parents and children, this generation of adults has faced many financial uncertainties and challenges.

This generation also has its own children's dreams to consider, as well. They still want to be able to provide their kids the comforts they grew up enjoying, whether it was summer camp, art, and music lessons, a college degree, or travel abroad. At least the dreams of the third generation are a bit more predictable for a parent as far as timing. For instance, you know that when your child reaches age 18, it's time to fund their college education. But baby boomers have become the financial jugglers of this new century because of their dual commitment to parents and children.

What can you do to plan ahead for such multiple, simultaneous dreamfunding? How do you stretch resources and collaborate with parents and children to keep everyone on a course of dream achievement? Let's see what several families have done to address these problems.

TINA AND HARRY: Siblings Cope Differently with Their Parents and Children

Tina loves her parents dearly, but she thinks they've done a poor job of planning for retirement. Her dad was in the garment business. While things were good, he and his wife lived well, bought nice homes and cars, and expected one day to sell their business to provide for retirement. Unfortunately, Tina's father developed Crone's disease, a debilitating chronic health problem; for years he could work only sporadically, so his garment manufacturing venture failed, leaving him and his wife with few assets other than their home and no retirement income beyond their government pension from Sweden, their country of origin. Tina's mom, age 63, is still working as a receptionist for a modest salary, and will have to keep doing so as long as her health lasts, because the aging couple needs her income. At one point, Tina's dad wanted to start another company and, needing some seed money to begin operations, he asked his thrifty, baby boomer daughter for a loan. Tina turned him down. She said she and her husband were saving for their one daughter's education and their own retirement and did not feel they could help her parents.

Tina's younger brother, Harry, stepped in to offer a solution. He had started working in a franchise business that helps restaurants keep track of employee liquor theft. The business was now getting enough clients that he offered his dad a job helping him promote the service. The extra income helped out a lot. Harry also told his parents that if it became necessary, they could come live with him, his wife, and two daughters.

The interesting thing is that Harry has two children, and he and his wife together make less money than Tina does on her own. Tina's husband also earns a good income, and they just have one daughter to educate, having decided they could not afford a second child.

It comes down to priorities, really. Harry took responsibility for helping find solutions for his parents' problems. Tina chose to put her child and husband's dreams on her front burner. Also, Harry is more willing to share his home with his parents than his sister; obviously his wife has agreed to that arrangement.

You may find that you feel differently than your brothers or sisters about your obligation to help your parents financially while stretching your dollars to fund your children's and spouse's dreams. There's no right or wrong solution here. In Harry and Tina's story, the family's intergenerational talks did result in sharing of money and other resources to solve a family problem. You probably cannot expect the financial commitment or sense of responsibility to be equal among your siblings. What you hope is that someone, like Harry, will be able to, and want to, step up to the plate and help solve a family difficulty. You should be thinking about whether that person is you. If not, then who?

SALLY AND CHARLEY: Trying to Keep Up with the Joneses

Neither Sally nor Charley have parents in need of financial help. Sally's parents are quite wealthy and have set up a separate property trust for their daughter. What is a concern to Sally, however, is that she feels pressured to live the prosperous lifestyle of her parents. Her mother tells her she and Charley should be able to live better than they do, given that Charley is an attorney and Sally has a job as a counselor.

So, Sally and Charley started out living in an expensive home, on the right side of town, with their two young children in private elementary schools. Their lifestyle cost about $17,000 per month. Even in a big city, that's living pretty high.

Their troubles began when Charley left one law firm to go to another, the work dried up, and he was suddenly out of a job. It was not so easy to find another firm quickly, at the hourly rate he was used to getting. Before long, the bills started to pile up, including their tax bills. When I met this couple, they were about to lose their house, owed the IRS more than $100,000, and were deeply in debt to credit card companies. They were fighting about money, near the brink of divorce.

Sally was desperate, afraid to tap her trust fund, because that money was there to pay for college for the kids. Charley was in denial that he had a spending problem—he spent first, thought second. Their situation looked pretty grim, except for two things: this couple really loved each other, and they didn't want to file bankruptcy—they wanted to work out of their financial hole and pay off their debts.

As their financial advisor, I made them sit down and provide me a financial statement and an income/expense statement detailing the income they could count on now and the expenses they were incurring each month. They'd already moved out of their house, leasing it to cover the mortgage, and moved to a less expensive part of town where their rent was considerably less than their monthly mortgage payment had been. They put their kids in public schools and didn't touch the college funds. By now their expenses were around $11,000 per month, a lot of it interest payments on debt. Looking at their income and outgo, it was clear they needed to cut their living expenses even further. I made them go through all the expense items until they could reduce their budget by a third. Next, we found a tax attorney to work with the IRS in trying to get a reasonable payment schedule on the back taxes. Then, one by one, Sally talked to each creditor to lower the monthly amount due; she assured them that she and her husband intended to pay off the balances eventually, but it would take time. To the one, they all agreed to work with her on lowering the monthly payments they required.

Three years later, I must say, I've never been more proud of a client. We've been able to address Charley's unconscious kind of spending. He now keeps tabs and reports to Sally all his weekly expenditures. She pays all the bills and deals with the creditors. He has found independent work in litigation and it turns out he can bring home enough together with Sally's income to cover their current lifestyle. No more debt is being incurred. They talk openly with each other about money, and they feel really good about how far they've come. Sally told me recently, "We're going to make it; I'm certain of it. And, you know, we realize we don't need to live on the West Side with that expensive lifestyle. We're happy with what we are doing to rebuild our lives." Sally also mentioned that she had a heartfelt conversation with her mother, where she explained that she and Charley were content living the way they were, and they had no intention of going back to trying to keep up with her parents or any other "Joneses."

Here is a baby boomer family squeezed between parents' dreams for their daughter and their own ambition to re-create for their children a lifestyle they thought they should have. Fortunately, they decided keeping up with the Joneses wasn't for them, and they dropped out of the economic rat race to build a better life for their family.

MYRON AND NINA: Playing Catch-Up

At age 50, Myron married his long-time girlfriend, Nina, who was age 35. The next year they became parents of a baby girl. Three years later, their son was born. Once they started this family, the couple decided Nina would work as a stay-at-home mom. Myron's career in real estate was going well, when suddenly prices plummeted in the California real estate market. A year later their condo was nearly destroyed by the 1994 earthquake in Los Angeles. Their income shrank to nothing, and they had to rent a home while the condo was being repaired. While Myron began looking for a new career, they used up savings to live on, then credit cards.

Nina had grown up in modest circumstances and was very frugal, but Myron was a true gambler—he had rolled the dice in life in general as well as in Vegas on a regular basis. But what he didn't want to gamble with was his children's future. He wanted to keep them in private school. Paying for it was a worry. Plus, Nina's mother, divorced and living in tight circumstances, had needed their financial help for some time. Myron wasn't sure how they could keep up her monthly stipend now that his career path had reached a dead end.

Nina, who wanted the best for her children and yet hoped to still help her mom, did her part to cut expenses. She started making all the children's clothes and began taking them to parks to play instead of her previous monthly outings to game parks and children's theater. An excellent seamstress, she made all her own clothes as well to save money.

Myron tried several other types of sales jobs, finally working as a promoter to help a budding young musician. He ceased all trips to Vegas and gambled on his own skills to make ends meet. For four years, he and Nina managed to keep their son and daughter in the private school and to keep their commitment to helping Nina's mom.

Finally, their luck turned for the better—the real estate market rallied. Myron went back to what he does best, and his income this year will be substantial. He got a friend to help him negotiate with creditors to create a long-term payment plan for his $70,000 in debts. The condo, mortgaged to the hilt to cover the last four years of expenses, is too small for them now, so it's rented out, and the family continues to rent a larger home with a big yard for the kids.

Weathering these tough times, Myron and Nina learned they could trim back their own lifestyle to help her parent and give their children priority. Now that Myron's income looks promising for the foreseeable future, they must play catch-up on saving for their future retirement and sending their kids to college. They had a late start to begin with, marrying when Myron was 50, plus the unforeseen career upheaval interrupted their investments for the future. What it didn't interrupt, however, was their investment in their family—both the older and the younger generations.

NEW RULES OF THE FINANCIAL GAME

As you can see from their stories, baby boomers face a changing financial world from what their parents knew. To stay financially savvy in the 21st century, you need to follow the new rules of the financial game:

- If you are not updating your career skills yearly, you're already behind the times. (In three years your knowledge and skills will be outdated.)
- Plan to live to be 100. You've got another half century of dreams to fund. (Where will that money come from? How much do you have now?)
- Your parents will live longer than you or they ever thought. (Will yours need your financial support?)
- Your children will likely have 10 to 18 jobs in their lifetimes, and more periods of unemployment than you could stand. (Will you be offering them help during transitions?)
- If you need financial advice, don't wait or feel embarrassed. Run, ask, look stupid, but get the answers. There's too much information available to stay in the dark financially.
- If you want to know your parent's financial status, if you want their input on your financial situation, ask.
- Your children need your financial training now more than ever before. Wouldn't you like them to know more than you did when you went out on your own?

- Your children also know more about computers than you do—they may understand how to set up financial software that can simplify your financial life. They'll certainly know how to search the Internet for financial Web sites you hear about.
- Whatever you've been saving monthly for your future, double it this month. And double that next month. In a few years, you may actually be saving the same percentage of your income that your parents did all their lives.
- Think about when you want to stop working. Then think about when you want to stop funding your dreams. Chances are you'll want to fund many dreams after you retire. So, save, save, save, and invest with a long-term horizon.
- There are more investments today than you can possibly study. The simpler your investment strategy, the better. Diversify into basic asset classes. You can always add more dollars to these. Educate yourself and read about the financial world regardless of whether you engage a financial professional.
- Great dreams don't have to be costly. Upscale your vision, but downscale your price tags. It lets you fund more of the dreams you really cherish.
- You have parents before you and children after you, but don't forget to fund your own dreams. Remember, the cream in a sandwich cookie is that sweet stuff in the middle—those are your dreams, sandwiched between the older and younger generations of your family.

INTERGENERATIONAL PLANNING IS CRITICAL FOR THE MIDDLE GENERATION

If you are a member of the middle generation, you need intergenerational financial planning the most of all the generations in your family. It's because you're in the middle, and more burdens fall on you than the bookend generations around you. You need to know if your parents, the grandparent generation, are OK financially. If they are not and might need your assistance, the sooner you and your siblings can start thinking about solutions, the better. A good time to ask is a few years before your parents plan to retire. They have some crucial decisions to make at that time, about everything from when to start collecting

Social Security to what type of distribution to take from their retirement plans, IRAs, or annuities. If you can have some input in that process, you may help them make good decisions, which might favorably impact your financial future as well. You need to know about their estate plans—all the things we discussed in earlier chapters—and how these plans might affect you, especially if you might have been expecting an inheritance and learn it won't be forthcoming. Or perhaps you'll be lucky and find there will be a substantial amount of assets that you will one day receive, barring some health disaster that uses up all the money.

Similarly, if your middle-school-age child thinks he's going to Harvard, you need to hear about that sooner than later and start planning for that extra-large private school price tag, or else give him a reality check that you can't afford to send him unless he can get scholarships or loans to help.

You've also got to do your own reality check as it relates to the elders and children. In the next chapter, you'll learn about your own preparedness for a secure financial future, and early on, beginning as a young adult, you need to look at your own dreams with a long-term view. Start out doing your family intergenerational meetings just with your parents, getting their input on some of the dreams you want to fulfill and hearing about theirs. If you have children, you can bring them into the discussions as early as age four or five. Start listening to them talk about the things they love and want to do.

HOW THE TIME VALUE OF MONEY CAN HELP

As you're creating your Final Family Dream List in these early years of intergenerational financial planning, keep the big picture in mind—knowing that there is better timing for some dreams, when your parents are still healthy enough to do them, or your kids are young enough to want to do them with you. If you can just start early in life doing this, the saving and investing part is so much easier, because you have the time value of money on your side. The premise of this concept is that you can get to the same financial end point (price tag) setting aside less money per month if you have more years (time) to save until you need the money.

Let's say you have the following dreams you want to fund ten years from today:

Dream	Price Tag	Needed By
Send John to first year of private school	$ 6,500	10 years
Visit grandmother/grandfather with kids		
for 40th anniversary party	$ 3,500	10 years
Buy myself new car	$20,000	10 years
Total Price Tags	$30,000	10 years

If you start saving and investing the money for the price tags right now, you need $150 saved each month at 10 percent return to equal $30,000 in ten years. However, if you wait five years to get started, you must save $388 per month at 10 percent to equal $30,000 in five years. Your monthly savings required more than doubled because you lost time and cut your saving period in half.

DECIDING THAT ENOUGH IS ENOUGH

Unless you're wealthy, most of us can't have all that we want right now. However, one of the great things about being the middle generation is that we've gained a certain perspective. We've seen our parents live conservatively, for the most part, having plenty for their needs without splurging much on extras. We see our children, on the opposite hand, who respond to media bombardment to buy every new gizmo and designer fad. We have bought them all these things, because we, too, indulged ourselves with most of what we wanted as young adults—prior to marriage, out in the exciting working world.

By now, most of us have accumulated enough stuff, too much in fact. There is a reason there are a gazillion books on organizing your life in today's bookstores—we have so much stuff, we need someone to help us organize it. Now you see creeping onto bookshelves another kind of book—about how to simplify your life. Many adult children today are starting to see the value in that. We're getting weary of washing, dusting, packing up, and unpacking all the material things we've accumulated. Sometimes living in a small place, with fewer things, sounds kind of appealing.

What it means is that, as we age, baby boomers are getting more discriminating about what we have to have and what we don't. We're willing to winnow down our shelves, garages, and wardrobes and simply do very well, thank you, with less. The great benefit to this is that now we can fund more dreams. Or perhaps I'll say, we're choosing different dreams to fund.

One reason this happens is that we're starting to lose our parents to death and our children to growing up and leaving home. Suddenly, we start to see that it's people that matter to us more, not things. Many of you may have also faced a sudden health threat, nonfatal, but nonetheless a wake-up call. We are starting to reevaluate what is truly important to us: whom we cherish, what we truly enjoy doing, how much money we really need to have to feel secure, and how we want to spend our time, now and into the future.

This kind of value analysis—figuring out what is the "juice" in life for you, is all part of knowing your passions (the first P of funding your dreams). It also helps you narrow your focus on your dreams, and probably do the same for the dreams you want for your parents and children. It may become a lot more important to you that they choose the dreams that matter most to them, and that you'll be happy funding those dreams. You might actually find you have fewer burdens than you thought, for their dreams might be more modest financially (cost less) than the dreams you've nurtured so carefully for them.

DREAMFUNDING STRATEGIES . . .

1. The key to middle-generation dreamfunding is to earn enough money to pay for your current lifestyle and have money left over for funding family dreams. Have you designed a career path that will inevitably have gaps of unemployment? Do you have emergency funds set aside so that you can cover these lapses in income? You should have six months of living costs in liquid investments that can be tapped. Do you have disability insurance? If not, and you can, buy it. You have a greater likelihood of being disabled at this age than of dying. Addressing these questions ensures that you have plans to stabilize your income no matter what happens in career upheaval.

2. Do your parents need your financial help? Have you asked about their financial situation? Have they done financial projections? Do they have long-term-care insurance, or are they self-insured with enough money to cover an expensive illness?

3. Ask yourself what parental expectations you are trying to live up to in terms of your own adult lifestyle. Do you feel your parents expect you to have more money than you have, or than you even want to have? Are you trying to keep up with the Joneses? If so, are you keeping up, falling behind, or sick to death of trying? Reconsider if your lifestyle goals are yours, or someone else's. What are your own ambitions in this arena? Are you satisfied with what you are doing with your life and your finances? If not, what areas still need work? Have you talked about this with your spouse? Take a weekend and sit down together as a couple and brainstorm on what you want to accomplish as a family for the next 10 years, 20 years, for life. Write down the dreams, the price tags. Make sure they are on the Final Family Dream List, when you make that list with your parents and kids.

4. What dreams do you have for your children? Are these dreams they themselves subscribe to? Which ones do you share in common? Are you helping them fulfill their short-term goals? What dreams of theirs do you need to add to the Final Family Dream List?

5. What about other members of your family—siblings, aunts, uncles, your own grandparents, if they are still living? Have you thought about talking with them about the dreamfunding you, your parents, and kids want to do? Perhaps one of them already has funded a dream like one you aspire to achieve. That person might have valuable input.

6. Total the price tags of the dreams you've listed for the next ten years. Select a rate of return on invested dollars that seems feasible with your own investment experience, current markets, and your comfort level with risk. It may be 6 percent, 8 percent, or 10 percent. Then work backward with a financial calculator (or ask your accountant) to figure out how much a month you need to save, starting today, to reach those dream price tags by their target dates. You'll have more than one target date, so you can figure out the monthly savings on each dream. Total the monthly savings needed for all the dreams. Is that an amount you are already saving, or

could save? Even if not, set aside as much as you can now. Add to it as your income goes up, or as you trim your expenses.

7. Reread the "New Rules of the Financial Game," listed in this chapter. Go down each rule and see how it applies to you.

8. In terms of helping the other two generations with their dreams, can you afford to pitch in financially right now and help them this year with a dream? If so, are you willing? Do they know that? Let your family know how much you can contribute to their dreamfunding this year.

9. If you need help with your own dreamfunding this year, have you asked for that help? Who would you ask? Call them, and start the conversations.

10. Take a look at your investments. Are they scattered, generating a mound of account paperwork every month? Could you consolidate or simplify your investment strategy? Are you diversified for better risk management? Do you subscribe to a financial newspaper or magazine to educate yourself about money?

11. Ask your kids how much they understand about the money world. What do they learn in school in finance or consumer education classes? Would they like to own a stock you could buy for them? Would they enjoy playing games like Monopoly, or using their computer to track their allowance and savings? For more ideas about expanding the financial education of your children, see Part Four.

12. How could you upscale your vision and downscale your price tags of your own personal dreams? This means taking a snapshot of where you are financially today. Complete the Financial Statement worksheet in the Appendix for a balance sheet of your assets and liabilities. Compare your savings and investments with the ten-year totals for price tags of dreams you have for you and your family. What is the gap between the dollars you need in ten years and what you have? What can you do about that gap, if there is one?

- *Upscale your vision.* This means doing your own value analysis, deciding what you have to have and what you don't, determining what you really want, and making your vision of the future focus on dreams you truly cherish. I don't mean upscale financially; I mean get a clearer picture of your most important dreams and those of your parents and children.

- *Downscale your price tags.* After brainstorming with your various family members, you may find ways to slash the costs of dreams you thought were unaffordable on first glance (e.g., pooling resources with other family members, seeking ways to lower the price tags such as bartering your services to help pay for a car, cruise, or school). That's another reason to review your marketable skills. You'd be amazed at how many people would give you a deeply discounted value on something you want in exchange for your talents. Also, think about that "simplified" mode of life, where you might be just as happy with a smaller house, older car, fewer and less fancy things, and that may cut down the cost of certain dreams you had in mind. You may find that, while you feel "caught between dreams," asking all three generations to upscale their vision and downscale their price tags may mean you can help your loved ones fund more of their dreams while also funding more of your own.

CHAPTER 13

Funding Your Retirement Dream

If you ask members of the baby boom generation at what age they plan to retire, you don't get a uniform answer. The usual gist of the response is, "I'm not worrying about *when* I retire, but *if* I can retire at all!" Some envision themselves working at fast-food restaurants way into their 90s; others fear they will be reduced to eating cat food for breakfast, lunch, and dinner. You get the picture.

This is the group of Americans who chose, in many cases, to extend their adolescence well into their late 20s. Having grown up in the postwar prosperity, not only have they been big spenders, compared to their parents, but also they started late as savers. Their stop-and-start careers have resulted in lower retirement savings rates, making retiring early a questionable dream for many.

What's more, baby boomers are looking down the long tunnel of longevity as medical advances lengthen life span. Even if they wait until age 66 to retire (the full retirement age to collect maximum Social Security for those born between 1946 and 1959—it ratchets up to age 67 for those born 1960 and later), this generation could well live 30 or more years in retirement. That's a lot of years of lifestyle expenses to fund with savings and investments.

So, as I discussed in Chapter 12, this group needs major catch-up strategies to pay their way to a golden age of financial independence.

Let's look at what some people are doing to make financial security an achievable dream.

PRISCILLA AND BURTON: Modest Retirement Dream

Priscilla and Burton believe that taking care of family first is the most important task they have as children of God. They have a deep religious conviction, and they live their faith. They have always been close to both sets of parents and have helped both Priscilla's and Burton's folks at one time or another—lending money when needed, and caring for Priscilla's dad in their home in his final year of life. They shared their resources often when money was not plentiful for themselves.

Priscilla, a teacher, worked when they needed her income; she mostly stayed home raising their three children, the last of whom went off to college this year. Neither of their two sons chose to go to college, so their daughter's educational expense is the only college funding they've had to do. But it is happening at a time when Burton had to close one business and go work for his competitor. The couple has moved several times, trying to find a better territory for Burton's commercial air-conditioning service; it just hasn't worked out too well. They've spent most of their savings on their children, their parents, or their own bills. At ages 50 and 52, they have only Paula's teacher's retirement plan and Social Security to fund their later years.

The one bright spot in their financial picture is that they've always been lucky at buying good real estate. From Oregon, to Kansas, to Arizona, they made money each time they sold their residential property. The 20-acre parcel and home where they live now will likely bring a good profit when they relocate to Wyoming, their state of birth, to retire. Priscilla and Burton hope to clear about $250,000 at that time and are planning to live modestly on a horse ranch in a remote area of Wyoming, where land is inexpensive. They figure they can buy a property with some acreage there for $150,000 cash and live on about $35,000 a year—derived from Priscilla's modest teacher's pension, their combined Social Security, and $8,000 interest on the remaining $100,000 of capital from the sale.

I know many people who would feel that $35,000 is not an adequate retirement income. But Priscilla and Burton are intelligent, resourceful people with simple needs. They've made choices in life that satisfy their hearts and souls, and, frankly, I think they've done the right thing for them. It's a reminder that we have lots of choices about how we live. A modest retirement lifestyle might be right for some of you, just as it is for Priscilla and Burton.

ABIGAIL: A Delayed Retirement

Twenty years ago Abigail, age 52, married a man 20 years older than she. They had two boys, who are now college age. Abigail never finished college, but worked in her mother's neighborhood retail business until the arrival of discount stores forced the family to close their store three years ago. Abigail has worked at several retail and sales jobs since but isn't trained in computer or other skills that would land her a decent job without a college degree. She needs to go back for more training, but funds are tight.

Abigail's husband never made much money. He dabbled at photography, then worked in the family store, then had a heart attack followed by two mild strokes. He's 72 now, collecting Social Security, and that's what the family lives on, supplemented by Abigail's modest salary. One big help is that the couple and their remaining son at home have moved in with Abigail's 85-year-old mother, who pays most of the household bills, except food.

While Abigail and her husband would like their sons to go to college, they cannot really afford to send them unless Abigail uses the $50,000 in an investment account her mother set aside for her, money that was targeted to help Abigail in her retirement years. Abigail's oldest son works part-time, hoping to figure out what area of academics and career he would like to pursue. Still, he's bright and probably will get student loans if he does go on to college. The second son plans to apply to the state university this year, and it seems that between Abigail, her brother, and her mother, the funds will be there to get him started in his first year. He'll live at home to eliminate school housing costs.

The real dilemma here is Abigail's long-term financial security. She doesn't have any, except whatever funds she may inherit from her mother, whose estate now is about $250,000. The family has talked about this issue—at least Abigail's brother and mother have talked about it. While Abigail's mother originally wanted to split her assets between her two children, the plan now is to leave all of the estate's assets to her daughter, since her son will have plenty of money of his own. Still, Abigail's mother, who lives on her investment income and Social Security, may have to dip into that asset base for medical care later on. It would be unwise for Abigail to count on having all that money as part of her retirement nest egg.

Clearly, Abigail needs to finance a good bulk of her own future security by going back to school and getting a career going, even at age 52. Once she gets a job with a better salary, she can start saving on her own for retirement. If she saves $200 per month at 10 percent for 20 years, that's still only an additional $151,873. Saving $350 each month would produce $265,779 at that rate of return over the two decades. That sum by itself would give her a modest retirement income of $21,262 (at 8 percent per year). Together with Social Security, and hopefully some assets from her mother's estate, she could get by. But look at how long she'll have to work—20 more years. If she finishes school in three years, she'll be working until she's 75.

One backup ace that Abigail has is her brother. Although the two don't always see eye to eye, he has told his mother that he will subsidize his sister's income if her resources are too meager in retirement. But, he insists, he wants to see her get her ducks in order and start facing her somewhat stark reality about her later years. He's not willing to foot the whole bill. Abigail's mother has suggested she use some of her $50,000 investment account to pay for completing her education.

These are the realities of some intergenerational and intrasibling dynamics. Not everyone gets along or approves of how someone else in the family may have chosen to live his or her life. Still, this family is pulling together to help one member whose plight looks somewhat grim. By offering money to help Abigail go back to school, they are trying to arm her with what she needs—better job skills—so that she can take charge of her own future and create a secure retirement. They are helping her fund that dream.

CINDY AND GIRARD: Early Retirement

Cindy and Girard have had good luck and bad. The bad luck is that Girard's academic career as a professor of history foundered when he did not get tenure. He loved being a professor, but he had to turn to a government job in historical research when no other teaching positions gelled. Cindy left her job at a government agency to become a newspaper journalist. They both earned modest salaries for their early years of marriage. Having married in their late 30s, they struggled with costly fertility problems but finally had two daughters. Eventually they left the big city for a smaller seaside community to raise their girls in a more child-friendly environment. Fortunately, Cindy became a local correspondent for a national paper. Girard found another city job that was OK, but nothing that stimulated him the way teaching did.

Another lucky stroke was that both Cindy and Girard share an attitude about money—they are thrifty. Having grown up in middle-class homes, they knew about investments and proceeded to sock away, both during their single years and also after marriage, a lot of money considering their individual incomes. Cindy was one of the first women I knew who bought her own condo. So, ten years after their marriage, this couple had saved a lot toward retirement.

They also are lucky in that their parents have been generous. Girard's parents died fairly young and left him $250,000. Cindy's father, a successful dentist, began gifting money yearly to Cindy, Girard, and the two girls, taking advantage of the annual exclusion that lets you gift to as many people as you want (the maximum tax-free gift is $10,000 per person per year). When Cindy's mother was alive, each parent gifted the maximum amount. (These gifts totaled $20,000 per person per year.)

The net result of their own thriftiness and this family generosity is that at ages 50 and 53, Cindy and Girard can now retire. They haven't done so yet, but they can. Now, I should say, they could almost retire on what they've saved themselves, for the children's trusts have been funded through Cindy's mother's estate as well as the money Cindy's dad continues to give each year. The gift money given to Cindy and Girard has been stashed away in their own investment accounts and will only make their eventual retirement lifestyle more comfortable.

What I admire about this family is that they were practicing intergenerational financial planning long before I coined that term—for more than 20 years. Cindy and Girard's parents taught them about money, shared their resources, and are contributing to the higher education of their grandchildren. Their gifting program has enabled Cindy and Girard to set aside the maximum amount for their own retirement, knowing that college funds are already taken care of by the older generation.

These adult children saved frugally themselves, learning from their parents, and providing for their future security despite career set backs. Even the granddaughters are being taught how to manage money through their allowances and are encouraged to shop carefully for their clothes and toys. This multigenerational sharing of resources fosters cooperation, financial training, and the option of financial independence at a young age for this family's "sandwich" generation.

THE KEY TO A SECURE RETIREMENT: Start Saving Now!

To win the game of financial catch-up, you must start to save more than you have in the past and invest that money for your retirement. I mean today, not next week, not next month—*today.* Whether you're 36 or 54, you've still got time to achieve the retirement dream. The older you are, obviously, the more you have to save.

Let's say you're 40 years old and want to retire with a million dollars. You'll target four possible ages of retirement: 50, 55, 60, and 65. Following are the savings you have to put aside to reach your retirement goal. (This is assuming you have nothing put away yet, or you want to add at least a million dollars to what you already have.) We'll assume a 10 percent growth on your savings:

Age Now	Years before Retiremeent	Required Yearly Savings @ 10 Percent	Retirement Age	Amount at Retirement
40	10	$62,745	50	$1 Million
40	15	31,474	55	1 Million
40	20	17,460	60	1 Million
40	25	10,168	65	1 Million

You can see that planning to retire in ten years with no current savings is not realistic at the million-dollar lifestyle. (At 8 percent, $1 million would generate $80,000 annual income from your portfolio.) To that, you would add any pension income and Social Security plus any outside income sources, such as rental income or part-time work.) So, you would have to rethink your plan—work longer, live on less in retirement, or find other sources of income in retirement beyond what you're planning for now.

What if you're 50 now, and you've got $200,000 in various investment and retirement accounts. What would you need to reach the million-dollar nest egg? To keep it simple, we'll assume your current portfolio is growing at 10 percent as well.

Age Now	Years before Retirement	Current Savings @ 10 Percent	New Yearly Savings @ 10 Percent	Retirement Age	Amount at Retirement
50	5	$322,102	$111,038	55	$1 Million
50	10	518,748	36,243	60	1 Million
50	15	835,450	5,179	65	1 Million

This should make you feel good, if you've already set this much aside and are willing to work until you're 65. But what if you're 50, and you have not started to save for retirement? Just look at the chart for the 40-year-olds, and add ten years to the retirement age column at each level, that is, at retirement you'd be 60, 65, 70, 75, and needing to save the amounts listed. If you could save the $10,168 per year ($847.33 per month) and are willing to work until you're 75, you can still get to that million dollars!

These numbers are not meant to scare you, but they should help light a fire under you. The next ten years are the most important years of your life, if you want to build toward a financially comfortable retirement. Yes, I know you will face other commitments in these years, such as educating children, helping your parents, fulfilling some other dreams of your own. However, you cannot wait any longer to save for retirement. The time is now, and waiting longer could jeopardize your ability to make your money last a lifetime. Also, the sooner you begin seriously saving toward retirement, the more options you'll have later on in terms of retirement age, retirement income potential, lifestyle choices, and, most important, peace of mind.

RETIREMENT PLANNING MADE EASY

What Do You Have?

It's the old truism: You can't get where you're going if you don't know where you are. You've got to get a handle on your financial picture. Use the Financial Statement Worksheet in the Appendix to review your assets and liabilities. Mostly, right now, we want to focus on liquid assets in both your taxable savings and investment accounts and in your retirement (tax-deferred) accounts. These are assets you've already saved for somebody's (yours, your children's) future. The next step is to assess how much of this money is set aside for your retirement, as opposed to savings for college funds or a vacation home fund, etc. Total all your assets currently earmarked for retirement.

What More Do You Need to Save?

Fill out the Cash Flow Statement and the Income/Expense Statement to compare your income and expenses (see the Appendix). What we want to determine is the amount of income over expenses that can be invested for the future. Let's say your combined income from all sources (total income) is $95,000, and your total expenses are $90,000. The difference of $5,000 is newfound money for investments. But how much do you really need to be saving each year?

Let's also assume you have $70,000 in combined IRAs plus another $25,000 in your company retirement plans. So, you have $95,000 current savings for retirement. You will need a financial calculator, such as the Hewlett-Packard 10B or an online calculator with financial functions. Here are the simple calculations:

1. Figure the growth potential of your current retirement savings. Take $95,000 as your present value (PV), 10 percent as your interest rate (I/YR), ten years as the number of years (N), and solve for the future value (FV). You should get –$246,405. (You'll get a negative number, but don't worry about that—it's the way the functions on the calculator work.) That's how much your $95,000 will grow to in ten years at 10 percent.
2. Next, figure how much you need to retire if you retired in ten years. Let's use the $1 million figure again. Subtract your current savings from that retirement nest egg amount needed:

$1,000,000
– 246,405
$ 753,595 This is "the gap" that you must still save.

3. Using your financial calculator once more, work back and use the $753,595 as the future value of what you'll need to save. Use 10 percent interest rate and ten as the number of years, and now solve for payment (PMT). You should get $47,285. So, you would have to save $47,285 per year for the next ten years to get to the $1 million. Sound a bit steep? It's a far cry from that extra $5,000 yearly net income that you found you could save.

How Will You Get There?

Go back to the drawing board and decide which of these financial factors you will change to alter your retirement picture:

- Retirement date
- Retirement income needed
- Current and future income
- Current and future expenses
- Monthly retirement savings

It's pretty simple: you'll have to change one, or better yet several, of these factors to achieve your retirement dream. Let's focus on a few of them to help you get started. Perhaps you won't be so discouraged when we're done.

RETIREMENT DATE

First, retirement isn't what it used to be. It's not like you're going to sit on a porch in a rocking chair drinking lemonade, or sun on a beach sipping martinis. Retirees lead active, vibrant lives. They do a lot, and in many cases they spend a lot. Some choose to start second careers, or work part-time. There are so many options and opportunities that you may want to think a bit ahead about just what you want to do in your retirement. Some people spend the 10 to 15 years before they retire planning for it—retraining to get some skills they'd like to use in a new career, choosing a community where they will one day resettle, taking fewer vacations, cutting expenses now, so they can retire earlier than they'd once planned. Others decide to work longer and retire later.

Moving your retirement date either way has pluses and minuses. There's no better time for you to think about these things than now.

Early Retirement

What most people mean by this is that they'll stop doing one kind of work so they can do something else they enjoy better. That could be paid work; full- or part-time work; leisure and recreational activities; and volunteer work. Setting yourself up financially to be able to retire early can open up a whole new chapter of life that absolutely thrills and delights you.

If you're planning to retire at 50, 55, or 60, you've got to save more each year as you saw from the charts. Also, you're going to need some investments that are not in retirement plans, especially if you will not be getting a pension income at retirement but rather a lump-sum distribution that you will roll over to an IRA (individual retirement account). IRAs and other retirement accounts restrict withdrawals before you reach age 59½. Although you can set up what are called *equally substantial payments* (IRS Rule 72(t)) to withdraw your retirement funds, you must adhere to specified limits for a period of five years, or until you reach age 59½, whichever is longer. Once you start these withdrawals, you have to continue them until age 59½. Otherwise you suffer a 10 percent penalty on your early withdrawals. Most people want to have outside investment accounts they can tap for income in the years prior to that age. Or you'll need other sources of income during "the gap" to pay your living expenses. If you're married, you may want one spouse to retire early while the other one works a bit longer.

Even if your company offers you an "early out" retirement package, be sure to read all the conditions before accepting the offer. In general, you take a smaller yearly retirement pension when you leave employment before the normal retirement, which varies from company to company. Some employers sweeten the deal and give you added years of service to bring your pension up to what you would have had at your normal retirement age. Also, be sure to take into account the fact that most pensions are cut substantially (usually in half) for the surviving spouse when the employee dies. See how your early retirement might affect your surviving spouse's income.

When you stop working may affect the age at which you want to start collecting Social Security. However, choosing the option to take

Social Security early will reduce your monthly benefits. Also, this "haircut" gets steeper as the full retirement age (FRA) pushes past 65. (FRA is the age at which you can receive your maximum Social Security benefits.) By 2005, the FRA increases to age 66 for individuals born from 1943 through 1959. With an FRA at 65, taking Social Security early at age 62 results in a benefit that is 80 percent of what it would have been if you had waited until 65. When the FRA goes to 66, the age 62 option will be 75 percent of the full benefit; and when the FRA goes to 67 (in 2022 for everyone born in 1960 or later), the age 62 benefit drops to 70 percent of the full benefit. So, there is an increasing cost to retiring early. Additionally, if you begin Social Security benefits before age 65 and then decide to pursue a second career or part-time work, the Social Security Retirement Earnings Test applies earnings limitations after which your benefits are further reduced. In 2001, the earnings limitation for beneficiaries *under age 65* is $10,680, after which your Social Security income is reduced by $1 for every $2 you earn over that limit during the year.

Another caveat of early retirement is that you have more years of inflation-adjusted expenses to cover. Let's say you retire at 55 and live to be 90. That's 35 years to fund. Consider what will be the inflation-adjusted value of your million-dollar portfolio, if that is your nest egg goal. I use 2 percent for inflation in my projections today, and assuming that inflation rate over 35 years means that your million dollars at the end of that period would be worth the equivalent of $548,696 today. Here's another way to look at this problem: If you want $80,000 per year (in today's dollars) for your retirement income, in 30 years, when you're 85, you will need $144,090 to pay for the same lifestyle. So, you have to figure in inflation.

Another issue is health care. If you retire early, you may have to leave behind your employer's health insurance plan, or you may have to pay fully out-of-pocket to stay in the plan. So, you may want to budget for health insurance until you're eligible for Medicare. I think it's advisable to keep private insurance even after you can apply for Medicare. As I said earlier, Medicare doesn't cover long-term-care expense for very long, and the high costs of health care can erode your carefully saved retirement dollars.

The big plus of early retirement, of course, is that you can do more of what you want sooner rather than later. If you have health concerns, perhaps you are better off stopping work early and enjoying the added retirement years of leisure and the pursuit of your favorite passions while your health is still good.

Retiring Late

There is no stigma to retiring late, if you love your work and don't want to stop. I have clients who wait until 70, even 75, before considering retirement. Some enjoy what they do. Others do it to benefit from the financial gain of working more years; they have more working time to save and invest in their retirement accounts, letting their assets continue to compound tax-deferred, before drawing on them to live in retirement. Their earnings often go up at their company during these later years, and most retirement benefits are figured on the employee's three to five peak earning years, which will likely be these last years of working. Also, older employees continue to enjoy the group benefits, including disability, life, health, and sometimes even dental insurance.

Taking Social Security late does not diminish your eventual retirement income. For anyone born after 1942, the delayed retirement credit is 8 percent for each full year that you do not receive your benefits, up to age 70, where benefits are capped. (Add that 8 percent yearly increase to the maximum monthly benefit, which is $1,536 for a retired couple in 2001.) In April of 2000, Congress repealed the Social Security Retirement Earnings Test for people who have reached full retirement age (65 in 2001). You can continue working after this age without any reduction in benefit. (Prior to this new Senior Citizens' Freedom to Work Act of 2000, a retirement test applied until age 70. However, if you turn 65 in 2001, there is a $25,000 cap on earnings for that year above which your Social Security income is reduced $1 for every $3 you earn over the earnings limitation.)

By the way, if you're worried that Social Security won't last long enough for you to collect, set that worry aside. According to the system's trustees, the retirement fund can afford to keep paying full benefits until 2037, at which time it can still cover 72 percent of the benefits promised. That gives Congress another three decades to work on the problem.

If you're a "late saver" playing catch-up, working longer may be your best option to secure your future. If you still have children to educate, a mortgage to pay off, or need to keep your group benefits until a younger spouse qualifies for Medicare, working longer may save the day. Let's say you're 54 and have only $150,000 in your 401(k) and you earn $70,000 per year. You're investing $3,500 per year in the 401(k). Your portfolio earns 10 percent, and in retirement you'll aim for an 8 percent return on your rollover IRA from the 401(k). Let's see what your retirement portfolio income would be if you retired at ages 60, 65, and 70:

	Age 60	Age 65	Age 70
Growth of $150,000 (at 10%)	$265,734	$427,967	$689,245
Growth of Yearly Savings			
($3,500/year at 10%)	27,004	64,859	125,824
Total Assets Saved	292,738	492,826	815,069
Portfolio Income (8%)	23,419	39,426	65,205

You can see that waiting five years, from age 60 to 65, increases your investment portfolio income by 68 percent from $23,419 to $39,426 annually. Waiting another five years until age 70 increases your income by 178 percent and gives you an annual investment income of $65,205.

It is obvious, then, that you can make a big difference in your retirement lifestyle by altering your retirement date. So, it is important to estimate how much income you want to have in retirement and, specifically, how much of that income must come from investments versus other sources. Based on your assets today and your potential net income from future investments, you can calculate when you can afford to retire in the style which you desire.

RETIREMENT INCOME NEEDED

You saw from our stories earlier that what each person feels is "enough" money for retirement varies greatly. Do you need $35,000 per year like Priscilla and Burton, or do you want $100,000 per year or more? This question is probably the most important one you have to answer. No one can tell you this. Perhaps you just want to keep living at the economic level you've already achieved, adjusted only for inflation. Some retirees will tell you they are spending more than they did before retirement—usually due to increased travel and recreational expenses.

You should plan on spending no less than 70 percent to 80 percent of your current lifestyle costs—that's about the average.

Obviously, the lower the income you need, the smaller your portfolio of assets must be to generate that income. Also, the more pension and nonportfolio income sources you have, the fewer savings for personal investments you'll need to make now, because you'll have less need for an investment portfolio altogether. Of course, when we're looking at setting aside money for the future, your monthly or annual contributions to your retirement plans are a key part of the accumulation effort.

Earlier in the chapter, I asked you to fill out the Financial Statement, Cash Flow Statement, and Income/Expense Statement worksheets in the Appendix. Look at the Income/Expense Statement to see what you're spending yearly to live right now. Do you want a similar income in retirement, adjusted for inflation? Could you live on less? Would you possibly need more income to incorporate higher travel expenses or the purchase of a retirement home?

Review your Cash Flow Statement worksheet to mark off any expenses that will not continue once you're retired. Think of ones you might need to add. Consider whether you'll have to buy health insurance once you quit working, if you cannot take your employer plan with you in retirement.

What kind of lifestyle changes might you make when you retire that would either increase or decrease your cost of living (income required)? Would you be traveling more, moving to a smaller community, moving an aging parent into your home or assisting them in paying for a residential care facility, letting an adult child move back home to help him or her during a life transition? All these would affect your need for income to pay associated expenses.

Now is the time to fill out the Retirement Income/Expense worksheet in the Appendix, if you have not done so yet. You'll need to examine every piece of income that you might be getting in retirement, including all pension and annuity benefits that come in the form of a monthly payment.

Also, it's time to review your Social Security Earnings and Benefit Estimate Statement (Form 7004). As of 2000, this document is now being sent to everyone age 25 and older. If you don't have a recent copy, call 800-772-1213, or your local Social Security office. You can also visit the agency's Web site at <www.ssa.gov>. It takes about five weeks after submitting the form to get your statement, showing the earnings that Social Security has on file for your working career and a projection of your benefit at different retirement ages. You should definitely plug this income into your worksheet, along with the Social Security income of your spouse. Use the income figures for the lowest age you might expect to retire—for example, 62. If you plan to retire early or late, calculate the alteration in benefit income such a change will produce, based on our earlier discussion.

As for potential income from a second career or part-time work, I suggest you leave that off. What if health interfered and you would decide not to work again after all? You don't want to count on potential income that is not definite.

Finally, take your liquid investments in both taxable and tax-deferred accounts and multiply by an average pretax rate of growth of 8 percent. Add that income to your worksheet. I would not add in any investment income you might derive from expected inheritances. Again, that windfall might not happen.

After filling in the expense section of the Retirement Income/Expense worksheet, you should have two critical pieces of information:

1. Your expected cost of living in retirement (required retirement income)
2. Total retirement income projected

If you have come up short, needing more than you're going to get, it's time to decide how you might change your plan for the amount of income you need. You could downscale your lifestyle budget. You could barter for vacation rentals by renting out your own residence, to save on vacation costs. You could tell your daughter that you'll provide $5,000 instead of $20,000 for her wedding, and she'll have to make up the difference. You could sell your current home that is larger and more costly to maintain and buy a smaller home or condo. You could sell your gas-guzzling car and just keep one car for the two of you. You can leave the country club and play golf on public courses.

Look again at your Cash Flow Statement and see where your current biggest lifestyle costs are—it could be that you spend $12,000 per year eating out, because you are tired at the end of the day and don't want to fix meals. That's a lifestyle option you could readily alter in retirement. Perhaps your wardrobe takes a lot of your cash now—buying it, dry-cleaning it, storing it off season. How might you simplify and reduce expenses here once you're retired? If you go down every expense item, from telephones, to publications, to entertainment, to automobiles, you may find that you can reduce your needed income by as much as 10 percent to 30 percent. That will make saving for retirement much less burdensome. So change your projected expenses in retirement accordingly.

CURRENT AND FUTURE EXPENSES

Do you know how much money you waste each year, each week, each day? Lots. I do it, too. Caffé lattes are my favorite treat during working hours, having lunch with a friend, or after a nice dinner out. I often choose where I'm going to eat out based on whether they serve lattes or at least whether they are near a Starbuck's, so I can stop by after and have a latte for my "dessert"! One time I figured that I was spending $25 per week, or $100 per month on lattes! Is that ridiculous, or what? At that rate, in ten years, I will have spent $20,484 on coffee! Humbled by my own calculations, I now drink one latte a week, partly because I'm giving up caffeine, and partly because I'd rather save that money for my own retirement.

You, no doubt, have something you're just as nuts about. So, why not go down the Cash Flow Statement list of expenses once again? Try carving out some money from at least ten items. Add the monthly total. Using your financial calculator, multiply 20 years of investments at 10 percent of that extra money, and see how much you would garner in new retirement capital. I bet it's somewhere between $50,000 and $500,000. Now, how badly do you need to spend that money on these expense items? Could you do without some of them?

My favorite item to have you assess is your current monthly payments for interest on your credit cards. Not principal payments, interest. Let's say you're paying $200 per month on your Visa or Mastercard. You may have gotten an introductory rate of 2.79 percent, but overall, you're averaging 12 percent, and you've been paying that amount for three years. That's $8,615 that could have been invested toward your future. And there are plenty of people who always carry credit card balances, often paying $400 to 500 per month. If you pay $500 for ten years at 12 percent, you've given the credit card companies $115,019 of your potential retirement assets!

The idea is simple. Spend less now and save the difference, investing it toward your future. You won't really miss the extras you're not buying, especially if you're buying them on credit, but you will miss the retirement cushion that redirecting those funds can afford, if you'll just be a bit more disciplined and selective in how you spend your hard-earned capital.

A friend I just visited in Hawaii, age 52, told me recently that she and her husband knew when they got married that they wanted to be able to retire at age 55. So, they've forgone taking major vacations over the past 20 years. Mostly they have visited her family on the mainland, taking their son to see his grandparents, or they've tacked on a few days of fun after her mainland business trips. Already, she confided, they have saved and invested enough money that they will reach their target date in three years, when she and her husband turn 55. She's not sure now that they'll both stop working then, but they can, if they want to. Regardless, they plan to take some fabulous vacations once they do stop working; they can afford to, knowing their future retirement income is secured.

DREAMFUNDING STRATEGIES . . .

Let's focus on increasing your monthly retirement savings:

1. Do one more run through of the Cash Flow Statement to see if you can cut 10 percent to 30 percent of your current lifestyle costs. Decide how you'll invest those savings for your retirement. As an incentive, calculate what those savings will grow to at a 10 percent growth rate over ten years.

2. For the next two months, try to save 10 percent of your gross income, even if you have to cut out some regular expenses. Pick the ones you care least about. Did you really miss having those things or experiences? More than likely, you didn't. Could you manage to continue this savings rate for another six months? A year? Next year, could you save 15 percent? You'll be able to afford to retire

much, much, earlier, if you keep increasing your percentage of retirement savings.

3. Check to see if you're maximizing the money you can save in your company's retirement plan—make sure you take advantage of any matching your employer offers.

4. Review your investments to see if you are willing to take a bit more risk to reach for greater returns on your investment dollars. What is your split between equity (stocks, stock mutual funds, variable annuities) and fixed income (CDs, Treasuries, municipal or corporate bonds, fixed annuities)? If you're in your 30s, are you comfortable putting 90 percent in the equity investments? In your 40s, how about 80 percent? In your 50s, 70 percent? Of course, you must pick an asset allocation that meets your comfort level, without risking your principal, to gain more return.

5. Review your Final Family Dream List, and see what years you have targeted to help other family members fund dreams. Increase overall savings rate to make sure you can help contribute to those other dreams and still continue setting aside retirement savings for this important dream of yours.

6. You need to decide your own philosophy of which savings priorities come first, second, third, and so on. Along the lines of the "pay yourself first" theme, consider saving for your retirement first, helping your parents second, and funding your kids' dreams last. Your parents won't always be here, so help fund their dreams now. Normally, your children will have lots of years during which you can help them make their dreams come true.

CHAPTER 14

Caring for Mom and Dad
Knowing How to Parent Your Parents

You get a call at work from your widowed mother's neighbor. Your mother has fallen and broken her hip; she's in the hospital. Can you please fly to Omaha at once? You drop everything and go. What else would you do? Your mother needs you.

Perhaps, as the adult child of an aging parent, you have already received a call like this one. If not, you likely will someday be summoned to handle a medical problem of one or both of your elderly parents. Or your sister may call to say that she was home visiting your dad for a weekend, she was shocked to see how messy his apartment was, and how forgetful he seemed. At one point, he had called her by your name.

One of the great sorrows and yet great blessings in life is to watch our parents live long enough to grow old and eventually die. We realize that soon the loved ones who took care of us when we were young and vulnerable will themselves need our helping hand. We are happy to give it, and yet we don't always know how, or we're not prepared with the right information. Sometimes this help involves spending our own money to help fund services for our parents. We may decide their financial needs temporarily must take precedence over our own. It could be that they can no longer handle the day-to-day management of their business affairs. Seeing this saddens and worries us. We feel even worse if we've been out of touch recently and did not even know these problems were developing. Regardless of how we learn of our parents' difficulties, we know we want to do everything we can to take care of them.

Here are just a few stories that may alert you to what lies ahead for you and your parents.

LINDA'S MOM: Assisted Living

Linda got her phone call in the middle of her busiest tax season ever. Her mother's best friend phoned, presumably to chat a bit, but soon expressed worry that Ada, Linda's mother, age 78, wasn't doing so well. She had fallen down twice that week, had failed to get dressed when her friend arrived to take her to lunch, and she seemed to not be eating much. Her friend was worried.

Linda phoned home, and her worst fears were confirmed when her mother told her she just didn't feel like cooking anymore, and getting dressed was too much trouble. She said she'd only fallen once, as best she could remember. The next weekend Linda flew from Albuquerque to her mother's home; the first day there, she realized that her mother could no longer live alone.

Fortunately, Linda knew of a wonderful assisted living center in Albuquerque, but it took a lot of convincing to get Ada to even consider leaving her home and community of 30 years, even though all but a few of her long-time friends had moved away or passed on. A month later, after Ada finally agreed to the move, Linda put her mother's house up for sale, packed up her things, and drove her back to Albuquerque.

It's been three years now, and Linda feels better that her mom is closer and getting good care. The staff at the assisted living residence help Ada with everything—bathing, dressing, eating, toileting, and straightening the room she shares with another woman. She's made a few friends already, and seems to be content. Linda visits her mother every few days, takes her flowers, does her laundry, and feels a certain peace of mind that her parent has caregivers who can watch over her every day, preventing further accidents like falls, and seeing that she has proper nutrition and grooming. She has found local doctors for her mom and takes her to the appointments herself.

The finances of this kind of residential care cost Ada plenty. She had no long-term-care insurance, so she faces paying the $2,400 monthly fee out of pocket, since Medicare will only cover skilled nursing care after a hospital stay and only the first 100 days of that. Proceeds from her house sale will fund the first five years of Ada's care. After that, Ada's Social Security ($1,160 per month) and small dividend income from investments ($440 per month) will pay part of the tab. Linda, who is single, may have to come up with the rest. She's looking into Medicaid to see if her mother will qualify, in case Linda feels the remaining $800 per month becomes too much for her to handle. Clearly, Ada will use up all her assets if she lives long enough, but at least she's getting good care.

The real strain will come if Ada requires skilled nursing care. Upgrading to that kind of facility could run about $4,000 per month. Linda is already looking into that problem and starting to check out facilities in case her mother ends up needing one.

LAURA AND KATEY: Caring for Parents from Afar

Laura and Katey had double trouble in caring for their parents. First, their mother had a stroke and was housebound for the remaining six years of her life. She needed help with all the tasks of daily living, except eating, which she could do for herself. While he was able, her husband provided most of the caregiving, aided by home care nurses who came daily to check vital signs and administer his wife's medication. Laura and Katey were in charge of finding the home care personnel. They went through several agencies before finding staff they liked. Their mother was depressed and ill-tempered; quite a few of the caregivers quit.

After about two years, the girls' father started to fail as well. He had congestive heart failure and got to where he could not climb the stairs. Soon he confined himself to the upstairs bedroom and refused to get dressed. He could no longer care for his wife, and now he needed assistance with bathing, cooking, housekeeping, and transporting.

Laura lived closest, about an hour away, so she went home to arrange more full-time help. The services were paid for by their parents' own assets, but costs for round-the-clock care for two people were astronomical, about $5,000 per month. After selecting new caregivers with skilled nursing credentials, Laura went home but came to visit twice a week for nearly three years. The last year, she would come during the week and go home on the weekends. Friction started to develop with her husband, who never saw her, and Laura started to resent that her sister, Katey, was off the hook because she lived so far away. Katey came home for visits every few months, but the burden of caregiving supervision fell to Laura.

The other twist here is money. While their parents had plenty of money to pay for their care, they had planned to leave a substantial estate to their girls. Katey, whose husband sold his company for millions, was not too concerned if her parents used up their estate to pay for their health care. Laura, on the other had, was very concerned. In a bad marriage, hoping to inherit enough assets to feel secure for her own future, she saw that hope dwindle as her parents' assets drained. Not that she didn't want her parents to get good care, but she was devastated at how fast the money was disappearing. She and her parents had talked about the estate, and she knew they also were worried that their care would drain the money.

Laura and Katey's mother died November of last year. Two months later, distraught over his wife's death and his own frailty, their father died. The six years of health care had cut the estate in half, and the strain on Laura and her relationship with her sister has taken its toll. Fortunately, her inheritance will give Laura a modest cushion to plan changes in her future.

Taking care of mom and dad often falls more on the shoulders of one adult child than the others. Proximity, willingness to help, and the closeness of the child-parent relationship all play a role in this inequity of caregiving burden. Also, even in a family that has done intergenerational planning, where parents hope to leave assets to their children, sometimes the funds are eroded in the final stages of the parent's life. That's why, as adult children, you really cannot count on your inheritance until you get it. Furthermore, you must understand that taking care of your parents may or may not result in any financial reward for your effort. It's part of being a loving child, parenting the man and woman who parented you.

LOREN AND JOHN: Why Written Consent Is So Important

Loren was very close to his dad, John, who as a young man had been blinded in a hunting accident. Loren was only a baby at the time, and all his life he admired his father's resilience and adaptability in living with his disability. A physician living in a state across the country, Loren tried to visit his parents often, and they were very close. One day, Loren received a call at his office that his dad had suffered a massive heart attack. He flew home at once and acted as a patient advocate for his father with his fellow physicians. John had to have bypass surgery; it was a tough case and a close call, but overall Loren concurred with the treatment given, and his father recovered rather well.

Three years went by, and a second heart attack landed John in the emergency room once more. Again, Loren flew home, hoping his dad would survive a second surgery. When he got to the hospital, his dad was in a coma, and surgery was critical. This time, Loren disagreed with the local doctors' game plan and wanted things done differently. However, John had never signed a health care power of attorney or a directive to physician, naming him or even John's wife, Loren's mother, to make medical decisions if he was incapacitated. The doctors proceeded to do what they thought best, against Loren's wishes. John lasted two weeks in great discomfort in the hospital and then died. I'm not sure Loren will ever get over his frustration that he felt so helpless to control the events surrounding his father's final weeks of care. He feels twice as bad because he is a physician himself, and even he could not act without the legal authority his dad had failed to put in writing when he could have done so.

More people today create these critical documents for health care. Too many, however, do not. How about your parents? Would you end up in a similar situation as Loren one day, unable to direct what you think your parents would want done to and for them? Ask your mother and father if they have taken care of this most important detail. It could make the difference in whether you and the rest of the family feel that you did all you could for your parents because you had the legal authority to make life-determining decisions in caring for mom and dad.

YOU NEED TO BE PREPARED

If you are the adult child of aging parents, you face many sensitive issues in the areas of health and finance as you begin the elder care of your mother and father. You may not want to think ahead to the day when your parents become ill, frail, or unable to take care of themselves, but that day will come, and you must begin to plan for this inevitable time in life. In too many families, these concerns are not addressed until a parent becomes ill or short of funds. You and your siblings, if you have any, may suddenly have to step in during a health crisis and select caregivers to assist your parents. You may become that caregiver yourself. Yet our culture does not give children a roadmap to deal with this transfer of caregiving—when your parents no longer take care of you, but you start to take care of them.

Such a crisis may cause turmoil in the family. Caring for parents is a family affair. You may face the situation where you and you brother or sister disagree about what is best for mom and dad. Who, then, makes the decisions? Also, your parents may insist on staying in charge of their financial affairs when you see they no longer can, or should, handle these tasks. These problems call for diplomatic intergenerational conversations; you must talk about the problems with each other and find a way for the family to reach consensus on what is best for your parents.

Increased life expectancy could mean that your parents might have to spend down all their assets to pay for their living costs or medical costs. They might even outlive their financial resources and need your help with their monthly bills or with funding some of their health care out-of-pocket expenses. These decisions force you to walk through emotional family minefields, fraught with difficult choices. Some of those choices may not make everyone happy, including your parents.

TRANSFER OF CONTROL

No one wants to give up control over their life, in any way—not in handling their money, making choices about where they live, deciding who helps them with what, least of all in determining how they are medically treated when they are ill, especially terminally ill. The truth is, however, all of us eventually must give up some control. It's part of growing old. However, we can have a lot more say in what happens to us in our final years, final weeks, final hours, if we plan ahead. This is what you want your parents to do, and do now.

As the adult child, on whom the burden of caregiving may fall, it is in your and your parents' interests to start the conversations about the transfer of control now. This goes back to my earlier request that you need to know as much as possible about your parents' financial situation. Not because you're prying to see how much you'll inherit, but because you want to know if they're OK. You want to know if they are financially comfortable paying their bills now, or if they are they starting to use up their principal. You want to know if they can afford to pay for their long-term medical care costs, or if insurance will cover those expenses. You want to know if their current income would cover the monthly costs of home health care or care in a residential setting such as an assisted living center or nursing home. You want to know where they would want to live if they could no longer live on their own— would they want to bring in professional caregivers to help them and stay in their current residence; would they want to come to live near or with you or another child? Would they consider an assisted living center or continuing care residential community, which offers all levels of care?

Some seniors are adamant about their preferences, but they may never have discussed these issues with you. They may think they'll stay in charge of their affairs until the day they die. You know they probably won't. Have they accepted that fact yet? It's time you strongly encourage them to look at these issues. In the long run, they will be grateful, even if at first they resist this reminder of their mortality.

I find the easiest way to start these conversations between the generations is for the adult children to broach the various "what if" scenarios with their parents:

- What if you had a stroke and could not do your own driving, cooking, or bathing? What kind of help would you like to have— assistance at home, or would you rather go to an assisted living center for a while, where everything is done for you?
- Mom, when Dad's pension stops at his death, will you have enough income to stay in the house?
- If you grow tired of handling your bank balancing or tax preparation, who would you like to have help you? Do you want one of us kids to assist you with that? Do you want to have a personal assistant come in once a month? If you could no longer handle your financial affairs, to whom do you want to turn them over? Have you given that person durable power of attorney?

- If you went into a coma and couldn't make medical decisions, have you filled out a health care power of attorney and appointed someone, perhaps one of us in the family, to make decisions for you?
- How do you feel about extreme measures such as life support or nutritional support to keep you alive? Would you want us to do that?
- Who do you want to take Tippy (dog) and Peaches (cat) if something were to happen to you?
- Where do you keep the information about your health insurance and Medicare, in case I would ever need to give that to a hospital or doctor?
- Do you have a neighbor or friend who would call us if they thought you were in trouble in some way? Could we call them if we were worried because we'd tried to call you, and you weren't answering the phone? May I have that person's name and phone number?

Now don't be surprised if you get some resistance when you first start to ask these kinds of nitty-gritty personal questions. But you can preface them by saying that you want to be of help to your mother and dad when they need you, and the best way to do that is to plan ahead. You might add that you feel some of this information would be helpful in case of an emergency, especially since you live so far away. When they see that you have their interests in mind, there is a good chance they'll cooperate and start to talk more openly about these delicate matters.

You may be lucky in that you or one of your siblings lives in or near the town where your parents reside. That means one of you can get there fast in a crisis and pitch in as part-time or full-time caregiver. However, if you are all geographically dispersed and far from your parents' home, preplanning becomes even more important. Have you and your siblings discussed who would go first to get the ball rolling with caregiving, hiring services needed, dealing with doctors, or finding a facility for rehabilitation or eventual residence for the ill parent? If both parents are still living, have you spoken to each spouse about what kind of help they might want in case the caregiving becomes too much for them? Talking about this early helps surface any disagreements that might be smoldering under the surface as to who should be on call first and how the other children will assist as well. If it looks as though financial support is required, then the children must agree on who will pay how much and when. Perhaps one of you simply cannot afford to help out your parents financially. Your siblings need to know that up front.

WHEN FINANCIAL SUPPORT IS NEEDED

I think most adult children have thought about what they would do if their parents needed financial assistance.

If you've never faced the dilemma of saying yes or no to such a request, you may still one day. Do you know what your answer would be? It's a good idea to think of this now. If you feel you either cannot or will not be forthcoming with financial support, you need to make a decision about this kind of thing. Otherwise, it's the type of family issue that can tear you apart inside. You feel guilty for not helping; you feel angry that you're put in this situation; you feel despondent that you are not able to give back in this way. Or conversely, you have the money to give, and you want to give, but you are not sure how to offer it without taking away your parents' pride.

The best solution, honestly, is to be honest with yourself first, and then honest with your parents. You have a right to say no, and you have no real obligation to say yes. Many of you will want to say yes, but I did remind you earlier that your first obligation is to take care of your own future—save for your retirement, and make sure that you won't someday be on the other end of this relationship, needing help from your own children.

Before you decide to provide financial assistance to your parents, you need to review your own financial situation. See how providing them a monthly stipend or paying some major bills will affect your own monthly cash flow. Perhaps you'll have plenty of money to spare some for these purposes and still be able to set your monthly savings aside. If the help they need is short-term, you may decide to trim your own lifestyle costs for a few months and give that money to them. If the need is longer term, you may want to decide on a "cap" on what you feel you can give, tell your parents what that is, and then both of you will know the limit you can supply.

You may want to approach your brothers and sisters to match your contribution, or decide that you'll each give according to your ability.

It may be that your parents have approached only you and may want you to keep this between you and them. Then you'll have to decide if that feels right to you. Secrets in families, especially financial secrets, have a way of backfiring if discovered later on. I think the best policy is an open one.

If it appears that your parents will run out of money altogether and you and your siblings cannot afford to support them, you need to check with the Department of Aging in the state where your parents reside and find out how they could apply for Medicaid. There are rigorous tests now for eligibility, and also stiff penalties for transferring assets out of the parents' names to meet those eligibility requirements. Still, the program is meant for situations where senior citizens cannot provide the basics of living, even with their Social Security benefits.

If your family does have ample resources to share, work together with your parents and those who can offer help. Set up a systematic way in which your parents can receive the income monthly. You might help them structure a budget so they and you know what it takes them to live comfortably. Keep in mind how difficult it is for them to have to depend on their children in their old age. Do all that you can to help them maintain their dignity by being sensitive to their feelings in this delicate matter.

THE EMOTIONAL TOLL OF CAREGIVING

The final years of your parents' lives contain moments of sadness, poignancy, discovery, and joy. Every time I saw my father in his last two years of life, I thought it might be my last time with him. I'd drive out of the driveway with a lump in my throat, aching already for the loss I knew would come. Yet some of my most powerful feelings of love for him came during these times. Another friend of mine spent seven months during her mother's battle with terminal cancer visiting her weekly, taking her food, and talking about all the old times when she and her brothers and sisters were growing up. She asked her mother to talk about her grandparents, and she tried to steep herself in as much family history as the time allowed.

Sometimes our parent is here, but not really. One of the great tragedies of old age is dementia, epitomized by Alzheimer's disease. I have a friend whose mother suffered with Alzheimer's for ten years. Her dad did his best to keep his wife, her mother, at home for five or six years. He had to sleep sitting up in their den at night, because his wife wandered about the house, and he was afraid she would trip in the dark. They covered the mirrors in all the bathrooms, because she was frightened of her own image. Ultimately she had to be placed in the custodial care wing of a nursing home. My friend said sometimes she was overcome with grief that her mother no longer knew her; at other times she was consumed with anger at the ravages of the disease that had robbed the family of this wonderful woman, whose personality had died long before her body succumbed.

None of us escapes the reality that one day our parents will be gone. Today and every day that you still have them are gifts—no matter what physical or mental shape they are in. Enjoy these moments, capture their goodness, and hold dear the memories you are building for the days when that is all you will have. Caregiving can be a burden, but it is also a privilege—one that you will not want to miss, for it is the ultimate form of love that you can give to those two individuals who taught you what love is all about. You will encounter numerous difficulties, days of discouragement, and times when you wonder if you are up to what you've committed to do—whether you've offered time or money. You will experience a wide range of emotions that the caregiving situation brings to the fore.

The ironic, yet comforting, cycle of living dictates that one day we will hold in our arms the parents who cuddled us as babes. The time you spend sharing your love, expressing your concern, guiding with dignity and understanding will be moments you will treasure for the rest of your life. The more planning you've done ahead to take care of the logistics of caregiving, the more you will be able to enjoy parenting your parents in their final years.

What you learn in taking care of mom and dad will stand you in good stead down the road. Someday you will be the senior needing attention and assistance. So, perhaps one of the best guidelines for you in helping your parents is to imagine yourself in their place, and think how you would like your own children, or someone, to take care of you. It is not so far away, you know—you should begin thinking about these same concerns for yourself.

DREAMFUNDING STRATEGIES . . .

1. Imagine that your parent suffers a short-term medical crisis a month from now, and your job is to coordinate relatives and create a game plan to help your parent through this situation. Be sure you have the answers to the following questions:

   - Which family member will drop everything and go to the parent and begin making arrangements for handling their affairs, including the medical services needed?
   - If your other parent is alive, what tasks can he or she handle, and which would you, your siblings, a neighbor, or outside professional need to handle?
   - How will your parent pay for the medical costs? Does your parent have liquid assets in checking and savings accounts to pay the balances once insurance claims have been filed? Are you or the other adult children willing and able to pick up part of the tab, if it comes to that?
   - If ongoing supervision may result from this medical condition, who can find, select, and coordinate this effort?

2. Imagine that your parent's medical problem is long term—he or she is suffering from a chronic condition and can no longer live independently. You're the only child living close enough to be an ongoing caregiver. Be sure you have the answers to the following questions:

   - Can your parent afford to pay for home care and stay living in his or her current residence? If not, what local nursing home or medical facility do you know that you feel is high quality and that you, and your parent, would want him or her to live in? What is the monthly cost for residents? Go check it out, and make a contact there with the community representative. Ask for a copy of the contract a new resident would be asked to sign. Look especially for clauses about financial requirements or deposits.
   - Find out about any continuing care communities near your own town. What does your medical condition have to be to get into them?

- How would your parent finance living in one of these facilities? Can he or she self-insure? Does your parent have long-term-care insurance? Does your parent have to turn over all assets to the facility in order to get in? What happens to those assets if your parent dies sooner than expected—does the contract provide for reversion of excess funds to the family?

- What would you need to do in terms of checking up on the care your parent receives to make sure he or she is being treated well, not only medically but personally? Check your local better business bureau to make sure no complaints are on file about the care given in this facility.

- Are there waiting lists to get into any of the facilities you visit? Under what conditions can you add your parent's name to that list?

- Would you be willing to have your parent come live in your home, with home care coming there and you footing part of the bill? Would your sister or brother agree to do that, if you cannot? It's important not to give a parent false hope that this is an option, if it is not.

3. Ask your parents the tough questions about what their fears, concerns, and preferences are in terms of extreme measures in an acute medical crisis. Find out if they've designated durable power of attorney, health care power of attorney, and directive to physician. Are you the one or one of several family members they have appointed? If so, what questions do you want to ask your mother and father about their wishes—how they want to be treated in a final illness. Ask if they've made burial and funeral arrangements. Where are the deeds to the cemetery plots? Do they want cremation? Have they bought a prepaid cremation plan? What kind of memorial would they want? Who would be the beneficiary—what charity or nonprofit organization? Do they have biographical information they would want in the obituary—what is it, where is it? Do they qualify for military honors or funeral expense benefits? Do they want a fancy coffin or a pine box? However grim this line of inquiry might seem, wouldn't you want to know the answers before something happens? Well, before is now.

4. Exchange phone numbers with a neighbor or friend of your parents so you can call each other about your parents' situation if something develops, or if you're worried because you cannot reach them by phone. Ask them to check on your mother or dad from time to time.

5. Suggest to your single parent that he or she devise some way to alert a neighbor in the case of an accident or illness. One suggestion: my uncle had an American flag that he put out on his apartment balcony every day. If his neighbors didn't see it out there by 8 AM, someone who had a key to the apartment was to come check on him. That person had our family phone numbers, as well. You could also get a beeper for your parent.

6. Ask your parents for a list of their doctors, accountant, house staff, and veterinarian (if they have pets). You would need all these numbers in a health crisis.

7. Call a family meeting of your siblings and your parents once you've checked out what your parents' feelings are about a health crisis and you've asked your siblings what they can or are willing to do to help out. Create a crisis connection game plan. With one phone call, you each know what to do, who will do what first, who will come later, and how to stay in touch with each other as progress is made to solve the situation. Make sure your parents like the plan; after all, it's for them.

8. Whoever your parents appoint to handle the money matters, urge that person to sit down with them and create or read the financial notebook discussed in Chapter 9.

9. Whoever is in charge of medical decisions (and it may be more than one person) should sit down with your parents and go over every question that would pertain to what they would want if they were no longer conscious, and you were making all treatment decisions. Review the health care power of attorney to make certain you have the authority to do all that they want. If you have the opportunity, speak with your parents' doctor, go on an appointment

once with them, meet him or her in person, and indicate you are the person to call when a crisis occurs and decisions must be made. Again, exchange phone numbers.

10. Think now about the financial support you are able and willing to give to your parents, should the need arise. Where would you find that extra money? What "cap" would you place on what you could give?

11. As for the emotional aspects of caregiving, sit down with a piece of paper and write down everything you can think of that you ever wanted to ask your parents about their lives, family history, even your own early beginnings that you don't remember. Next time you see your parents, start to ask some of these questions. Don't think you have forever to do this.

    Also, write down everything you want them to hear from you—that you love them, that you appreciate them, that there was a particular thing they did that made you know they loved you, or that increased your own self-esteem. Imagine how you would like to convey these feelings to your mother or father—on what kind of occasion, and whether you'd like to tell him or her in a letter or in person. Take precious pictures now, of your parents, of you with your parents, of their home—memories you want to capture for the future, once they're gone and the old family home is sold. Simply, imagine that your parent will pass on in a matter of weeks—what is left undone, unsaid? Do and say those things now. Now is all you have for certain, and you don't want to live with regrets.

Educating Your Children
Funding College Dreams

If saving for retirement has some baby boomers in "price tag panic," paying for their children's college education has no less of a sticker shock. They've known it was coming; they thought about it when their child was born, but a recent study conducted for *Money* magazine shows that parents of college-bound high school students today typically have saved only $11,000 for their child's college bills. That's about 13 percent of the average $82,700 price tag of four years tuition at a private college, 21 percent of the $53,200 cost for out-of-state students at a public school. It's wake-up time; you've got more catching up to do. Still, you and your child have plenty of opportunity to do a quick study in college funding, take advantage of many sources of financial aid information, and create a strategy for funding that precious dream—the lifetime benefit of higher education.

It is obvious, and probably worth repeating, that the earlier you start your college strategy the better. Infancy or grade school would be great; while your child is still in middle school is good timing. If you've waited until high school, well, it can be done, but you'll have to pull out all the stops and probably go into debt to do it. Planning earlier helps not only because you have more years to invest your savings for growth, but also because getting into the college of choice, vying for the attention of financial aid officers, and figuring out how to finance your part of the college price tag take a great deal of effort and lots of intergenerational planning. While you may feel that the burden of college funding is mostly on you, as the parents, don't fail to look to both the older and younger generations in your family to help foot the bill or at least contribute to increasing your child's chances of getting financial aid. Fully 41 percent of undergraduate students in American colleges and universities get some form of financial assistance. Yours could be one (or two or three) of them!

Let's see what some other families have done to fund the college dream.

MEGHAN AND STAN: Grandmother's Help and Student Loans Pay the Way

Meghan and Stan married in their early 20s, and had three children right away. By age 27, Stan was diagnosed with multiple sclerosis. Meghan, who had never finished college, asked the doctors for the frank truth about her husband's condition. They told her his disability would progress rather rapidly and ultimately end in early death. With three children to raise and educate, Meghan knew she'd have to go back to school, complete her own college degree, and find a good job. In four years, while Stan could still work, she got a Bachelor's in Accounting and an MBA. Still, fresh out of school, her income was modest, and most of Stan's salary went to cover his out-of-pocket medical expenses that weren't covered by their health insurance. In short, the college funds they had planned to save just didn't get saved.

Fortunately, Meghan's parents started their own college funds for the three grandkids, and these savings were enough to pay for the first two years for each child. Another favorable fact—all three kids were smart and did well in school. Early on, Meghan knew they might qualify for merit scholarships and financial aid. Because she had taken a job as an accountant at a local private university, she had the ear of financial aid officers, asked a lot of questions, and learned the ins and outs of financial aid applications.

Sadly, Stan died at age 46 while his first child was just heading to college. His life insurance was used largely to pay off medical bills and make needed house repairs. $20,000 was left to help the oldest child, a daughter, start undergraduate school. She and the couple's two boys all used the funds from their grandparents and also applied for and got merit scholarships (based on grade point averages and test scores) as well as federal loans (based on need) to pay the rest of their college tab. The grandparents' savings did not count against them in the financial aid formula for loans, because aid officers only look at assets in the parents' or child's names.

Seven years later, all three children have completed their college degrees, and two have gone on to graduate school, all paid for with loans that the kids will have to pay back. The daughter is an attorney, making over $100,000 a year as a new associate. One son completed his master's in chemical engineering and has a good job lined up. The second son just completed a five-year program in landscape architecture.

Meghan is proud that her three children were resourceful enough to help figure out how to win the financial aid game and pay the balance of their college costs that the grandparents and she could not afford. She feels they've gotten a good start in life and that they can well afford to pay off their student loans with the increased earnings their education has garnered them.

SANDRA AND PETER: Upper-Middle Class Parents Hit Hard

Sandra and Peter are a well educated, upper-middle class couple. Peter has a Ph.D. in physics and an undergraduate degree in petroleum engineering. Sandra is a lawyer. They both make a good living, but in the early years, they struggled like most baby boomers to get started in life, buy a house, raise two kids, and simultaneously save for college as well as their own retirement. They took less expensive vacations and always flew in the wee hours of the morning anytime they took airplanes to get the discount fares. They did a lot of house repairs themselves. In short, they were frugal, worked hard, and saved and saved to send their boys, first to private middle and high schools, and then to the finest colleges.

There was no doubt in Sandra's or Peter's minds, nor in those of their sons, that the two boys would go to college. It was a given, an expectation. However, when the couple started looking at the cost of the Ivy League schools, they both blanched. It would cost more than $100,000 per child to obtain the educations they wanted for their sons.

Sandra's parents knew the boys were bright and that their daughter wanted to send them to the best schools. So the grandparents began a gifting program of $10,000 per year to both Sandra and Peter, to be used as they saw fit, knowing the money likely would go into the college kitty. These intergenerational gifts made the difference in whether the couple could send their boys to the top schools, or send them to local universities.

Still, Sandra felt her sons' academic achievements should count for something, so the oldest boy pieced together three scholarships to Stanford. Because he was class valedictorian, he qualified for the Phi Beta Kappa award given to every valedictorian by the local chapter of that society. He applied for and got a National Merit Scholarship and a third one given by Peter's employer, a company scholarship of $500 awarded each year to the most outstanding students of employees. These merit awards, however, amounted to less than 10 percent of the first-year tab of $22,000 at Stanford, and they were only for one year. Fortunately, the son was also state computer champion, and this honor got the attention of Stanford's Computer Science department. They offered him a work-study opportunity to trade working for a professor for a tuition discount.

The second son, five years younger, went to Northwestern University. Although his grades were even higher than his older brother's, he failed to get any scholarships because he didn't apply. When asked why, he said he didn't want to have to write the essays. Also, by the time he even considered it, application deadlines had passed.

So, for upper-middle class, or even middle-class parents whose income and assets disqualify their children for need-based financial aid, the only relief comes from intrafamily gifts, earnings by the student himself or herself, or through merit-based awards, for which there is stiff competition. If your son or daughter wants to win one of these merit scholarships, he or she had better apply early.

MOLLY AND DANIEL: Special Talents Make a Difference

Molly and Daniel are lucky. Both their daughters are competitive swimmers who've won regional and national medals. Even before they started looking for colleges, colleges started looking for them. While Molly and Daniel make too much money to qualify for financial aid, their daughters may well get their whole way paid through sports scholarships. There are plenty of fine universities, even private schools, looking for talented athletes and willing to pay handsomely to get them to sign on.

We've all heard of basketball and football stars who get the red carpet treatment, even when their grades are not very good. But there are many talents that garner financial support in colleges today—artistic, musical, mathematical, scientific—and your child might qualify for this kind of award.

Despite her love for swimming, Sarah wants to eventually become a doctor, so Molly and David are doing Internet searches to see which universities with medical schools also have outstanding swimming programs. Sarah is just in eighth grade, but the family wants to be prepared so that before too many more colleges approach them, they have a good idea where Sarah might want to go to school. If they can match the academic future she wants with a good swim scholarship, her college funding worries are over—at least for her undergraduate premed degree. Medical schools are a different story. Far fewer grants of "free" money are available for graduate students in professional programs such as medicine and law; mostly these grads have to arrange a package of student loans, which will take years to pay off. Some universities, however, help you shorten the professional study track by combining your senior year of premed with your first year of medical school. Sarah is considering one of these.

Another piece of good news for Molly and Daniel is that despite their level of financial comfort, sometimes schools will provide financial aid if you have more than one child in college at the same time. When Sarah is a junior, her younger sister, Cindy, will be starting her freshman year. This is one angle Molly and Daniel are exploring to see if they can get some relief with the simultaneous, double college price tag for their children.

PAT AND BARRY: Lower Cost Doesn't Mean Second-Rate

While $100,000 is not an unusual price tag for a four-year private college degree, there are plenty of less expensive routes to go—with a fine education as the result. Pat and Barry have a daughter who wants to be a teacher. Kit is a bright young woman with a love of children and great patience and compassion. During her junior year of high school, the family was back in Pat and Barry's home state of South Dakota for a family funeral. They decided to visit Black Hills State University in Spearfish, South Dakota, because it has a good reputation as a teacher's college. Kit fell in love with the campus, and liked the small size of its student body (about 3,500), as well as the look of the small community in which the college is located. Kit recently finished her freshman year at Black Hills State and described it as "The best year ever!"

One of the best things for Pat and Barry is the reasonable price tag of Kit's college tuition—$8,500 per year for an excellent education that will prepare their daughter for the career of her dreams. This comes at a good time, since Pat and Barry are saving for retirement right now, and lowering the cost of Kit's education by selecting a well-priced teacher's college makes it easier for them to retire sooner. Indeed, they may retire back in South Dakota themselves.

WILL YOU PAY THE FULL PRICE TAG FOR COLLEGE?

The answer to this question depends on a number of factors at the time your child applies to college, including:

- Family income
- Parents' assets
- Child's assets
- How many children you have in college at one time
- Special talents or areas of interest of your child
- Availability of financial aid at the particular college to which your child is applying
- Whether your child is a minority (including being a woman)
- Your child's grade point average in high school and tests scores (SAT, Scholastic Aptitude Test, being the most important)
- Whether the family has special hardships at the time
- How early your child applies to the college in question

As you can see, some of these factors are within your control to manipulate in your favor—such as amount of assets in your name versus your child's name and how early your child submits his or her application. Others, such as your child's aptitude or availability of funds at a particular college, are not. Another aspect out of your control is rapid inflation in the total cost of attending college today. According to a 1996 *Newsweek* article, the tab for attending private colleges and universities grew 95 percent between 1984 and 1996, more than twice the rate of overall inflation. Although this rate has slowed in recent years, playing catch-up requires skillful, focused planning. Assuming 5 percent annual increases in college costs, by the year 2018, a four-year education in a private college is expected to cost an astounding $260,620; public school will cost $80,395, as shown in the chart.

Years in College	Average Four-Year Cost of Private School	Average Four-Year Cost of Public School
2000–2004	$138,212	$42,635
2003–2007	159,998	49,355
2005–2009	176,398	54,414
2008–2012	204,203	62,991
2010–2014	225,133	69,448
2013–2017	260,620	80,395

Don't let these numbers discourage you. First of all, you and your child have a choice about what schools he or she will apply to, so to some extent, you can control the total outlay for college costs by self-selection of the kind of school (public or private) your child will attend. Next, even if you aren't sure your family will qualify for financial aid, you can still do a lot of homework to find the answer to that question, and the result can make a huge difference in the savings rate you need to implement. Also, if you're getting a head start on dreamfunding with some years to go before your child graduates from high school, your monthly investments, as well as your total outlay to fund the price tag, will be lower than if you start late.

Here's an example: You and your spouse decide that your eight-year-old son should go to a private university when the time comes, and you'll target paying $100,000 for the four years of college. (The school may cost more than that, but you think your son will get a music scholarship because he is a gifted violinist. So, you're figuring on $100,000.) You've got ten years to save the money, since he turns 18 and heads off to college at the end of that period. Look at the following college goal chart. See what your monthly investments need to be if you start now, or if you wait. Also, notice what it would have been if you had started saving by his first birthday.

College Goal: $100,000
Assuming an 8 percent annual rate of return, compounded monthly.

Years until College	Monthly Investments Needed	Total Outlay
17	$ 230	$46,920
15	287	51,660
12	413	59,472
10	543	65,160
8	742	71,232
5	1,352	81,120
2	3,831	91,944

You can see from this chart that starting to save with less than ten years before college really escalates the monthly savings rate needed. Also, note that the total outlay with only two years to go is just about double that if you had started when he was one year old.

STEPS IN FUNDING COLLEGE

Besides buying your home, paying for college will likely be the most costly "service" you ever buy. You don't want to approach this purchase haphazardly. Be a smart consumer, do your homework, involve your whole family in the process, and you'll be amazed how you can trim your out-of-pocket expenses for college and yet provide your children with the lifelong benefit of higher education.

Step One: Save as Much as You Can This Month, and Every Month

While you're steeping yourself in the intricate journey of learning about how financial aid administrators determine if your child gets some help, start your own college savings fund now. Even if you have to start small, with $25 per month, begin.

One important decision to make as you start these college accounts is whose name should be on the account—yours or the child's. To start off, I suggest you keep it in your name. There are pluses to that in the financial aid formulas, as discussed below, and you can always open an account later for the child and transfer the money.

Step Two: Make College Planning a Family Affair

You are not in this alone. You have two generations minimum who will likely help you. Your parents, the children's grandparents, may very well want to help out with paying for college. So, right away, open the conversations with your parents about whether they want to or can contribute to their grandchildren's educations. Also, there is a definite bonus to college funding coming from grandparents. It's known as the "granny account." In the financial aid formulas used by colleges and universities, assets in a grandparent's name do not count against you when determining your child's eligibility for scholarships, grants, or loans. They only look at your assets and the child's assets. So, your parent can sock away a ton of money for your child's education, and he or she could still qualify for financial aid.

The other generation that's going to help you pay for college is your children themselves. By the time they are in middle school, if college is your goal for them, then start talking about it. Start talking about how vital grades and test scores are, and the importance of being a well-rounded individual as well as an academic achiever. Let them know it's going to cost a lot of money. You might suggest that in high school they may get a part-time job to help set aside money for their college education.

When it comes time to apply for college, your son or daughter will have to fill out the lengthy applications, write essays, shop for colleges of their choice, investigate financial aid information from their high school, on the Internet, and from the 300-plus books out there on financial aid. The sooner your children realize the importance of the college dream and that they are integral to the process of funding that dream, the more engaged they will become in "owning" this dream and their responsibility in making it happen.

Step Three: Start Looking at Schools Early

With more than 2,000 four-year colleges and universities to choose from, you've got your work cut out for you. Start sifting. Check first with your child's college advisor, as well as the library for directories on schools, and start reading. In preparing for this chapter, I found several good comprehensive guides to colleges, including Kaplan/ Newsweek's *How to Get into College,* which comes out with a new edition each year. Also, check out *U.S. News & World Report America's Best Colleges 2001.*

Step Four: Begin to Study the World of Financial Aid

No one wants to pay more for a purchase than they have to, and, even if you're pretty sure you make or have too much money for your child to get financial aid based on need, look into it anyway. You may find that you have certain circumstances that do let you get a tuition break, and many scholarships are given based on merit to students of affluent families.

The best way to start is to talk with a high school counselor or college financial aid officer and have him or her run you through the numbers, as your situation is today. It's just a ballpark estimate, but you'll start to see how it all works. Ask about the formula financial aid officers use to determine your "expected family contribution."

Also, you should be aware of a recent trend of parents who haggle over financial aid offers. If you feel that your situation involves specific hardships, or your child has special talents, excellent grades or test scores, or any marketing plus that you can use in your child's favor, by all means write or call the aid officer at the college where your child has applied and try to negotiate for more money. To do this more effectively, a lot of parents are having their children apply to multiple schools of the same caliber, and pitting one college against the other when the financial aid packages come in. Most schools, who really want your child, will reconsider their offer if given enough good reasons to do so. After all, they're in competition for students. You have a certain amount of bargaining power.

One caveat about applying for early acceptance: Some students have a number-one favorite school and apply early in hopes of getting accepted and knowing that they've gotten the school they wanted. However, most schools require that if you're accepted on such a basis, you guarantee that you'll take the offer. This certainly undercuts your ability to bargain on financial aid, because they've "gotcha," so to speak.

Types of Financial Aid

There are two basic types of aid: grants or scholarships (you don't pay them back) and loans (you do). Other forms of borrowing exist, as well.

1. Grants
   - *Government grants* are for the poor. If you're middle class, forget about getting one of these.
   - *College-based grants/scholarships,* however, can be based on financial need or on merit. At least 1,300 schools give merit scholarships. They take the form of tuition discounts, and are often used by the colleges to lure students they really want. Ask the schools where you're applying what criteria they use to offer their grants.
   - *Private scholarships* are granted by various organizations, foundations, or individuals. Your child's high school college placement office should have databases on scholarships. The local library or bookstore will have a wide range of publications on the subject. Have your child also search the Internet for information. The FinAid Web site at <www.finaid.org> links to 42 scholarship databases, where your child can search for scholarships that match his or her individual interests and qualifications.

2. Loans
   - *Federally insured student loans* allow freshman students to borrow up to $2,625 and larger amounts in later years. If you qualify as "needy" (i.e., your total college tab amounts to more than your family's "expected contribution") the government will pay the loan interest while your child is in school. Otherwise, you owe the interest, but it does not have to be paid until the student is out of school. Although the interest rate is variable, by law it is capped at 8.25 percent.
   - *Federally insured Parent Loans to Undergraduate Students (PLUS).* After subtracting other aid, you, as the parent of a college undergraduate, can borrow up to the full cost of your child's college, if you have good credit. You pay a variable interest rate, capped at 9 percent. To show the cleanest possible credit report, it's a good idea to pay off your credit cards before applying. For more information on federal loan programs, you can call the Federal Student Aid Information Center at 800-433-3243 or look up <www.fafsa.ed.gov>.

3. Other Forms of Borrowing
   - *Borrowing against your life insurance* is something parents have done for years to help fund their children's college edu-

cations. Indeed, many of them bought life insurance to pay for educating and raising their children if the parents died at a young age before their children were grown. You should compare the interest rates on these policy loans with those on student loans.

- *Borrowing against your IRA or 401(k)* lets you tap retirement funds on an interim basis to pay for your child's college education. In both cases you can borrow without the normal 10 percent penalty on withdrawal of retirement savings before age 59½. You will pay income tax on the withdrawals, so figure that in when you decide how much you need to withdraw.

- *Home equity borrowing,* whether through a second mortgage or a home equity line of credit, is a way to tap otherwise illiquid funds to pay for college. However, this may be the most expensive way to go in terms of interest paid; you may be looking at one and a half points over the prime rate, although interest is generally tax deductible.

- *State-sponsored college programs* are now offered in 40 states and come in two forms, varying state to state:
  - *Prepaid tuition plans* let you pay for your child's college costs at rates set today. You usually get a guarantee that your child will be assured of an education paid in full at the time of registration. The money can be used at either a public or private school, in or out of state.
  - *Savings trusts* let you set aside money in a state-sponsored, professionally managed investment account. You can invest up to $100,000 or more and use the proceeds at any school in the country. The earnings are taxed at the student's income tax rate. You should know, however, that you have no control over how the state invests the money.

Step Five: Set Up Long-Term College Fund Accounts

By now you've estimated the price tag of the type of college your child may want to attend, you've checked out what federal and state financial aid might be available to a family with your financial means, you've investigated personal borrowing, and now you know about how much money you want to provide yourself for your child or children's education.

You have three personal sources of money to pay the balance of the college costs that need to be covered:

1. Money you've already set aside in investments for your kids that can continue to grow until it's needed
2. New savings you need to take from your current earnings
3. Money from other members of the family (grandparents, siblings, your own children)

Types of College Accounts

It is important to figure out in what types of accounts these savings should be placed for growth, what tax advantages each type has, and what specific investment vehicles you should use, given the length of time until your child's freshman year of college begins.

Accounts in Child's Name

- *UGMA/UTMA (Uniform Gifts to Minors Act, or Uniform Transfers to Minors Act) accounts* can be set up at banks, brokerage firms, and mutual fund companies by parents for their college-bound youngsters. The parent is named as the custodian of the account and manages the investments for his or her minor (under age 18) child or grandchild. The first $700 of income on these accounts is tax-free. Income from $701 to $1,400 is taxed at the child's rate. Until he or she is 14, any income above $1,400 is taxed at your tax rate, but reverts to the child's rate after age 14. An additional tax break is that any growth on these accounts, if held more than a year, will be taxed at a favorable 10 percent capital gains rate (half that of the normal 20 percent rate for long-term capital gains).

    You should be warned, however, that once you put assets in this type of account, technically they are no longer yours; they become an irrevocable gift to the child, which you control until they reach age of majority (18 to 21, depending on the state). Also, remember that financial aid officers may ask a child to contribute a greater percentage of his or her own assets than the college would require of the parents.
- *The Education IRA* is a tax-exempt custodial account created exclusively for purposes of paying for qualified higher education

expenses of the trust's beneficiary (your child). Annual contributions are limited to $500, must be made all in cash (not in other assets), and can only be made until the beneficiary reaches age 18. The contribution limit is phased out for single taxpayers with adjusted gross incomes of more than $95,000 and less than $110,000 and for married taxpayers with an AGI of more than $150,000 and less than $160,000. Contributions to Education IRAs, unlike regular IRAs, are not tax deductible. When distributions are made to pay for an eligible education institution, the money is excluded from the owner's gross income to the extent that the distribution does not exceed the expenses incurred by the beneficiary during that school year. Monies held in an Education IRA can be rolled over to another Education IRA for the same beneficiary (to change investment firms), or to one for another minor beneficiary of the same family (another child, for example).

- *Trust accounts* may be set up for your children for estate planning purposes. These trusts may last well into adulthood, and monies from these accounts can be spent for their education, as long as the trust document itself does not exclude such a purpose. Most have a phrase allowing income and principal distributions for the minor beneficiary's "health, education, and welfare." You or some other adult would have to be the trustee of the trust for the benefit of the child until he or she reaches the age of majority. Many grandparents set up gen-eration skipping trusts for the express purpose of funding higher education as well as other lifetime benefits for their grandchildren.

Accounts in Parents' Names

You can set aside funds for your child's college in any investment account bearing your name without adding the child's name. I've already mentioned the financial aid formula bias to ask for a smaller percentage of funds from parents' accounts than from those in the child's name.

Grandparents' College Funds

I've already discussed "granny accounts"—investments in the grandparents' names, which are favorable for maximizing financial aid to the grandchild, since they are not counted in the financial aid formula. Usually, I think this is the best way to go, rather than putting money in an UGMA or UTMA for the grandchild. First of all, the grandparent keeps control of the money, so if a child decides not to go to college but would rather buy a Porsche with the money, you can control whether that happens or not. Second, if the grandparent is not in a position to give all the money when the grandchild goes to college, the account is still in the grandparent's name to be handled as he or she wishes. Of course, if you have to change your intentions, be sure to let your children (the grandchild's parents) know immediately, for they'll have to make up the difference that you were going to provide.

Another estate planning tool that benefits grandparents and helps fund their grandchildren's educations is to make direct tuition payments to the educational institution the student plans to attend. As long as the payments go directly to the college, not to the grandchild, the assets can be transferred without invoking federal estate and gift taxes. This move will reduce the estate size and thereby lower future estate taxes.

Accounts of Other Family Members

Any family member who wants to save for future college expenses for a student in the family may want to consider Plan 529, formally referred to as Internal Revenue Code Section 529. Originally, these plans were quite restrictive, set up primarily as prepaid tuition plans run by the state. Several national financial institutions, however, have now set up plans that can be used in any state and for any accredited institution of higher learning. The person who sets up the account is the participant, the child for whom the account is set up is the beneficiary.

Tax benefits of this type of account are significant:

- Contributions are excluded from gift and generation-skipping taxes.
- The balance in the account is not included in the participant's estate. So, it's a way to move money down to future generations early.
- Many grandparents love Plan 529 accounts for funding their grandchildrens' future educational expenses. Indeed, if the child is ten years or more away from college, gifting annually or in a lump sum using the five-year special provision can nearly provide an entire education price tag. But if the grandchild doesn't go to col-

lege, the beneficiary can be changed to another member of the child's family.

Tax Aspects of College Funding

The federal government and many states have created tax incentives for college savings, whether through specific programs, investment vehicles, or tax breaks. It's important that you learn about them while making your college funding plans.

- I've already spoken of the income tax advantages of Education IRAs and UGMA and UTMA accounts, mostly derived from the taxation of the money at a child's lower income tax rate with certain restrictions.
- Interest paid on college loans may be tax-deductible on a graduated scale that reaches to $2,500 per year by 2001. This provision is driven by level of income.
- IRA withdrawals are allowed to pay for qualifying higher education costs without incurring the 10 percent penalty for early withdrawals before age 59½. (Income taxes on the distributions may still be due.) Check your company's 401(k) withdrawal policy as well.
- Federal income tax credits: The Hope scholarship credit gives you a tax credit of up to $1,500 per student for their first two years of college. After that, a $1,000-per-family lifetime learning credit may be used. This program is limited to individuals earning less than $50,000/year or to families with incomes below $100,000.

YOUR CHILD CAN GO TO MORE THAN ONE SCHOOL

If it's still a financial stretch for you to send your child to their first-choice college right away, consider having him or her go to a local community college for the first two years and then transfer to his or her favorite college or university. Fully 30 percent of undergraduate students graduate from a different school than where they start. In many cases, this strategy can help you cut the total college price tag by nearly a third. Also, course work in the first two years of college is pretty standard. It's when your child begins to work steadily on his or her major in junior and senior years that the particular department becomes more critical.

DREAMFUNDING STRATEGIES . . .

1. Do a trial run on college funding by selecting a school, investigating current costs to attend this year, and applying a 5 percent inflation rate to get the future value of sending your child to this school.

2. Take a look at your current liquid savings set aside for college. Calculate the future value of those assets at a 10 percent rate of growth by the year your child will start freshman year of college. Subtract this number from the answer to strategy 1, and arrive at the difference—the money you must save or find to pay the difference.

3. Call a "college funding meeting" of your family—grandparents and you and your spouse. Find out if the grandparents have or plan to contribute funds to your child's or children's educations. If so, put your heads together to see what the rate of growth is now on those funds and what the future value will be by the time your child goes to college. Subtract this number from the answer to strategy 2. This balance is the new "gap" you're trying to fund.

4. Meet with the college placement officer at the local high school your child will attend, and ask him or her to run the numbers for you regarding your family's ability to qualify for financial aid. Also search libraries, bookstores, and the Internet for information on federal, state, and private scholarship, grant, and loan programs. The closer your child is to graduating from high school, the sooner you must gather this information.

5. Sit down with your child to discuss colleges and college costs, and ask how he or she might be able to earn some of the money to pay for college. What about working part-time after school or during summers while still in high school? Would your child consider participating in a work-study program in college? Indicate the cost of

several colleges in which he or she has expressed interest, and start to enroll your student in his or her responsibility to help fund this dream.

6. Send off for the T. Rowe Price "College Planning Kit," (call 1-800-678-5660), and look for the college guides mentioned in this chapter. Read everything you can about best college buys today—those schools where you get the most for your college price tag.

7. If you work for a company, ask what scholarship programs the firm offers to college-directed high school graduates who are children of employees. Find out when your child would have to apply.

8. Look at your overall family saving and investment program. Are you setting aside enough for college for each child while still funding your retirement accounts? Are your investments allocated in such a way that when the college years arrive, you'll have cash to pay tuition and other college costs? If not, consider gradually shifting your investments to types of assets that will accomplish this goal.

9. Examine how you and your child feel about starting off school at a local community college and then going to the college of choice after sophomore year? Is this a cost-saving measure you want to consider? Would you want your child to live at home and go to a college in your community? What special talents or academic interests does your child have that might influence which college or university is the best choice? What scholarship programs are available for such students? What is the deadline for application?

10. Discuss with your child the reasons you feel a college education is important. Tell about your own college experience, if you went. What difference has it made in your life? Explain why you have this particular dream for your son or daughter, and how he or she might find value in earning a college education.

CHAPTER 16

Funding Your Fun Dreams

You might think as a financial planner that I advise my clients to save everything for future dreams. Not so. While planning for a rainy day helps secure an adult child's long-term financial independence, it is just as important to enjoy the journey—to travel and share recreational experiences with your parents before they are too old, and with your children before they leave home. Leisure activities and adventures often create invaluable riches for our families—time spent together that builds the "emotional capital" of family wealth. With short-term intergenerational planning, you can fund today's recreation passions while planning for longer-term goals.

My first comment about fun dreams—those that involve travel, adventure, or the pursuit of avocational interests—is that you should take them seriously beginning this very moment. These passions can profoundly alter your perspective on life, bring you enormous joy, assist you in sharing more of who you really are with your loved ones, and make your life interesting. You should dream big, far, and wide—take the lid off your expectations or limitations about what travel and adventure should encompass. Delve into your favorite hobby or sport with verve and commitment. Be willing to take your children out of school and go on an archeological dig in Peru or visit the great battlefields of the American Revolution and make that period come alive for you and your family. Take an extra week off so you can go on an extended "roots" trip with your first-generation American parents and visit their homeland and the village where they were born, and where they met and married. Begin a language immersion program, then go spend a summer living with a family in that country. Enroll yourself, your spouse, and all three children in a scuba diving course and make this year's family vacation a trip to Cozumel to explore one of the most beautiful offshore reefs of the underwater world.

My second recommendation is to think creatively about how to fund these recreational dreams. You'll need a financial strategy—your passport to adventure. There are countless ways you can afford to travel and explore the world and the plethora of interests that fascinate you. You have a lifetime of adventure to cram in. Take your cue for the variety of fun and insight that awaits you from the adventure dreams these people have made come true.

THE BROWNS: Dream Vacation

Mary and Greg Brown suffered a terrible blow when their 13-year-old daughter was diagnosed with a rare form of stomach cancer. Devastated, the family rallied to help young Candy through the ordeal of surgery, radiation, and chemotherapy. To make it easier, Greg decided the family needed a goal—a carrot held out in front of them to keep their eye on through the dark days of battling the disease. He promised Mary, Candy, and their other daughter, Cara, that when the doctors said Candy could travel, the whole family would go on a Caribbean cruise followed by a private boat trip to go scuba diving in the Cayman Islands. All four members of the family loved diving and had been licensed for this underwater sport several years earlier. Greg asked his travel agent for any posters they had showing the Caribbean waters. Rallying to the cause, the agent found lots of posters, which the family plastered on the walls of Candy's hospital room and then later her bedroom at home.

The great news came when Candy's doctors said the surgery was a success; they'd gotten all the tumor, the margins were clear, the cancer had not spread. They also assured the family that the cure rate of this kind of cancer following results like Candy's was over 98 percent. The time for celebration had arrived! That Christmas, only six months after the diagnosis, Candy and her family went on that cruise. With huge medical bills facing them, they opted to forgo holiday presents that year—

the trip was their gift to each other. To this day, ten years later, Mary and the girls look back on those two weeks as the happiest of their lives— they look back with special poignancy, since Greg died only a year ago, the victim of an unfortunate car accident. His wife and daughters re- member how he was the one who championed the travel experience that got all three of his loved ones through a most difficult time. Candy says it was the thing about her dad that she loved the most—his insistence that they, as a family, had dreams ahead to achieve and that this "carrot" trip was just the first of many adventures they had yet to share and enjoy.

DAVEY: Taking His Kids Out to the Ballparks

Ever since he hit his first home run in Little League, Davey had a passion for baseball. As a young boy, he collected every baseball card he could find. He knew the players, their batting average, on-base average, runs batted in, and number of home runs. For birthdays, his parents would take him and his friends to the ballpark. One year, on a family vacation at New York's World's Fair, Davey thought he had died and gone to heaven—he got to see Whitey Ford pitch at Yankee Stadium. Then and there he made an important decision. One day he would take his own son to see a game at every major baseball stadium in the country.

Davey is now 46, and every year he takes his son and daughter to one of the great ballparks during their family vacation. This dream doesn't take a whole lot of money; at less than $15 each, baseball tick- ets are still one of the great entertainment values. The family drives cross-country, camping out in national park campgrounds, and packing picnic lunches. Sometimes they stay with relatives who live near or on the way to their destination. They've driven from Los Angeles to Chicago to watch the sport at Dodger Stadium, Comiskey Park, and Wrigley Field. Next year they're headed for Pacific Bell Park to watch the San Francisco Giants.

What's wonderful about this kind of family recreation is that Davey has shared his passion with his wife and children, creating a bond of shared interest that may well go on for the duration of the children's lives. The younger generation may even pass on the tradition to their own children. Davey's daughter has become a baseball trivia expert. She throws out questions on baseball minutia that stumps even her dad as they caravan across the miles on the way to the next ballpark. Her dream is to start the first women's major league baseball team. Time, and passion, march on.

INTERGENERATIONAL RECREATION: Creating Memories That Last a Lifetime and Beyond

From these stories, you can see how adventure and travel can create some of the best memories of your family life. Sharing your passions and enjoyment of the outdoors or some special interest, teaches young family members that the world is a vast and fascinating place—a place they will want to explore.

This storehouse of adventures comprises the emotional capital that constitutes some of the true wealth of your family. Wealth is not just dollars and cents. It is experience, a life filled with adventure that helps each person know more about his or her identity and capabilities. This is why I challenge you to make travel and adventure a most important part of your dreamfunding efforts. You can afford to do this—indeed, if you want to live life to the fullest, you cannot afford not to do this kind of dreamfunding all of your life. And another promise, you will never regret a single dollar invested in emotional capital.

CREATIVITY IS KEY WHEN FUNDING FUN DREAMS

I will warn you that you're about to have some of the most fun financial planning that you've ever encountered. You will be amazed at how creative your "recreation dream team" can become. The greater the passion, the more inventive your kids, your parents, and you will get in finding ways to pay for these adventures. Here are just a few ideas for trimming the price tags of travel dreams:

- Travel off season to get discounts on hotels and air fares. Travel in off-peak hours (between midnight and 6:00 AM) to get the best transportation ticket prices.
- Be willing to travel at the last minute to a favorite destination, taking advantage of cruise or trip cancellations.
- Consider being a courier to transport anything from small packages to cars and get your way paid for doing the favor. Remember, though, you'll have to trim your own baggage to do this.

- Take advantage of group tour prices, which can reduce your price tag as much as 50 percent from doing the trip on your own.
- Take advantage of using frequent flyer miles, AAA, company, or other discounts on everything from plane flights to hotels to rental cars.
- Seniors (people over age 65, sometimes 50), should ask for their special discounts, too. You can buy senior travel booklets, which let you purchase two round-trip plane tickets at once, saving substantially on both fares. Check with the American Association of Retired Persons (AARP) for the discounts they offer members. Get on the mailing list for their magazine, *Modern Maturity*, which includes many articles about recreation and travel.
- Students of all ages get breaks on travel prices. Even adults attending continuing education courses at local colleges and universities qualify for many of these discounts.
- If you have an area of expertise, consider packaging a trip you want to take, advertising for other travelers to join you, and charge your fellow travelers just enough extra to pay the way for you and your other family members to go along.
- Join a home exchange club and swap your home during a vacation with someone else across the country or the ocean. Your hometown may be a destination resort to someone else. Make sure you select a home exchange group that screens applications for suitability and ability to pay.
- If you're really a travel bug, consider working part-time as a licensed travel agent so that you're in the loop of learning about all the great trips you and your family might want to take. Plus, you'll get certain free "reconnaissance" trips as a professional travel agent.
- Get on the Internet and start exploring all kinds of travel companies—those specializing in exotic or adventure travel, or that focus on types of transportation (cruise ships, clipper ships, cargo ships, rail, bicycles, etc.). Look up a country and see all the information you can get on your own about lodging, sightseeing, and travel tips.
- If you travel on business, find out how you might tag on extra days for personal pleasure travel before or after the business portion of the trip. Your company likely will pick up the tab for a good portion of the price tag of getting you to your destination.

- Consider studying or working abroad for a while, and then travel your socks off on weekends to see as much as you can, since you're already there. Check out special discount train passes.
- If you're in the science field, consider signing on an expedition, offering your expertise and work in exchange for having your full way paid to a place you've always wanted to explore.
- Team up with another family or relatives to share housing costs for everything from holiday trips to summer vacations. You could swap houses with a relative as well as a stranger.
- Decide what about travel you have to do "first class" and what aspects you don't mind doing on a strict budget. You may be perfectly happy with the Motel 6 variety of accommodations, packing picnic meals, and spending your vacation dollars on entrance fees to museums, concerts, theme parks, and an occasional meal at fancier restaurants.
- Check out if you're better driving your own car, cutting down on real vacation time with travel days, or spending the extra money on flights and rental cars to maximize pleasure time at your destination. The shorter your trip, the more likely you'll want to do the latter.
- Pack carefully, taking only what you need, but everything you need, so you don't end up buying items left behind at inflated prices in tourist areas.
- If you sign up for a group trip, or even when booking hotels, be sure to ask about their cancellation policy so you don't get stuck paying for amenities you never used because you had to bail out of the vacation. That's the very reason travel vendors take deposits on your credit card in the first place.
- Before leaving on a trip, confirm your flight, hotel, and rental car reservations. Buying last-minute tickets and hotel rooms can be extremely expensive.

KEEPING YOUR DREAM FROM TURNING INTO A NIGHTMARE

The worst travel nightmare is to plan a terrific vacation and then have something go wrong, causing you to cancel your trip altogether or to go home early. One of your best vacation buys may be trip insurance, which can cost as little as $200 for a $5,000 trip. This can be a cancellation policy that would reimburse you for prepaid airfare and other trip costs. The mother of a friend of mine had bought this protection for a trip to Hawaii. One week before she was to leave, she was diagnosed with breast cancer and had to forgo the trip to have surgery. She got all but the $150 trip insurance back, that is, she was reimbursed for the $3,500 that she had paid for the trip ahead of time. Travel insurance also can cover medical emergency treatment and evacuation while on the trip. When I discovered that it could cost me $40,000 to be transported out of remote areas on my Nepal trek, I figured $200 was a good investment to cover that rare, but costly, misfortune, should it happen. Happily, I didn't need to use the insurance.

Whatever your travel plans, check with the airlines, hotels, and group tour agents to find out their cancellation policies and what proof of reason for cancellation you would have to provide. Note deadlines for cancellation in your calendar so, if you have to cancel, you do so without suffering a partial or full penalty of the money you've already paid.

INTERGENERATIONAL ADVENTURE PLANNING

Whether your travel is domestic or international, you want to think ahead to which family members will join you on the road and who will pay for the trip's price tag. Although your parents may no longer feel up to a long journey, they might want to help finance a special trip for you and your children. Also, you may observe in your family travel planning meeting that perhaps there is a place or type of vacation your parents yearn to experience, but they don't feel they can negotiate the planning, change planes at big airports, or handle all the logistics of carrying luggage, arranging transportation, or traveling on their own. They might be more than willing to foot part or all of the bill for the whole family if you take responsibility for supervising the details.

Remember, too, your parents are getting older. When you start talking with them about vacations they would like to take now, you may realize that you don't have that many more years to enjoy these times together. Perhaps you'll choose to put one of your own travel dreams on the back burner and coordinate plans to make sure their dreams get funded first. Likewise, your children will grow up, leave home, and go on with their lives. You have a window of about 13 years, from age 5 to

18, when family trips will work into their schedules. The earlier you do these, the better, for high school kids often want to spend their summers with their peers, not their parents. Don't miss the opportunities to build closer bonds with your children during time away from the rigors of homework and busy schedules of day-to-day life at home.

When you're planning your family adventures, I invite you to think about areas of interest you might wish to explore, many of which may take you to diverse places. You can orient a whole summer or a particular vacation to let family members expand their experiences with everything from art, archeology, history, language, sports, or music. Whatever your passion, you may be able to combine it with travel or an immersion experience that allows you to delve deeply into something that fascinates you.

There are no age or sex barriers to these experiences. Sometimes letting a child do something adventuresome away from home even as early as age five or six can be an exhilarating occasion to build confidence the child might not have gained for years to come just doing normal kid stuff. Or a family member who has faced a personal crisis, such as a major illness, divorce, or loss of a job or loved one, can undergo a soul-search and subsequent renewal through some adventure you encourage, allowing them to move on to a new chapter of their life. Observe your different relatives—parents, siblings, grandparents—and ask yourself, then ask them, what great adventure would they like to experience next. No matter what they say, seriously entertain the notion of helping them fund that dream.

CAN'T AFFORD A FUN DREAM? THINK AGAIN

Too many people cut their adventure dreams short by being too practical, especially with the issue of funding these experiences. Let's face it—there are no guarantees that you'll live to be 80, or even 65. What if you wait to do things until after you retire, but you have a stroke at age 59? Or you suffer a terrible accident and are never again able to climb another mountain or hike another trail? Adventure belongs to the adventuresome, and these individuals don't wait until even middle age to start being that way.

You can afford adventure now, this year. You only have to think of which of your many passions you're going to give yourself permission to pursue without another day's delay. You can figure out the most important priority activity, research its price tag, plan to fund it, pooling resources at your disposal, and then live the richness of experiencing your dream—the prosperity of adventure accomplished. Nothing in life gets better than that! So, if you don't have travel/adventure/recreation as a line item on your yearly budget, make room for it! Create a Top Five Adventure Dream List that you plan to start funding now. Prioritize these dreams and begin today to work through the six Ps on adventure dream number one.

DREAMFUNDING STRATEGIES . . .

1. Write out your Top Five Adventure Dream List. These are the fun dreams you'll start saving for now. Then create a list that includes every leisure activity, sport, vacation idea, and travel adventure you can think of that you would like to do. I don't care if your list has 100 or more items, write them all out. It's easiest if you categorize by topics, such as the following:

   - Sports to pursue
   - Hobbies to start or expand
   - Educational opportunities and programs
   - Family outings near home
   - Vacations in the United States
   - Trips abroad/countries to visit
   - Passionate interests to explore
   - Ways to challenge yourself

   I want you to dream far, big, and wide. Think of areas in which you know you need to grow—gain a greater perspective, test your physical limits, push the edge of the envelope in becoming more courageous, more sensitive, more enlightened. I am sure you will come up with many other major areas of recreation and adventure than those I have listed.

   Now go through this list and, within each category, prioritize the list numerically, number one being the activity you want to tackle doing first. Do that for all your categories. Now look at your number ones in each category. Do they include your Top Five Adventure Dream List items? If not, you need to redo that list, making sure your top five are number ones in your categories.

Now estimate the price tags, in both dollars and time needed for your top five recreational must-dos as well as any additional number-one items, if you have more than five categories.

Next, list your top five number ones by year in which you hope to accomplish these recreational dreams. They may go out as far as five years. I think your top priority dreams, however, should not be put off longer than five years. Remember, you've got to enjoy the journey year by year, not a decade out into the future.

Finally, total the price tags for each year, in dollars and time, and you're ready to begin planning how to accumulate the price tags by your target dates.

2. Have each member of your family go through the first exercise. Even your young children. Then call a family dream team meeting and create the Final Family Adventure Dream List; make sure it contains the number-one fun dream for each family member. Total your family price tags and see what kind of time and money is needed to accomplish the number-one dreams for all. Review your family budget to see where you can carve out the money to fund these adventure dreams. Do your kids need to work a bit during school or the summer to help pay for their dreams? What can your parents contribute to the family dreams? What can you and your spouse contribute, while still setting aside your retirement funds and education funds, if that is still in the picture for your children? Also, see if any dreams dovetail and might be accomplished on one vacation; for example, if your son wants to visit Gettysburg and your daughter wants to see the White House, both can be done on one trip.

3. Now have each of your family members brainstorm ways to slash the costs of your family recreational dreams. Who has access to discounts on lodging or rental cars? Who has a lot of frequent flier miles that can be donated? Who is willing to travel at a moment's notice? Try to cut your recreation dream costs by as much as one-third. See how many more dreams your family can then afford with just a bit of creative price-tag slashing?

4. Take a look at the Final Family Adventure Dream List and think about which dreams include opportunities for individuals in the family to stretch their boundaries of personal growth, challenge, and risk-taking. Can you build into your family vacations some element of challenge to add excitement and transformation into the trip package? What would you personally like to accomplish in this arena yourself? What do you think would benefit your children, even your parents? Chances are you can add a bit of thrill to an already attractive recreational adventure without adding much, if anything, to the cost.

Each summer, hold your family adventure planning meeting to review your Final Family Adventure Dream List, reviewing the recreational dreams you have targeted for the following year. Does anyone want to change the priority of the dream he or she most wants to have funded next year? If so, make adjustments, add up the price tags, and start brainstorming for how to find the time and money for those future dreams. Finally, look over your current budget, figuring in changes you'll make for next year, and see where you can carve out money to spend on next year's recreational dreams.

CHAPTER 17

Teaching Children about Funding Their Own Dreams

YOUNG CHILDREN (AGES THREE TO FIVE)

Even the youngest members of the family can learn about money—where it comes from, what it's used for, the continuum of earning, spending, saving, and investing. You'd be surprised how these very early lessons can start a young person off down the road to financial responsibility. You can start small, with a child's allowance; even a child age three to five can begin learning the lessons of financial management. Here is how a few families have begun educating their children about the world of money.

Jim and Sara: A Dollar for Every Year

Jim and Sara have three children, two years apart: ages one, three, and five. They believe in giving their children some money to learn with, and their system is to give each child a dollar a week for every year of age—the five-year-old gets $5; the three-year-old, $3, and they even set aside $1 per week in a piggy bank for their infant, who just celebrated her first birthday.

This couple believes that allowances must be earned with household chores. For kids this young, they assign making their beds and putting away toys as the "conditions" for earning the allowance. The baby doesn't have to start until age 18 months, however, and mom will help her with her chores. Jim says that when their son, the oldest, is seven years old, they will encourage him to do odd jobs around the house and yard to earn extra money. The idea is to instill the concept that you have to work to make money.

The couple also wants their kids to become smart consumers. Sara has taken the two older children on shopping trips to let them spend some of their money as they want. She tries to show them which toys or candy are better buys, but she lets them make mistakes, too. "How else are they going to learn, really feel the pain of making a bad buy, without making a few wrong choices?" she asks.

Jim and Sara also believe in teaching their kids about helping others. They belong to a church, and once a month at Sunday school these three children donate $1 each to the food fund for the needy. Their parents explain that it is important to give some of what you have to help those less fortunate. These very young children already are learning about charitable giving, a habit their parents hope they will continue for a lifetime.

Matt: Learns Money Lessons the Hard Way

I sat with Matt at his brother's birthday party one day. He was looking rather glum. When I asked what was wrong, he started to get tears in his eyes and reluctantly explained that he'd spent all that week's allowance on a plastic truck that broke two days after he bought it. He had asked his mother to buy him another one, and she had refused, telling he should have selected a better-made toy. With red eyes and a pout on his lips, he said he hated her. My, the life of a five-year-old can be really tough.

Later I spoke with his mom and realized she was letting her son learn a money lesson the hard way. Lots of parents would give in and buy the kid another truck, a more expensive, longer-lasting model. Not this mom. She said her son would probably be a wiser shopper in the future for this hard-won lesson, and she felt she would undercut his education by giving in. I happen to agree with her, but it sure is difficult sometimes to let our children make mistakes that are valuable lessons in disguise. I wish more moms and dads would do that, though. You can bet Matt will be a lot more choosy when he buys his next toy, and the next, and the next.

Allowances: Do's and Don'ts

It's an old debate among child development experts. Should you just give a child an allowance because he or she deserves to have some of the family money, or should the child earn it? After all, mom and dad don't get paid without working; why should the kid get a free ride?

I'm in the latter camp, along with three-quarters of American families who offer their kids allowances. We believe that it helps children learn that you have to earn money. I think every family member, children included, should take care of certain chores because they live in a household with other people and they need to contribute effort to make the household run. I believe if you don't do your chores, you shouldn't get your allowance. However, I do think that a child should be able to work for extra money by doing additional tasks, much like Jim and Sara plan to offer their oldest child. This lets a young person take initiative and have some say in earning more money to fund his or her own dreams.

The amount of allowance is up to you as the parent. It's based on your financial circumstances and your local cost of living. Going to a movie in Waterloo, Iowa, costs a lot less than patronizing a cinema house in New York City. Also, as your child goes off to school and has to buy school supplies or sports gear, you should adjust the amount given accordingly, so your child can afford what he or she needs to participate in school activities.

Another issue is frequency of allowance. Very young kids have trouble waiting to buy things and probably should get their allowance weekly. Otherwise, they'll blow it all too soon. Older children, though, need to learn about spacing their expenditures. I got a weekly allowance through age 14, and then it went to monthly, with a checking account, and I had to learn to manage my money carefully, making it last for 30 days.

Finally, you need to show prudence in the freedom you give a child in how they spend their allowance. Neale Godfrey, head of the Children's Financial Network, an education and consulting group, and author of several books on teaching children good money management skills, recommends the "four jar system":

- Jar one is for charity. Tell your child that it is important to help people who are less fortunate. You and the child can decide who should receive the donation.

- Jar two is for instant gratification. This "quick cash" should be the child's discretionary money. You may set some ground rules—no live animals and only one-third can go for candy—but otherwise the children can choose what they want to do with this money.
- Jar three is for medium-term savings. Here you teach them to stave off "instant gratification" and save up for more expensive dreams like Rollerblades or designer duds.
- Jar four is for long-term savings. This is money put away for really big-ticket items—summer camp or college.

The concept you're teaching is that money is used at different times for different purposes, and sometimes it's not spent on you at all, but on other people you want to help—family or members of the community.

One big no-no about allowances: Don't dock your kid's regular allowance for bad behavior. Why? Because it doesn't happen in adult life. People act inappropriately and still get their paychecks. Also, your child still has to operate in the money world, buying things at school, for example, even after an incident that you want to punish. A more effective means of showing your disapproval is to withdraw social privileges, such as going to an overnight sleepover or playing with friends after school. You can insist on verbal apologies to the people involved or isolate younger children through "time outs" for short periods. *Don't withhold their money.*

Money Lessons for Young Children

Consumer Education

Like Matt, most young children need some guidance in how to become wise consumers. Don't forget that your toddler TV watchers are bombarded with more advertising messages in a single day than you probably hear on the radio, see on billboards, or read in magazines. Children have no idea that they shouldn't, and can't, buy everything. They don't know that manufacturers produce shoddy goods and retailers overprice their wares. It's your job to take them to discount stores, discuss the concept of seasonal sales, show them catalogs, and explore shopping on the Internet. The best way to do this is an imaginary shopping tour, encouraging your child to pick out a few items he or she wants to buy; then you compare the price tags of these purchase dreams at the different shopping venues. Let them see that at one place they can buy only one of their three favorite toys; at another place they can afford two; at still another their same allowance will buy all three. Also, point out items that are poorly made—the kind of toy that won't last because it is designed to self-destruct before long.

Delayed Gratification

This important lesson teaches them how to save for something they want, such as a tricycle or Barbie doll. You might get them started by saying that you'll match every dollar they save with your dollar, so that together you save the price tag of their dream purchase. Then make a big deal of it the day the child has enough money to walk in the store and buy it.

Living within Their Means

This is the great spending lesson for individuals of all ages. That means no bail-outs when the child cannot make his or her allowance stretch for the whole week. You simply must not give in. Life won't provide your child a bailout later when he or she is an adult. Don't you do it now! Next week, or next month, eventually, the child will get the message—live within your allowance, now and for the rest of your life.

How Money Works

You also want to teach your child about coins, paper money, and financial institutions. Visit a bank and explain that this is where you save money for them and for the entire family. You can even open an account in which the child can put his or her savings, and show him or her how the money grows each month, because the bank pays interest. You can tell the child that some things cost a lot of money, like going to college, and tell them about the investment account that their grandparents or you started for their college fund.

Most important of all, teach your children about dreams. Help them discover their own passions. Tell them about some of the family dreams they can share in enjoying—like an upcoming vacation or a surprise anniversary party for grandma and grandpa. Ask them what they want to do right now, next month, and when they grow up. You'll be amazed at what they reveal is important to them. Don't discount these yearnings a bit. Help make some of their dreams come true, so they get the experience of planning for something important and then getting to fulfill that wish. Add their dreams to your Final Family Dream List. Even if their goal costs little and easily can be afforded. Let them see that the whole family values their dreams and wants to see them funded. You're starting a small child out on a journey to dream accomplishment; they can start small and later dream big.

SCHOOL-AGE KIDS CAN START EARNING AND INVESTING (AGES SIX TO FOURTEEN)

Teaching your family's younger generation about the value of the dollar and engaging them to work for money in the family and in their community are just a few of the important lessons you can give your children to help them build a firm financial foundation. Earning some money, however little, gives a child self-esteem, self-confidence, and a sense of autonomy. However, you do want to strike a balance and not overemphasize money as the end goal of all productive activity. School-age kids can learn these distinctions. Earning and investing money are among the best ways to provide them this rudimentary financial training.

Danny: Allowance for Extra Chores Buys Delayed Dream

Danny, age ten, wanted a boogie board in the worst way. His mother suggested he start saving his allowance to pay the $50 for the board. Danny did the math and realized that, on his $5 weekly allowance, it would take him ten weeks to get his coveted boogie board. By then, summer would be over. So, he asked for extra chores around the house to earn more money. He weeded the garden, took out the trash every day, babysat for his younger brother, and washed the dishes three nights a week. His mom assures me there were some bitter complaints when his added chores cost him a TV basketball game he wanted to watch, or he couldn't go out to play with friends until the weeding was done. Nonetheless, Danny's work efforts accomplished what he wanted—in four weeks he had the $50 and bought his boogie board. He was ecstatic, and every day he was out there learning how to ride his new mode of transportation. I asked Danny later that summer how he felt about working for his boogie board. He said, "It's great! I saved my allowance for something that can last my whole life, instead of buying a bunch of little tchotchkes or baseball cards that you just trade around or other small stuff!"

Jake: Teenage Investor

Jake, age 13, is my youngest client. He studied about the stock market in an economics class this year, and he decided he wanted to buy stock. His mother, who already had an account with me, asked if she could open an account for Jake. We did that, putting his $100 in savings in an UGMA (Uniform Gift to Minors Account), with his mother as the adult custodian. She made it clear, from the beginning, however, that she wanted me to deal directly with Jake so he and I started discussing what stock he'd like to buy. He scans the business section of the local newspaper daily, and, having read an article about GTE, he decided that would be his first stock pick. He held the stock for about six months, and then when the stock market started its gyrations in the spring of 2000, he sold. Now he's sitting on the sidelines, studying his next investments.

One hard lesson for Jake is that buying and selling costs a bit of money for the transaction fees. He still came out ahead, but he told me that next time, he'll try to hold the stock longer, so he won't get "eaten up" by trading costs. Smart boy. He's learning about the risk of stock investing, the way transactions are done, and he's already building a small investment portfolio for the long-term. When I asked him what he was going to use his investment capital for, he replied, "Oh, I'm not going to spend it; I'm going to keep adding to it!" Now that's an ideal investment client, at any age!

Work for Pay Pays Off, Inside and Outside the Home

Paying your kids for extra chores around the house or helping them get "outside" jobs during summer or the school year provide your children with their first work opportunities—opportunities to learn about the real world of earning money. They see how much work goes into earning a dollar; they learn money doesn't grow on trees. Also, whether working for you, performing neighborhood jobs such as baby-sitting, lawn-mowing, and leaf-raking, or holding down a part-time job at a local business, your son and daughter start to learn that working for pay involves a lot more than just the money. They gain experience in how to get along with people, how to take responsibility, and how to upgrade their job skills. They get to pursue their early passions and try on careers that have intrigued them. Working early helps young people eliminate what they don't want to do when they grow up, as well as reaffirm a type of work that does appeal to them.

Perhaps the best lessons youngsters learn through working are about the valuable character traits of honesty, punctuality, reliability, self-discipline, resourcefulness, patience, courtesy, and compassion for people. Through their work in the community, they meet a whole group of people they may not have seen in person before. When they encounter the old, the poor, the disabled, the helpless, they start to gain an appreciation of their own comforts and opportunities, and they begin to evolve into young people with empathy for others. When they are faced with a disgruntled customer or employer, they learn how to deal with difficult people. When they see an employee fired for theft or misconduct, they start to understand that they had better be honest and responsible if they want to keep their jobs. When they come home with tales of discovery, you have a golden opportunity to remind them of the values and work ethic you hope they will practice in their own lives.

And don't overlook the job training, expanded knowledge, and technical skills a teenager can acquire through work. Colleges today look at your child's nonacademic education and breadth of experience, including work, when deciding whom to accept for enrollment.

How Much to Work and Earn

As for how much money is wise for a young student to be able to earn, whether through household tasks or at a job, I think it depends on your family finances and what you feel in your gut is right for your child and your family. You can always limit the amount of earnings a child can actually spend at his or her own discretion, just as you did with the allowance jars earlier. So, if your child earns $400 per month doing summer lawn services, you can have him or her put $100 in his or her own bank account, and you might put the $300 balance into the child's college fund account.

I will also say that I don't think it's wise to let your child work so hard that he or she never has play time with friends. Socializing and learning people skills with peers is every bit as important to success in later life as making money. Building friendships and working out conflicts that arise when you play together are very important tasks for a child to undertake. So, keep the work balance in perspective. Also, make sure your child has time to do homework.

As for income levels, you may not know there is a minimum wage for children as well as adults. For adults, it's $5.15 per hour; for children up to age 20, it's $4.25 per hour. As soon as your child works for pay, or opens any kind of financial account that earns interest or growth, the child must have a Social Security number. Up until age 14 your child's income, whether earned or investment income, will be taxed at the parents' income tax bracket. At age 14, the income is taxed at the child's tax bracket.

Young Earners Should Learn to Pay Themselves First

This lesson alone might be the most important result of letting a child work for money. A seven-year-old who gets $3 for weeding the garden should be advised to save 75 cents (25 percent) for their intermediate-term dreams—maybe for a pair of ice skates, or to go to next year's Christmas cookie-making school—and 75 cents for their long-term dream of a high school car. As a parent trying to instill the idea of planning for the future, encourage your child to think beyond next week, even next month, and to continue allocating their earnings, whether from allowance or job money, for the "four jar" categories. You want your children, early on, to understand the idea and the benefit of paying yourself first—saving for your later needs and wants. You can help them think of particular purposes for these future dreams. If they are willing to save for their college, you could match them $2 for every dollar saved. When they start to see their education fund growing, they'll not only be proud of their own discipline, they'll come to appreciate that an education is very important—so important that the whole family wants to save for it, including them.

As your children approach high school age, you can start to share with them how you are saving for your own retirement, too, and that you have a certain amount of money deducted from your paycheck, just like they are doing with their allowance or job money. They start to see how one day you will be able to afford to stop working, and they get the idea that investing in their future makes a lot of sense. As soon as your children earn outside income, you can start an IRA for them as well. They need to understand that they cannot touch this money for a very long time. Forty years (until age 59½) may sound like forever to them. Just tell them that if together you and they save $158.14 each month in their IRA, at a 10 percent growth factor, in 40 years they'll have $1 million. See if that doesn't get some wide-eyed looks of amazement. See, you've just taught them about the eighth wonder of the world—compound interest!

Investment Accounts for Kids

Opening an investment account in a child's name, such as an UGMA or UTMA account with you as custodian or an account in your name but earmarked for each child, is a sure-fire way to make kids feel part of the greater world of money. You can start with a single stock. Then introduce the idea of mutual funds, where your child will see that he or she can own pieces of a lot of individual companies. Many mutual funds allow initial investments of as low as $25 in custodial accounts as long as you plan to do some form of regular investing—it could be as infrequently as four times a year, for example.

When the market is choppy, you can show your children how the value of their account will not always go up, and they can begin to understand how risking their money feels. After the first year, if the account has grown, help them figure out their rate of return on their investment. Show them how leaving the money to invest over several years can take advantage of the time value of money and compounding of growth. You can also share how you're investing their college funds and about your plan to make sure the money is liquid—available—for the years they will be in college. This may lead into a discussion of growth investments (stocks and stock mutual funds) versus income investments (CDs, money markets, bonds, and bond mutual funds).

Also, encourage your child to read books about money. You might buy them a subscription to *Zillions,* a money magazine for kids. There are Web sites to visit as well that get kids involved in money concepts. (See <www.fundingyourdreams.com> for references.) The more familiar young people become with financial terms and concepts, the more they will begin to feel a part of the larger money arena, in which they will have to learn to survive as they grow up and leave home.

Dreamfunding for School-Age Children

One thing about this age group, you don't have to work hard to get them to dream big. Once a child gets into school and gets exposed to history, geography, biology, literature, and sports, he or she develops very specific passions—heroes and heroines to emulate; places to roam; professions to pursue like those of a favorite uncle or some visitor at school.

Try your best not to brush off, crush, or dampen these wild hopes. You just never know how these dreams will evolve into something quite different and wonderful. It's best if the child comes to the conclusion that a particular dream is not what he or she wants after all, rather than you predetermining that the child should not have the chance to explore it.

By this age, your children should be participating fully in your family dream team meetings, listing their favorite dreams on the Final Family Dream List. You may have trouble getting them to select their top 5 dreams, for they may have 20. Still, this winnowing down experience will help them focus and realize they cannot possibly have time (or the money) to go after all their dreams at once. Still, you cannot imagine how important it makes a child feel when the whole family turns and listens to what they are so passionate about. They come to understand deeply that their dreams are valued by every member of their family.

DREAMFUNDING STRATEGIES . . .

1. Set up a regular allowance program in your family. Decide the following:

   - Will you give the allowance without regard to chores, or will you make one of your money rules that allowances must be earned?
   - How much allowance should each child get? Will you base it on age, numbers of chores completed, or give all kids the same amount until a certain age?

- What restrictions will you place on how your kids spend their allowances or the money relatives give them? Are there certain things you will not allow them to buy? Must they save some money for charity, short-term, intermediate-term, or long-term goals? Will you fork out more money if they run out? (I hope the answer to this last one is "no.")

   Once you've decided on these allowance guidelines, have your children sit down to a family "allowance" meeting and explain the new rules. Answer all their questions, and tell them what day (this week) you will begin the new allowance program. If you expect your kids to earn their allowance, negotiate the chore list now. Get their agreement, making them understand that if they don't do the chores, they don't get the allowance. Ask your children if any one of them wants the opportunity to earn extra money doing additional chores. You may want to put a cap on how much in total you would give any one child in a month.

2. Set up a weekly *chore scoreboard* with each child's name and expected duties listed. The first evening of the new program, take each child to the scoreboard and see who has done what. Check off the tasks done, and explain how the program works again—chores not done, no allowance that week. The next day, ask about the chores earlier in the day, so your child won't get in the habit of procrastinating until the last minutes before bedtime. At the end of the first allowance period, pay according to chores done. Don't be tempted to cheat to make your kids feel better. Be consistent every week in your resolve to be fair and tough-minded about each child earning his or her keep (and allowance).

3. With your spouse, make a list of *money values* you want your children to learn at different ages. Write the list down and post it on the chore scoreboard for all to see. Think of ways to teach these values in discussions or outings with the kids. Make the shopping excursions and other lessons fun—children love the "game" aspect of learning something new. When an incident comes up that exemplifies one value, talk about it that night at dinner. After your kids have had several years to handle their allowances, or perhaps

earn money outside the home, ask them to write their own money values lists. See if they come up with new ones they didn't learn from you.

4. Teach your child how to count money. Explain where money comes from, and show the difference between coins and paper denominations. Explain how you save money to do things for the family—like a vacation, or to buy a new home. Decide on some form of jar system to separate out the money your child gets— some for immediate purchases, some for buying a special thing later on, some for charity, some for really long-term goals like college. Suggest that the longer-term money could go into the child's very own savings account.

5. When your child first wants to buy something, help him or her look at different toys, books, games, or even food items that he or she might want to purchase. Show the child how some items seem well made; others do not. But let the child ultimately choose how he or she wishes to spend the discretionary money.

6. Have a *dream discussion* with your children. Talk about your dreams—dreams you have for yourself, for your parents, and for the children. Ask each child to describe the dream he or she most wants to make come true right away. Add those dreams to the Final Family Dream List and invite your kids to come to the next family dream team meeting. They may just sit and listen, but that's OK. They'll start to see the family working together, and they'll hear that their dreams are important to the whole family. Start them young participating in intergenerational financial planning.

7. Have a *fireside money chat* with each child once a month. My dad used to do this with me and my sister, separately. We'd each go over our allowance and how we had spent it, and we would talk about different money values or topics that he thought we were old enough to understand. I had the chance to ask questions about everything from how much money he made to why I couldn't have more allowance. We even talked about one of my aunts who could not control her spending and how difficult that was for my uncle.

Dad's candor was a real eye-opener for a 12-year-old who had trouble making her allowance last for two weeks! Sometimes I used to dread these meetings, because I had "blown my wad"; other times I proudly reported that I had $10 left over. Most of all, this open forum of money talk introduced me to a lot of ideas about what does and doesn't work in managing my money. I learned a lot from my dad during these sessions—lessons I still apply today.

8. By the time your children are 12 years old, they can learn to manage money over more than weekly allowance intervals. Try paying the allowance only twice a month. By age 15, pay them monthly. Give them a checking account, too. Help them create their first budget using the Child's Budget worksheet in the Appendix. Make them list everything they have to spend money on that first month—school supplies, meals away from home, birthday gifts for friends, etc. Next, ask them to list their *wish list* items that they want to spend some of their earnings on. Add up both lists for the spending total. The next step is to have them add up all their earnings for the income total. Now have them subtract the spending total from the income total. Do they have money left over? Or are they in the red? Explain the concept of deficit spending. If this is their situation, they must go back to their wish list and trim the heck out of it. Finally, make sure there is a savings/investment line item in their budget—they still have to keep setting aside some of their earnings for later. By now they should have both a bank savings account and some type of investment account. They can make regular monthly deposits into each.

    You'll be reviewing their budget at each monthly fireside money chat. Discuss their successes and failures in sticking to the budget. When necessary, as their circumstances change, you may need to revise the budget, probably annually.

9. Start telling your children more about the family finances. Talk about your entire family's monthly budget, what it covers, the amount you set aside for savings for such future dreams as next year's vacation, college in four years for the oldest child, or retirement. Also, make a future budget list of the expenses each child will encounter when he or she becomes independent—car insurance,

health insurance, rent, utilities, food, clothing, gas, and car maintenance. (Use the Child's Future Budget worksheet in the Appendix.) Give the child a round number of what it might cost to live independently—just so he or she starts to appreciate all the costs you cover now and why the child needs to save for the future.

10. Start to really train your kids to understand borrowing and credit. Show them your mortgage statement and let them see how much of the cost you pay each month is interest on your home loan. Show them a credit card bill, point out the interest rate, and give them an example of how much interest you would pay in a year if you didn't pay off your balance each month. The idea here is to teach them the high cost of borrowing. Also, tell them about credit bureaus, credit reports, and what happens to your credit standing if you don't pay your bills on time. Explain that there is a limit on what you can charge on a credit card—it is not an endless supply that can be tapped. Impress on them that any money borrowed must be paid back—the sooner, the better.

11. If your parents, the kids' grandparents, want to give money to your children, decide up front how much you will let each child take for spending now and how much is to be saved for later. You might encourage your parents to set up savings accounts directly for the kids and put their donations into these accounts. Discourage lavish material gifts from well-intended relatives, and suggest that college funds would be welcomed in their place.

12. Encourage your children to participate in the dream team family meetings. Let them observe that other people in the family have dreams that are just as important as their own. They'll begin to get the idea of pooling the family money resources to help everyone fund their dreams.

CHAPTER 18

Prepare Teens and Young Adults for Financial Survival

One of the best ways for teenagers and young adults (ages 15 to 22) to become financially savvy is for them to know the nitty-gritty specifics of your own family's finances. You've already started showing them your family budget and mortgage payments, talked with them about credit, and helped them create a monthly budget. Now you need to get into greater depth about your total financial picture. During their high school years, they should get a good idea what kind of financial shape you are in and learn that your money picture may change somewhat based on your and your spouse's earnings, job stability, and your total living expenses, including unexpected extraordinary expenses you hadn't planned on.

Your children should feel comfortable talking with you about what you earn, how much you have in savings for their college years, and what you've set aside to date for your retirement. They should also be clued in to whether you're on target for important dreamfunding, or if you're behind schedule. Don't try to hide from your kids when financial times are tough. They'll sense something is wrong anyway. If you share your financial truths, they can learn to adjust their own money habits to what is going on in the family financial arena. In lean years, they can learn to cut back and spend less, as you do. They may even take on a summer job or after-school work to help with their own expenses and dreamfunding. In better times, they should also be able to share in the plenty, along with you, their parents.

A good way to clue in your kids is to show them your financial plan, if you have one. (By the time you come to this chapter, you should have done one.) Explain the process you went through with your advisor to create the plan. You gathered financial information, you discussed your short-term, intermediate-term, and long-term goals (dreams). You estimated price tags of those dreams. You looked at the financial assets and liabilities you had when the plan was generated, and then with your financial planner, you figured out how much you needed to save and invest to reach your targeted dreams. You can tell your teenagers how well you've done to meet your deadlines, such as how much money is set aside for their college and the size of your retirement accounts. You can review the kinds of investments in which you have the childrens' and your own money, and why you picked these types of investments.

One great benefit of this disclosure is that your child becomes more fully aware of the steps he or she will need to take to help fund future dreams. The child also will know early in high school if you have enough money set aside for his or her college education. If you are off the mark, then you can discuss how the child may need to help contribute more savings to his or her college funds, seek student aid in the form of loans or scholarships, or even postpone college and work a few years to go to the university of his or her choice. This information is sobering stuff for a teenager, who may have been sailing along thinking everything was set for college the fall after high school graduation.

Kids need to know a lot about how finances work and their relationship to money. This first look at family finances gets them thinking about what you will be able to afford for them and what they may have to fund through their own initiative. Even as they head off to college, young adults have to fast-track their financial education to set out on their own with a firm financial footing.

Let's see what a few high school students and grads have learned from their parents and how they've had to smarten up to pay their way.

SYBIL AND AMY: Single Mom Urges Daughter Out on Her Own

Sybil is a divorced parent whose 20-year-old daughter, Amy, has no clue about how to become financially independent. Amy is a sophomore in college and wants to go to New York City to finish school. She knows a few friends she can room with, but other than having worked as a waitress part-time, she has no real job skills and no idea about how to make her way until she graduates. Her dad will pay for tuition and books; the rest she's got to provide on her own. Sybil will help out some, but she's told Amy that by her junior year, she needs to be paying her own expenses. Sybil is saving 25 percent of her salary for her own future nest egg, hoping to retire from her consulting work in another three years. There is nothing left over from her earnings to pay Amy's way any longer.

Sybil's first step was to bring Amy to a meeting with me. We talked about Amy's goals—to be a print journalist right out of college and then to marry and have a family. She plans to work all along, but doesn't know how much she'll earn in her chosen career field, and she has no inkling what it costs to live in New York. She plans to wait until her late 20s to start a family, and she wants to have at least three children.

Actually, I was pleased that Amy had this many specific goals. Most 20-year-olds have only a vague idea of what they will do after college. Few have thought ahead to how many children and when they want to start their family. Still, Amy needs to find out rather quickly what her expenses will be during college, whether she can get living expenses covered through student loans, and whether she can work during school to help pay her expenses.

The first assignment I gave her was to call her friends in New York City and find out what they spend each month to live. I gave her a checklist of items to cover. Next, she had to call the school, Columbia, and find out about work-study opportunities, talk with the financial aid officer, request aid application paperwork, and apply for any merit scholarships for which her grade point might qualify. I suggested she ask her dad for flight funds to visit the campus, her friends, solidify the housing situation, and come back with a better idea of total living costs, potential aid, and the amount of "gap" money she needed to provide. She also was to check with professors in the journalism school to see if any wanted to hire an assistant or help her find work in the department.

After her scouting trip and homework, Amy found that her out-of-pocket living costs would be $15,000 per year and she was about $3,000 short in terms of aid or outside income she thought she could generate. She had landed a work-study stipend and an after-school waitress job. Sybil and I discussed the matter, and she agreed to loan

Amy $3,000 per year, borrowing on her home equity, and charge her daughter the 11 percent interest she would have to pay on the borrowed money. She will do this for two years. Amy will have to fund any graduate school years on her own.

In this case, it took some outside counseling for mother and daughter to agree on a game plan for funding Amy's college dream in New York. It also took some homework and planning on Amy's part to understand the exact price tag of her dream. It might have helped if Sybil and Amy's dad had told Amy earlier that she would be responsible for a significant part of her educational funding. Also, Amy could have sought financial aid much sooner in her college career with perhaps a better chance of gaining full coverage of her expenses for all four years. Finally, this family should have taught their daughter back in high school about the array of expenses her college dream entailed and had her do some budget projections for what it costs to live out on your own once you've left home.

FRANK:　Founderer Finds His Future

To call Frank a screw-up would be a little harsh. He was always a good kid—warm, fun-loving, but a poor student. A child of divorce, Frank had a few emotional problems, which got him into trouble in high school. He flirted with drugs, even petty theft. His dad decided to pull him out of public school and send him to a private high school with a campus near his greatest passion at the time—skiing. The kids would study in the morning and then have free afternoons on the slopes. With this carrot to stay in school, Frank graduated from high school, barely.

Frank's dad is quite wealthy, and his son knows that one day he will inherit a bundle. Still, Frank wanted to go to college and try his hand at something to earn a living. Problem was, he didn't know what. He went to a community college but left after one semester. Then he worked at a pizza restaurant. He even tried his hand at being a gaffer in Hollywood. Finally, when he had just turned 21, his dad told him that in two years he would be out on his own, sinking or swimming—no more financial support. That's when Frank started getting serious about his future. His mother lived on the coast of Mexico, near a famed barrier reef. Visiting her, Frank enrolled in a summer scuba class and fell in love with the sport. He found a local dive shop where he could train to become an instructor. While teaching scuba, he lived at home with his mom and her husband, and decided to finish school at a local business college. He graduated, formed a business partnership with his former scuba instructor, and now has a thriving business taking tourists on private guided scuba excursions. He loves what he's doing—scuba is now his greatest passion. It only took a little time—until age 27, before he discovered a way to make his living at something he truly enjoys, and it's a reasonably well-paid living at that. Now in his own apartment, he's saving money to buy a condo on the beach. His father has started teaching him about investments, and you couldn't find a prouder dad. Sometimes forcing a young adult to get out from under the family paycheck, letting him or her discover his or her interests and talents by trying a number of jobs, is the best financial education you can provide a floundering child.

WELCOME TO ADULTHOOD

I think the worst thing you can do to teenagers and young adults is to shelter them from the facts of life, including the financial facts. Soon enough, your son or daughter will be out of the house, forging his or her way in the adult world, armed only with what you've taught and the little he or she has learned in the few short years since entering school. One of the great voids in our educational system is the lack of comprehensive financial training for children in public or private middle schools and high schools. Parents are the main source of financial instruction for your teenage children. The onus, and the opportunity, to teach kids about money is on you.

FINANCE 101 FOR YOUNG PEOPLE

Besides acquainting your teenagers and young adults with the facts of your family finances, there is so much you can teach them before they venture too far out into the money world. Let's start with the basics: the continuum of earning, spending, saving, and investing.

Earning

While your children may have worked at summer or after-school jobs, and certainly that is a good place to start learning about making a living, most young people have no idea how to scout out careers they might want to consider. I've mentioned helping them explore their interests as young children, or even in middle school, enrolling them in extracurricular workshops, sports, art classes, something that sparks their excitement. In high school, you need to rev up your efforts to educate children about career development and earning an income.

One way to open the conversation is to talk about the idea that someday they'll be out on their own, working for money, and they need to think about what kind of a career they would like. It also is a good idea to tell them how you arrived at your own career decision. Maybe share some mistakes you might have made, adding whatever insights your learning curve taught you. You might have a conversation about the relationship of career choice to income opportunity, letting them know that their choice of career can greatly impact their lifetime earnings.

It's also important, though, for young people to realize they have many decades in which to build their income throughout their career. They won't be making forever what they earn in their early, lower-paying years. Also, acquaint them with the startling statistic that a person leaving college today can expect to have an average of seven jobs and three careers in his or her working lifetime. Your children need to anticipate possible periods of unemployment, the need to go back for retraining, and job upheaval that can cause interruptions in income and periods of financial instability. Most kids today know that the work world is a fast-changing place, and that they need to be adaptable to move with the currents of career transitions and change.

Spending

By the time your kids are in high school, I hope you've given them a lot of experience with spending their allowance and some of the money they've earned through work. You've taught them that they should not spend every dime they get, and that they must be selective in how they allocate what they do spend. They've had to do their monthly budget for several years. Now it's time for them to do a future budget for their first year out of high school. Walk them through the process of figuring out what it will cost them to live at college, or out on their own if they don't go to college right away. Take the Child's Future Budget worksheet (see the Appendix), and let them take a stab at guessing what each item will cost. Call a college financial aid officer at the school they've chosen and ask about living expenses for a typical student in that area. If your child is not college-bound but wants to live at home, figure out what costs you will ask him or her to pay while going out and beginning to work. If the child is going to move away from home, find out what average apartment rents, utilities, and food cost; decide if you can keep your child on your insurance for a while longer, or whether he or she must buy auto and health insurance. Help your child determine what he or she should allocate for recreation, entertainment, travel, taxes, and even beginning savings for long-term goals.

Once you and your child have filled out the future budget, total all the expenses and point out that this is what it will cost him or her to start living independently. If you can see that the expected income is substantially less, you as parents must decide if you're going to subsidize your fledgling adult the first few years until his or her income matches the cost of living you've outlined.

Talk about credit cards again now. Discourage your children from taking on debt as a way of life just to bridge the gap between their wants and their starting income. Go over the cost of credit and remind them that keeping good credit is a financial prerequisite if they want to finance a car or obtain a home loan on their own.

Saving

When your child first starts work, think of a novel way to remind him or her to start saving for the future. Find out when the first paycheck arrives and send a telegram to arrive that day. The message is short and simple "pay yourself first." This phrase should ring a familiar bell if you did your parent homework earlier in the financial education game.

Remind your children about dream funding and making savings an important line item in their future budget. Help them prioritize some of the big dreams most young people want to take on right away—a car, nice vacations, paid-off student loans, and eventually a first home or condo. Refresh their memory about setting aside $158 per month at 10 percent for 40 years to accumulate that $1 million dollars. That will trigger the incentive they may need to begin long-term savings. Help them open an IRA, if they haven't. Suggest they participate in their employer's retirement plan at work.

Investing

Here's where you pull out the big guns of motivation. Send your children notes now and then with a new investment idea that intrigues you. Clip articles of investment advice by professionals to continue your child's financial education. Consider paying for two hours of a financial planner's time to meet with your son or daughter by age 20 and let a third-party expert champion the cause of lifelong investing. Challenge your child to work with that advisor to create a financial plan for his or her first ten years after college. Ask the child to talk with you later about the ideas they came up with and the goals they set. Ask what monthly commitment your child plans to make toward investing.

If your parents or other relatives want to help your adult child get a financial start in life, suggest that they give your child an investment, such as stock or a mutual fund, as a birthday or holiday gift. If they want to do regular gifting, suggest that the donor set up an account in their own name, make the investments, and not turn it over to your child until he or she reaches a certain age of maturity—maybe age 25 or 30. By then, the amount will be considerable; it could fund the down payment on a home, or help pay for a wedding plus honeymoon.

Invite your child to attend investment seminars with you to help expose him or her to investment strategies and products. Involve your child in conversations during family get-togethers, and test his or her understanding of basic investment concepts. Give a subscription to an investment newspaper or newsletter, and then ask what he or she has learned from it. You'll find that some kids will be open to such financial coaching. Others will resist your well-meaning guidance and want to search out investment information on their own. All you can do is try to educate the coachable ones. The others will learn one way or the other, hopefully not the hard way.

NET WORTH VERSUS SELF-WORTH

This is one fundamental financial truth you want to be sure to impart to your children as they mature. Maybe as your child heads off to graduate school or to a first job away from home, you'll want to give a reminder that a person's value has little to do with income or net worth. Sure, you're proud that your child has taken the education you helped provide and discovered a career path to follow. But the emphasis on making money, getting ahead, and being successful is so prevalent in our culture, sometimes we forget to tell our children that we love them for the people they've become, for the character they've developed, not for the amount of money they can or will make. They are valuable to us as people first, as loved ones, not as money machines.

MONEY IS NOT THE END GOAL OF ALL PRODUCTIVE ACTIVITY

Another important money value for young people to learn is that individuals may do some very important work for which they do not get paid. Pro bono contributions of their professional talents, such as serving on boards of nonprofit organizations or offering time and expertise in volunteer community work, are valuable, productive activities in which young adults may want to get involved from the beginning of their careers. Many high school students learn about nonpaid work through volunteer hours spent at local hospitals, senior centers, and agencies for the homeless or as tutors to younger children.

Money is not the end goal of all productive activity, and young people who participate in their communities in this way go on to become the adults whose efforts help thousands of organizations provide the multitude of services needed by so many. Encourage your children to explore this kind of opportunity to serve others. They will find the experience very enlightening and rewarding, and will come to understand that we get paid in many valuable and satisfying ways besides in dollars and cents.

CHILDREN OF WEALTH

Children of wealth often have special problems dealing with the real world of money that most other people have as a frame of reference. Often affluent families fail to teach their young that many of their fellow students or colleagues at work do not have the kind of money at their disposal that they do. This can make for insensitivity to the financial means of others, often leading to embarrassing situations for them or their friends. If you're in this category of the very rich, educate your youngest family members about the financial limits of others. Your children need not hide the fact that they come from wealth, but they should not flaunt it either.

Parents with a lot of money have the additional task of preparing their young adult children to manage their current and future assets. Don't assume that because your children have heard your table talk at dinner they are well informed or have received public education that prepares them for their fortunate financial state. Whether you care to disclose the extent of your net worth to your maturing children is up to you. Eventually, however, they must learn how to handle their wealth, and I think the sooner you clue them in to their special responsibilities in this area, the better money managers they will become.

RICHES MONEY CAN'T BUY

No financial education is complete without passing down this final important notion: We all have many blessings in life that cannot be purchased or paid for with money. As your children grow into adulthood, teach them this very important lesson—that among their riches are those that have nothing to do with financial assets. These include their loved ones, friendships, natural talents, the beauty of nature, the variety of animals and other living species, the diversity of things to be learned, and their vitality and good health. I think to be truly happy, everyone must appreciate these treasures. It's part of your job as a parent to add to your children's joy in life by teaching them to count these blessings as part of their abundant riches.

DREAMFUNDING STRATEGIES . . .

1. When your children turn age 15, consider putting them on a monthly allowance with a checking account. This will force them to learn to budget their money for an entire month at a time—a good practice to begin before they're out in the real financial world. Show them how to balance their checkbook, and if you're one of those many adults who doesn't balance yours, keep that to yourself. Young, enthusiastic earners and spenders just might make this good habit part of their financial ritual for the rest of their lives. Stress the importance and sense of security in knowing where you are financially at

all times, seeing when you're close to running out of cash, and doing your level best to never bounce a check.

2. In one of your fireside money chats, have your high school–aged child come up with three versions of his or her monthly budget: the luxury version, where money is allocated for all the child's wants (within reason, of course); a moderate budget, with its mixture of wants and needs; and a bare-bones version, stripped down to basic necessities. Explain that this three-budget system will come in handy when the child first starts working, especially if his or her income fluctuates. Once a young person recognizes that income production is not always an upward trajectory and that there will be lean as well as fat times ahead, he or she may learn to adapt financially when conditions change.

3. Challenge your 16- to 18-year-olds to rethink their savings programs in terms of their dreams. Start with the charity portion. Ask them to consider which group(s) of disadvantaged persons, sick people, or worthy causes they most want to help with their donations. Suggest that they volunteer some after-school hours to work with this group, observing where the greatest need lies in that nonprofit organization. Suggest that they revisit their amount of donation and come up with a specific giving dream that they can commit to sponsoring. It may be helping to buy clothes for battered women in a shelter. It might be to pay for and help organize a pet visitation program at the Alzheimer's unit of a nearby nursing home. The idea here is to get your children to see their donation dollars at work supporting a cause they strongly champion.

   Next, look at the dreams and goals they have listed for their quick cash, intermediate-term, and long-term savings accounts. If they have too many dreams to fund now in each category, get them to reprioritize each dream list.

4. Over dinner one night throw out the question, "What is net worth? Do, you, Linda, have a net worth?" If she looks dubious, explain that she has savings accounts and a college fund, and these are part of her assets. Then discuss liabilities and net income versus gross income. Finally, bring up the concept of self-worth versus net worth.

Invite your children to tally up their wonderful character traits that comprise their self-worth. It's really enlightening to ask one child to describe the positive attributes he or she admires in a sister or brother. Boy, does that get the attention of the child whose worthy traits are being lauded. Sometimes this exercise alone can turn sibling rivalry into sibling bonds that make family life much more enjoyable for kids and parents!

5. When your high school children approach graduation, think of ways you can send them out into the world armed with the financial know-how you wish you'd had at the same age. If you feel there are important lessons you've not had time to explain, sit down and talk about them now. Think back to the major money mistakes you have made. What advice might have averted them?

6. If you have a lot of money, ask yourself if you've sensitized your children to the reality that they have more financial resources than many of their peers. If you see your kids flaunting their money, pull them up short and ask them how they might feel if the situation were reversed and some uppity rich kids kept showing off their wealth. Also, begin to educate your children about their personal and family responsibilities to protect and add to the financial resources you now have. Unless you don't want them to go out and work, but rather sit on boards of community organizations and contribute in that way, urge your children to develop careers they can enjoy and through which they can earn their own money. Many times children of wealth feel unworthy of their "easy ride" and would welcome the guidance to create some value and earnings of their own through hard work and utilization their education and talents.

7. Have an "I am rich" discussion with your high school kids. Talk to them about the many riches that you as a family and they as individuals possess. These are the blessings that have no monetary value—good health, a loving family, friendships, etc. I'm sure you can come up with a long list. You want your children to think of a long list, too. Give them ideas, and then see who can come up with the most riches. You can dub that child the "wealthiest" member of the family. Ask for a copy of each child's list and save them. Then

one day, when your fledgling young adult is bogged down in graduate school, anxious to get out and make some money, or speaks woefully of the piddling starting salary she is earning, send a loving cheer-up note and include the I am rich list, written years ago. It's bound to give your child a boost in spirit. In fact, you'll probably get a "Thanks Mom, thanks Dad" phone call. Your child can't help but appreciate the reminder that we all have many treasures that money can't buy.

CHAPTER 19

Teaching Adult Children How to Make the Most of Their Inheritance

Perhaps you know the saying: Shirtsleeves to shirtsleeves in three generations. Often a hardworking generation will create and pass down considerable wealth to their adult children and grandchildren with no real instruction in how to manage or utilize this financial windfall so early in life. Sometimes by the third generation the wealth is gone. If you have a sizable estate to leave, do you really want your children to squander this hard-earned money? Are you tempted to leave it all to charity so they won't have a chance to blow it?

Whatever financial legacy you want to leave your heirs at death or gift to them during life, help your adult children anticipate these family resources. Advise them to make financial plans for themselves and their own offspring; encourage them to take the family money and use it with care. Be the lead example of an intergenerational financial planner in your family; share your wealth of financial information with your loved ones along with sharing the wealth.

SONIA: Still Looking for the Money

Sonia is a 45-year-old accountant and a qualified one at that. Still, she was financially ignorant of her parents' personal finances. They told her nothing; she didn't ask. When she lost first her mother to cancer in November, and then her dad to a heart attack two months later, she not only was emotionally devastated, she was clueless about their finances. When the executor, a local estate attorney, read the will, she did find comforting its simple directive that she was to inherit all her parents' assets. Then she tried to find out more details. Glancing through the mail she saw monthly statements from a brokerage account, two savings accounts, and her parents' joint checking account. These assets totaled about $150,000. A few weeks later, her dad's pension and Social Security checks came in, as well as her mother's nominal Social Security payment (she had worked only a few years). Thinking that this income and accounts were the sum total of their money, Sonia did the legal paperwork to have the account balances given to her. She sent back the post-death retirement checks and wrote the employer and Social Security that her parents were deceased. Nine months later she filed the estate tax return. Subsequently, having looked over her parents' previous year's tax return and finding no other income sources, Sonia prepared and submitted their final joint personal income tax return for the year of death. She figured at last she had closed the chapter on her parents' finances.

Eleven months after her dad's death, however, some of her parents' mail was forwarded to Sonia's address. Included was an annual premium notice on a life insurance policy of her father's. The death benefit was $350,000. Sonia was floored. The executor and she had not known to include this asset in the estate value; the Form 706 (estate tax return) would have to be amended. Since the total estate was under $675,000, still no estate tax was due. Seven months after this first discovery, Sonia got another surprise. She was notified by the state (somehow they got her address) that her parents had a safe-deposit box, the contents of which were about to be escheated (given over because the owner had not claimed them) to the state treasury. After proving she was the rightful heir, she went to the bank, opened the box, and found two more insurance policies, one on each parent, totaling death benefits of $400,000. This time, it was good that she was sitting down. The new total of estate assets now surpassed the $675,000 asset cap for filing an estate return without estate tax due. She would have to amend the return once again and pay the tax. Nonplussed that her parents had squirreled away all these assets without her knowledge, Sonia began to wonder what other money or accounts she might not have yet found. Although nothing additional has turned up, she won't be surprised if something does. Her parents were very private about their money. It must not have occurred to them that their daughter, trying her best to put closure on their death and their estate, might still be looking for all their assets, two years after they are gone, wondering what else lies undiscovered in some financial institution's lockbox.

Sonia is not alone among adult children who are left with a messy estate to sort out because their parents did not educate them about the family finances. Estate attorneys tell me they've seen cases where assets are not uncovered for more than a decade. What a needless frustration and waste of time. Think what opportunity loss these missing assets represent as they lie fallow. In Sonia's case, the $400,000 of newfound life insurance benefits, invested at 7 percent during that year they were "lost," would have provided her an additional $28,000 of income. Think what total value would be after ten "lost" years of growth at 7 percent—$786,800! This assumes the estate tax was paid out of other estate assets.

BONNIE: Grandma Skips a Generation but Shares Her Game Plan

Bonnie, vibrant and active at age 80, is a smart investor. Left a sizable estate by two husbands, she's built the family assets substantially since her second husband died. Now she is looking way ahead to how to disperse the family wealth among the younger generations and to train her offspring to make the most of their inheritance. All of her children are from her first marriage. They've given her six grandchildren, five boys and a girl. Bonnie is financially savvy, and she hates the idea of paying estate taxes. So she and her second husband had formed a marital trust—to preserve both his and her lifetime estate tax exemption ($600,000 for him; hers will be the graduated amount above that, which could be as much as $1 million, if she lives until 2006). Furthermore, Bonnie has added a generation-skipping trust, preparing to pass down an additional $1 million in her estate to her grandchildren estate tax–free.

Some adult children might get upset that their own kids will inherit this large amount of money, having the assets bypass them. Bonnie has taken care of that problem, for she has plenty of other assets to divide among her son and two daughters. All the money she's leaving is in trust. The children get their inheritance outright at her death to use as they see fit. The grandchildren won't get their money until age 25.

Bonnie's estate is not really that complicated, but it took some forethought and tax planning. What is important to know about this family is that all three children have copies of Bonnie's estate documents, including all trusts plus her powers of attorney, directive to physicians, and codicil listing the allocation of her personal property, such as cars, jewelry, and a special fan collection. There are no secrets—no undisclosed money or insurance policies. What's more, Bonnie has instructed that each of her grandchildren be told by their parents about their inheritance when they reach age 21, a full four years before they get the money.

Meanwhile, Bonnie has opened separate UGMA/UTMA accounts for each grandchild's college education (to remove the assets from her own estate), and she's informed the parents of the amount and type of assets in these accounts. Indeed, the parents are the custodians of the money. Looking down the road to their future, Bonnie wants to help educate her grandchildren and then give them a lump sum when they're more mature.

Just as Bonnie has been educating her three children about her finances, she has talked with her grandchildren about money, careers, and investments. Taking her cue, the adult children have started telling the grandkids more about their own family finances. So we have three generations whose dreams are being funded, and the tradition of financial disclosure and training are firmly in place. These six grandchildren will inherit money and are receiving guidance in financial management long before they receive the bequest from their grandparents. This is intergenerational family-finance education and dreamfunding at its best.

INHERITANCE PREP 101

If you want your children to value and care for the financial resources you pass to them, don't wait until you're dying to start preparing them. Here are some steps to take to guide your adult children in making the most of their inheritance.

Step One: Give Them the Big-Picture Financial Snapshop of Family Resources

Start by showing your children the most recent version of your financial statement (it should be updated yearly). This is the financial snapshot of your assets, liabilities, and net worth. (See the Appendix for the Financial Statement worksheet.) Explain where the assets are located, how they are titled, a bit about each investment, including information on the cost basis and unrealized capital appreciation. A more comprehensive approach is to show each child your financial notebook, going though each document, describing its importance in your total financial plan. Included in these papers should be your estate documents, detailing who are your executor, successor trustees, and holders of your durable powers of attorney and health care powers of attorney. If you have several children, it may make sense to call a special meeting and inform them all at once.

Step Two: Explain Your Estate Plan in Detail

Through a series of discussions, disclose to your heirs why you've set up your estate the way you have, especially if there are any inequities in how your assets are distributed. Go over all wills, trusts, and designated agents. If you've selected only one of your children to be executor or successor trustee, you might explain how you came to this decision. Discuss how assets are to be distributed among family members, when they will get these assets (during life or at your death), and in what form (lump-sum distribution, stream of income from current assets, or both; or as benefits from life insurance or retirement plans, either in the form of immediate cash payments or an annuity income). Out of these discussions, you may find that your children would rather you leave their part of the inheritance to their children, because of their own financial status. They may have suggestions about the naming of beneficiaries on your insurance policies, employer retirement plans, or IRAs. Review any charitable giving you have done in advance and how you have replaced these assets with life insurance (as in a life insurance trust), if you did so. If you have created trusts (marital, QTIP, generation skipping, spendthrift, life insurance, to name a few), detail how they work and why you've selected these estate planning instruments. Distinguish if your trusts are living trusts (in force now while you are alive) or testamentary trusts (created at the time of your death).

Step Three: Have Your Heirs Meet Your Financial Planner or Investment Advisor

I am always delighted when clients introduce their children or other heirs to me, because doing so makes financial transitions so much easier, and often more economical, for all members of the family. It is extremely helpful for the financial advisor to get a sense of the financial savvy of the younger generation members and to observe the family dynamics in action. Often times, I've discovered "problems" that we eventually addressed through changes in the estate plan—such as sibling dissent on some aspect of the distribution of the estate or discovery that the way the plan is set up may cause major estate tax or income tax problems for one of the heirs. If not remedied, these errors can be costly in terms of the family's total financial picture. It's best to do this intergenerational financial planning while both parents are still alive and mentally capable of making changes in the estate plan. Obviously, it is better to bring your children into the estate planning process before irreversible decisions are made, such as charitable gifts or establishment of irrevocable trusts, which cannot be changed even by the creator (trustor) of the trust.

One thing to consider, however, is that there may be conflicts of interest among family members regarding an estate plan—differences of opinion that can cause rifts in family relations. Your financial advisor is just that, your advisor. You are his or her client, and the advisor in good faith can represent only one client (which may be a husband and wife together). Therefore, your children may want to have their own financial advisors or attorneys representing their interests in these discussions. Clearly, all the professionals have one goal—to see that the family resources are preserved and distributed to the best advantage of the family as a whole and to see that all parties are treated fairly. Still, when it comes to money, you can get into some hairy disagreements before the final estate plan is established. Even if some family members are disgruntled about the resulting plan, the person whose estate is under discussion has the last word on what will be done.

Step Four: Warn against Consequences of Blowing the Inheritance

As the older generation, you have the wisdom and foresight of experience. You also remember all the hard work it took to create and grow the assets of your estate. Young adults often do not have this perspective and, frankly, may not truly appreciate their inheritance windfall, unless you do a bit of scenario "what-if" projections for them. You want to show the benefits of wisely managing the family money and the painful consequences of blowing it.

One simple way is to take the estimated amount of each child's inheritance, factor in a prudent rate of growth (I would use 7 percent after tax) and calculate for that individual what the money would grow to in, say, 10 years, then 20 years, then 40. Let's say your daughter is 30. A $200,000 inheritance at 7 percent would become $393,430 in 10 years, $773,936 in 20 years, and $2,994,890 in 40 years.

Then cut the inheritance amount in half—she might decide to upgrade to a bigger house and use $100,000 of the inheritance to fund that dream. Show her that $200,000 will be $196,715 in 10 years, $386,918 in 20 years, and $1,487,445 in 40 years. Now your daughter can see that buying the bigger house might mean she'll need to keep working an additional five years because her nest egg will be that much smaller and she'll have to set aside more of her income over more working years to arrive at the same level of financial security at retirement. By looking at this scenario now, she can think ahead about which way she might want to spend that inheritance when she gets it.

Most young people have no concept of the incredible boost to financial security a lump-sum inheritance represents. A good way to get that point across is to ask your son, "How many years would you have to work to save the $100,000 you'll inherit from me and your mother?" That's not how long to *make* $100,000; it's how long to *save* $100,000. This query will get your point across—you want your children to realize that if they maximize the opportunity of such a gift by investing most or all of it for the future, then their future dreamfunding—be it early retirement or the purchase of a vacation home for younger generations to share—will be achieved much sooner.

A few words about the meaning of *blowing it:* One man I know was left $3 million in life insurance proceeds when both his parents were killed in a plane crash. He was 21 at the time. He decided to quit school and travel, and over a seven-year period of gallivanting about the globe, he managed to spend the entire inheritance. He told me it was only after the money was gone that he started thinking about what his future career should be. He had to go back to school on student loans, went on to get a Ph.D., and now lives a comfortable lifestyle that he built from his own efforts. He admits that getting this windfall at such a young age, without any preparation, literally cost him millions.

Clearly you would hate to see your own children blow your financial legacy in this way. Yet, while you want to admonish young adults from squandering their inheritance, you also don't want to scare them off and make them think they can't touch a dime. This gets us back to short-term, intermediate-term, and long-term savings. Remind them that you hope they will fund many of their dreams and those of their own children all along the way—allocating some of the money they get from you at different times for funding specific dreams. Just as I encouraged you to enjoy the journey, part of your dreamfunding legacy is to impart the concept that they shouldn't stockpile all the family money once you're gone. It's a fine balance we're after—marshalling the family resources to provide for long-term financial independence and funding important dreams year to year. Perhaps sharing how you've done that during your lifetime will help guide your heirs in finding the right balance after you're gone.

Step Five: Optimize Value from Your Family Business, Plan a Smooth Transition

If a family-owned business is part of your wealth, you want to prepare your children to get the most value out of it for future generations. Fully one third of family businesses do not survive to the second generation, mostly due to poor succession planning.

You may have a child or children who now work in the business you created or inherited, and they look forward to taking over the business when you retire or die. If you have business partners, turning over your share of the business requires careful planning and legal documentation for transfer of ownership. Also, if some children will be active in the business and others not, you need to make certain the latter ones are compensated for their share of the business interest.

If none of your children has an interest in the business, then you have a much more complex task to provide a smooth transition of obtaining the family's value in the business at the time of your retirement, disability, or death. You need some form of buy-sell agreement in place so that when one of these events occurs, your partners (or employees) can buy out your interest in the business. In the case of death, this can be done through a buyout contract supported by a life insurance policy on your life. At your death, the death benefit proceeds pay to buy out your family's interest, removing them from the business, and paying them for the sale of your share.

Most business succession plans also have clauses to remove a permanently disabled or retiring owner with some form of payout of his or her business interest. If you're looking ahead to retirement, you need to double-check with your children to make sure no one has suddenly developed an interest in becoming involved in the business. If not, then you need to put a succession plan in writing where you and your partners agree to a payout, whether a lump-sum buyout, or a series of installment payments.

If you are a sole proprietor, you will need to look for a buyer for the business. Don't wait until the last minute; this could take some time. Seek professional advice about valuing your business; you don't want to underprice this substantial family asset.

If you plan to work until you drop, it's prudent to sit down with your children and explain what happens to the business at the time of your death. Give them the names of your partners as well as the details of the buyout arrangement. If you die as the sole business owner, give them an idea of what you think they should do to liquidate or sell the business to maximize its potential as a family financial asset. Give them the name of a business attorney you trust who can help them through this rather complex transaction.

Step Six: Share Your Vision of Passing Down Family Wealth

In all likelihood, by this time in life you have saved and invested your money for long-term dreams. You've raised and educated your children and have gotten them out into the world of work. Perhaps now they are building their own families. Do you have some vision of what you would hope they might do to continue utilizing and building the family financial resources for future generations? If so, it's important to share that intergenerational dream with your heirs. They might have some vague of idea of your philosophy of money, and I hope they have a clear idea of the assets you've accumulated, where they are located, and what kind of inheritance they might expect. Still, they don't have your perspective or life experience. It's up to you to express these views through conversations, perhaps even as part of your estate documents about your intent and interest in how your estate funds will be used— for what purposes and what dreams. If you look at the large family dynasties—the Rockefellers, Mellons, Fords, and Kennedys—there is no doubt that grandparents passed on to parents, who passed on to children and grandchildren, the family legacy of values. The younger generations of these families have a mission—for each family it is different, but it is part of the expectation that parents place on their offspring—to carry on the family intention, be it public service, preservation of wilderness, support of the arts, expansion of medical research on a particular disease, or foundations to fund various service entities. Think about your own intention with the family money. Have you talked about this with your heirs? If not, begin to do so now.

DISCLOSURE CAN SAVE MONEY AND HEARTACHE

As in Sonia's story, leaving your kids uninformed about your money can cost dearly in terms of heartache and opportunity loss. If you're going to pass down the assets to them anyway, why keep your heirs in the dark? In particular, if your distribution of the family finances may be uneven, isn't it better to explain your reasons while you're still alive, rather than die with the beneficiaries wondering why you did that?

Also, without these intergenerational discussions, how will you share your intent and relate the money to the dreams you want to still fund, even after you're gone? This is another occasion when you can tell your children more about your money values, your charitable interests, and your hopes for their future.

Finally, if you've raised your children to be financially responsible adults, trust them with this knowledge and trust that they'll use it and the money wisely. Inevitably you will have to relinquish control and pass the mantle of financial stewardship to your heirs. The more you can educate them about their inheritance in advance, the better they'll be able to carry on dreamfunding for their own generation and those to follow.

DREAMFUNDING STRATEGIES . . .

1. If you, or you and your spouse both died today, how prepared are your children or heirs to receive their inheritance and manage it well? Do they know much about what assets they'll get? Have they

seen a recent accounting of family financial assets or your most current financial statement? Do they know where the various estate documents and assets are located?

2. How long has it been since you reviewed your estate plan? Does it need updating, given any changes in your financial circumstances in the past year? Have any of your heirs had changes in their financial status that might affect the estate planning you've done so far? Perhaps their tax or income situation warrants some rethinking of the way you pass down your assets. Your children might rather you give their share of the inheritance to their children, skipping the first generation. Do you have a child with professional liability or debts that concern you? You might need to consider asset protection measures in these instances.

3. Are you planning to distribute your estate equally among your children? If not, do they know that, or would it come as a surprise at your death? Do you think it might cause less problem if you disclosed that now and explained your reasons for allocating the money the way you've planned? If so, make this part of your family estate plan discussion.

4. Do you plan to leave your assets outright to your children, or will you place restrictions on the form, conditions, and timing of their inheritance distributions? If so, don't you want to include this information in your estate plan talk with family members as well? It will cause less confusion and perhaps less dissatisfaction if you explain why you're setting things up this way.

5. If you have a lot of wealth, do your kids have any idea how much money they'll come into one day? Who will train them to handle this inheritance? Are you the best person to do that? Have you started educating your children to maximize their inheritance opportunity? If not, when will you begin to do so?

6. Do you have a financial planner or investment advisor you would like your children to meet? If so, set up an appointment when they can all attend, or have each child meet that person individually. You

might want to have a discussion with the advisor in advance to go over any sensitive or important topics you want the advisor to address at such meetings.

7. Do you have a physically or mentally disabled child who will need a guardian of person or property? What arrangements have you made for this situation? Do not waste any time in setting up this part of your estate plan. It's imperative that you help secure this child's future.

8. Do you have a formal succession plan for your family business? Have you designated and invited any of your children to run the business if you retire, become disabled, or die? If you have several children and not all will participate actively in the business, what arrangements have you made to compensate the "silent" siblings? Have you decided how the business should be disposed of eventually (liquidated or sold)? In the case of sale, have you identified the buyer and established a buy-sell agreement? Would your partners buy out your interest at your death, and if so, has the company purchased a life insurance policy on your life so that your heirs will be paid for your share of the business value? Make certain you create a smooth transition by creating an airtight business succession plan.

9. What is your vision of passing down family wealth? Be sure to share it with your heirs. Start these conversations now.

We've looked at three generations of many types of families, and we've seen what happens when these generations work in isolation or without the support of their elders and the young—the result is that fewer dreams get funded and each generation struggles harder to accomplish dream achievement. We've also seen what happens when grandparents, parents, and children work together through intergenerational financial planning to fund the dreams of all. Using the six Ps of funding your dreams, individuals experience the magnified potential for reaching their life goals. They have more ideas, more energy, more financial resources to call on, more emotional support, a greater sharing of values, and closer family ties. Who wouldn't want to experience the three great opportunities of intergenerational dreamfunding: being closer to your family, showing your love for your individual family members, and being appreciated and remembered as a generous and loving person within the family? This happens when you begin to use money as a family resource to be shared by all the generations.

I am hoping that some of you already have started dreamfunding work in your own family. After reading this book, my great wish is that you will do even more. If you had never learned or practiced the communication techniques and financial strategies outlined here, you can see that they are not that difficult to implement. It takes courage to approach your parents, even your children, and grandchildren to open a dialogue about dreamfunding. That's probably the biggest hurdle you'll face. Once you've done that, I think you will be amazed at the enthusiasm, support, and cooperation you will get as each family member begins to understand that by pooling mental, emotional, and financial resources, you all will benefit by getting more of your own dreams funded and by seeing those of your loved ones given proper attention as well. Even if you are skeptical that your family will be receptive to the idea, experiment—give it a try, and see what happens. The greatest risk is never to begin trying your hand at working together, generation to generation.

I've had some people tell me that they come from a family where money definitely is a "taboo" topic, and there is no way, they say, that they would dare approach their parents to get involved in this kind of dream team work. They are afraid of being turned down, or of seeming too interested in the family money. What I suggested was that we do this together. If I can get them all to an initial meeting, they begin to open up the communication lines about money. You could draw in a financial advisor to do the same. The key to motivating and enrolling your family in this process is very simple—it's the dreams themselves. Not many people can say no to the questions I pose: Would you like to have more of your life dreams come true? Would you like to have more dreams come true for your parents, children, and grandchildren to come true? When I put it like that, most people get it. It's not about giving up too much of their time, their money, their own dreams; it's about getting a whole lot more than they're getting now.

I don't know the particular money dynamics in your family. I don't know how courageous you feel about reaching out to achieve more of what you want in life, for yourself and for your loved ones. But I do know this: If you expand the intergenerational financial planning and dreamfunding in your life, you will be happier, richer, more loving, and more loved than you are today. I have seen it happen for many clients and friends. I know it can happen for you. I wish you luck, and I hope to hear about your family dreamfunding successes as the years unfold, generation to generation.

I would love to learn about your family dreamfunding success stories. Please send them to me at:

Funding Your Dreams
Carol Akright
15332 Antioch Street, #518
Pacific Palisades, CA 90272
Or e-mail to:
Akrightcr1@aol.com

For more resources of intergenerational financial planning, visit this Web site: <www.fundingyourdreams.com>.

At every Crossroad,
Follow your *Dream*
It is Courageous
to let your
Heart lead the way

—Leland Thomas

PPENDIX

Worksheets

FINANCIAL STATEMENT

ASSETS

Home	$_____
Vacation home	$_____
Rental real estate	$_____
Savings	$_____
IRAs	$_____
Deferred compensation plan/401(k)	$_____
Other retirement accounts	$_____
Investments	$_____
Miscellaneous/ Personal property	$_____
Total Assets	$_____

LIABILITIES

Home	$_____
Vacation home	$_____
Rental real estate	$_____
Auto loans	$_____
Credit cards	$_____
Personal loans	$_____
Miscellaneous	$_____
Total Liabilities	$_____
NET WORTH (Assets – Liabilities)	$_____

INCOME STATEMENT

Salary (husband)	$_____
Salary (wife)	$_____
Interest	$_____
Dividends	$_____
Capital gains (losses)	$_____
Real estate net cash flow (loss)	$_____
Miscellaneous	$_____
Total Income	$_____

EXPENSE STATEMENT

Federal income taxes	$_____
State income taxes	$_____
Other taxes	$_____
Social Security	$_____
State disability insurance	$_____
Savings and investments	$_____
Miscellaneous	$_____
Nonrecurring expense	$_____
Living expenses (See Cash Flow Statement, annual expense total minus income taxes and savings and investments.)	$_____
Total Expenses	$_____

RETIREMENT INCOME/EXPENSE STATEMENT

MONTHLY INCOME

Pension (husband)	$_____
Pension (wife)	$_____
Social Security (husband)	$_____
Social Security (wife)	$_____
Interest	$_____
Dividends	$_____
Real estate net cash flow (loss)	$_____
IRAs (self-directed)	$_____
IRA rollovers (from employer plans)	$_____
Other	$_____
Total Gross Income	$_____
Federal income taxes	$_____
State income taxes	$_____
Net Income	$_____

MONTHLY EXPENSES

Living expenses (See Cash Flow Statement.)	$_____
Nonrecurring expenses (wedding, car replacement, other major purchases)	$_____
Total Expenses	$_____
Retirement Income over Expenses (net income minus total expenses)	$_____

CASH FLOW STATEMENT

A. Fixed Expenses	Monthly Expenses	Annual Expenses
Home mortgage/rent	$_____	$_____
Other mortgage	$_____	$_____
Real estate taxes	$_____	$_____
Maintenance fees	$_____	$_____
Auto insurance	$_____	$_____
Homeowners insurance	$_____	$_____
Life insurance	$_____	$_____
Disability insurance	$_____	$_____
Health insurance	$_____	$_____
Other insurance	$_____	$_____
Newspapers and magazines	$_____	$_____
Dues, licenses, fees, etc.	$_____	$_____
Bank loans and other loans	$_____	$_____
Credit cards	$_____	$_____
Support/Dependents	$_____	$_____
Pets	$_____	$_____
Other	$_____	$_____
Total	$_____	$_____

B. Variable/Fixed Expenses	Monthly Expenses	Annual Expenses
Food (at home)	$_____	$_____
Heat	$_____	$_____
Gas, electricity	$_____	$_____
Telephone	$_____	$_____
Water, sewer, and garbage collection	$_____	$_____
Laundry, dry cleaning	$_____	$_____
House help (garden, cleaning, child care)	$_____	$_____

	Monthly	Annual
Clothing	$_____	$_____
Medical, doctors, and drugs (out-of-pocket)	$_____	$_____
Cars, gas, oil, and parking	$_____	$_____
Auto repairs and maintenance	$_____	$_____
Home repairs and maintenance	$_____	$_____
Cable/ Internet services	$_____	$_____
Federal income taxes	$_____	$_____
State income taxes	$_____	$_____
Savings and investments	$_____	$_____
Other	$_____	$_____
Total	$_____	$_____

C. Discretionary Expenses	**Monthly Expenses**	**Annual Expenses**
Entertainment (include restaurants)	$_____	$_____
Vacations	$_____	$_____
Education	$_____	$_____
Books, tapes, CDs, videos	$_____	$_____
Contributions	$_____	$_____
Recreation	$_____	$_____
Health care, beauty care	$_____	$_____
Incidentals	$_____	$_____
Cash (unallocated)	$_____	$_____
Other	$_____	$_____
Total	$_____	$_____
Monthly Expense Total (A+B+C)	$_____	

Annual Expense Total (monthly total × 12) $_____

CHILD'S MONTHLY BUDGET

INCOME

Allowance	$_____
Earnings	$_____
Gift money (from relatives)	$_____
Other	$_____
Total Income	$_____

EXPENSES

Have to Spend

School supplies/sports gear	$_____
Meals away from home	$_____
Other entertainment (movies, etc.)	$_____
Gifts for family and friends	$_____
Savings/Investments:	
Short-term savings	$_____
Intermediate-term savings	$_____
Long-term investments	$_____
Charitable donations	$_____
Other	$_____

Want to Spend

Clothes/Grooming	$_____
Car (gas, maintenance, license, insurance)	$_____
Big purchases (computer, stereo)	$_____
Travel/Vacations	$_____
Other	$_____
Total Expenses	$_____

CHILD'S FUTURE MONTHLY BUDGET

INCOME

Earnings $ _____

Family support $ _____

Gift money $ _____

Other $ _____

Total Income $ _____

EXPENSES

Household:

Rent $ _____

Utilities (gas, heat, electricity, water) $ _____

Telephone $ _____

Cable/Internet services $ _____

Renter's insurance $ _____

Other $ _____

Food $ _____

Clothing/Grooming:

Clothing purchase $ _____

Laundry/Dry cleaning $ _____

Grooming/Beauty care $ _____

Auto/Transportation:

Loan payment $ _____

Gas, oil, and parking $ _____

Vehicle repairs/maintenance $ _____

Other transportation costs (fares) $ _____

Health:

Health insurance $ _____

Nonreimbursed expenses $ _____

Gym membership $ _____

Entertainment (movies, restaurants) $_____

Vacation/Travel $_____

Publications, Books, CDs $_____

Dues, Licenses, Fees $_____

Disability/Life Insurance $_____

Student/Other Loan Payments $_____

Credit Cards $_____

Savings/Investments:
   Short-term savings (emergency cash) $_____

   Intermediate-term savings $_____

   Long-term investments $_____

Charitable Donations $_____

Other $_____

Total Expenses $_____

TOTAL INCOME $_____

LESS: TOTAL EXPENSES $_____

NET INCOME $_____

S OURCES

The following people provided technical research for this book through personal interviews:

- *Estate planning:* Kathryn Ballsun, Esq.; David Grady, Esq.; Raymond E. Makowski, Esq.; and John Rooks, Esq.
- *Long-term care:* Linda Keegan and Larry Lite, LUTCF
- *Financial planning:* Douglas W. Baker, CFP
- *Psychology of money:* Avie Engel, MSW; Elizabeth Gong-Guy, Ph.D.; and Bob Mauer, Ph.D.
- *Children and money:* Neale S. Godfrey

Original materials for worksheets in the Appendix were provided by Gael S. Kennedy, CFP, courtesy of the estate of Gael S. Kennedy. Retirement planning sources consulted:

- *Secure Retirement,* National Committee to Preserve Social Security and Medicare, Washington, D.C., January/February 1999 and November/December, 1999.
- *The Money Guide to Living Well in Retirement,* by Lisa Ellis and the editors of *Money,* Time, Inc. Home Entertainment, New York, 1999.

- *The Ultimate Retirement Guide, Money,* Time, Inc., New York, July 2000.

Estate planning sources consulted:

- *Generations: Planning Your Legacy,* by Robert A. Esperti, Renna L. Peterson, Karl W. Adler, and Raymond E. Makowski, Esperti Peterson Institute, Denver, Colo., 1999.
- *The Elder Law Handbook,* by Peter J. Strauss and Nancy M. Lederman, Facts on File, Inc., New York, 1996.

College planning sources consulted:

- "Those Scary College Costs," by Tom Morganthau and Seema Nayyaz, and "Save First, Then Borrow," by Jane Bryant Quinn, *Newsweek,* 29 April 1996.
- *How to Get into College,* Newsweek, Inc. and Kaplan Educational Centers, Inc., Medford, N.Y., 1997.
- *How to Get into Graduate School,* Newsweek, Inc. and Kaplan Educational Centers, Inc., Medford, N.Y., 1998.
- *Money Magazine's College Guide for Best College Buys on 150 Schools,* Time, Inc., New York.
- "America's Best Colleges," *U.S. News & World Report 1998 Directory of Colleges and Universities,* Washington, D.C., 1998.
- *T. Rowe Price College Planning Kit,* T. Rowe Price Investments Services, Baltimore, Md., 2000.
- *Picture the Future: A Step-by-Step Guide to Financing Your Child's College Education,* MFS Fund Distributors, Boston, Mass.
- "The 529 Plan: A Tax-Saving Way to Pay for College Expenses; Will It Work for You?" by Roger Carmody, *The NSBN Advantage,* Winter 1999–2000, Nanas, Stern, Biers, Newstein and Co., LLP, Beverly Hills, Calif.

C

Car ownership, 53
Career
  achievement, 30–33
  change, 36–37
  dreams, of children, 49–50
Cash Flow Statement, 176, 182, 278
Certified Financial Planner, 99
Charitable donations/legacy, 24–25,
  142–43
  children and, 254, 256
Children, 33–34
  budget worksheets for, 280–82
  chores and, 242
  disabled, securing future of, 270
  dreams of, 45–61
    allowances, 45–46
    careers, 49–50
    car ownership, 53
    entrepreneurship, 50–51
    financial independence,
      51–53
    helping parents in tough
      times, 54–55
    pets, 47–49
    popularity, 56–57
    possessions, 46–47
    to be best at something, 55–56
  education of. *See* College funding
  financial self-sufficiency, 42–43,
    147, 246–58
    earning, 250–51
    dreamfunding strategies,
      255–58
    investing, 253
    net worth vs. self-worth,
      253–54
    saving, 252
    spending, 251–52
    wealth, 254–55
  fostering responsibility in, 48
  funding their own dreams, 231–45
    allowances, 233–34, 241–42
    consumer education, 234–35
    delayed gratification, 235
    dreamfunding strategies,
      241–45

investing, 236–37, 240–41
jobs, 237–39
saving, 239–40
gifts to. *See* Gifting
money training session with, 74
socialization skills in, 56–57
Children's Financial Network, 233
Churchill, Winston, 86
Clothes, children/teens and, 47
College funding, 33, 202–19
  accounts in child's name, 214–15
  accounts in parents' names, 215
  community college option, 217–18
  dreamfunding strategies, 218–19
  family planning and, 210–11
  financial aid, 211–13
  gifting and, 146
  grandparents' college funds,
    215–16
  long-term college fund accounts,
    213–17
  scholarships, 205, 206
  steps in, 209–17
  tax aspects of, 217
"College Planning Kit" (T. Rowe Price),
  219
Communication. *See also*
  Intergenerational financial planning
  care of aging parents and, 200–201
  college funding and, 218
  of estate plan, 263, 269
  financial, xi, 7–8, 10–13, 122–35.
    See also Financial
    communication
  health care directives, 121
  of values, 141–42
Community college, 219
Community contributions, 24–25
Comparison shopping, 46
Compound interest, 43, 240
Consumer Credit Counselors, 1
Consumer education, children and,
  234–35
Continuing care communities, 198. *See
  also* Aging parents, caring for
Control, loss or transfer of, 41, 192–95.
  See also Aging parents, caring for

Financial communication, 122–35, 247
  business succession plan, 129–31
  children's involvement in, 244–45
  dreamfunding strategies, 133–35.
    See also Dreamfunding/
    dreamfunding strategies
  estate plans, 132. *See also* Estate
    planning
  financial notebook, 125–26
  funeral plans, 132–33
  location of assets, 127–28
  powers of appointment, 128–29
  residential/living costs, 129
  taxes, 131–32
Financial education, 10–11
Financial Engines Web site, 99
Financial health questionnaire, 4–5, 12
Financial independence, 16–18, 91–109
  adult children and, 36–37
  asset allocation, 105
  capital preservation, 100–105
  children and, 42–43, 51–53
  determining adequacy of
    retirement income, 99
  monitoring investments, 105
  projecting retirement figures, 98–99
  retirement expenses, 97–98
  sources of retirement income,
    96–97
Financial notebook, 125–26, 127
  tax information in, 131
Financial planner, 263–64
Financial self-sufficiency, 147
Financial Statement Worksheet, 175–76,
  275
Fixed annuity, 102
Fixed-income investments, 101–2,
  103–4
Four jar system, 233–34
401(k), 44
  borrowing against for college
    expenses, 213
Frequent flier miles, 38, 224
Friendships, 21–22, 38–39
Full retirement age (FRA), 178
Fun dreams, funding, 220–30
  creativity, 223–25
  dreamfunding strategies, 22–30

  intergenerational recreation, 223,
    226–27
  travel insurance, 225–26
Funeral plans, 132–33

G

Generation skipping trusts, 215, 261
Gifting, 145–53
  college funds, 205
  determining amount of, 151–52
  dreamfunding strategies, 152–53
  gifts vs. loans, 151
  helpful kinds of, 147–48
  hurtful kinds of, 148–50
  timing of, 150–51
Godfrey, Neale, 233
Grandparent generation, dreams of,
  16–29
  community contribution, 24–25
  enjoyment of friends and family,
    20–22
  financial communication. *See*
    Financial communication
  financial independence, 16–18
  good health, 18–19
  to help adult children/
    grandchildren, 23–24
  investment and estate, 25–27
  legacy of values, 27–29
  leisure and entertainment, 19–20
  love and respect, 29
  travel and fun, 22–23
Grants, college, 211–12. *See also*
  College funding
Great Depression, 54–55

H

Health, 18–19
Health care
  anticipating costs of, 110–11,
    114
  early retirement and, 179
  inflation and, 115
Health care power of attorney, 116, 117,
  191
Health insurance, private, 114